Karl Jaspers' Philos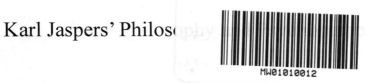

Thomas Fuchs • Thiemo Breyer • Christoph Mundt
Editors

Karl Jaspers' Philosophy and Psychopathology

Editors
Thomas Fuchs
Psychiatric Department
University of Heidelberg
Heidelberg
Germany

Christoph Mundt
University of Heidelberg
Heidelberg
Germany

Thiemo Breyer
Clinic for General Psychiatry
University of Heidelberg
Heidelberg
Germany

ISBN 978-1-4614-8877-4   ISBN 978-1-4614-8878-1 (eBook)
DOI 10.1007/978-1-4614-8878-1
Springer New York Heidelberg Dordrecht London

Library of Congress Control Number: 2013951810

Printed on acid-free paper

Springer is part of Springer Science+Business Media (www.springer.com)

Preface

The name of Karl Jaspers represents a particular constellation of thought which characterized the cultural life in Germany at the beginning of the twentieth century. Philosophy, humanities, social sciences, and medicine conjoined to enter into a dialogue. In this intellectual environment, Karl Jaspers first studied medicine from 1906 to 1909, then worked as a psychiatrist at the Psychiatric Clinic of Heidelberg, headed by Karl Wilmanns, until he took a chair for philosophical psychology in 1914. As early as 1913, at that time being a 29-year-old clinical assistant, he published his "General Psychopathology", a pioneering achievement in overcoming the disciplinary boundaries. Although moving more towards philosophy later on, Jaspers attempted to combine psychiatry, medicine, philosophy, and the humanities throughout his life. Thus, he also supplemented his approach to psychopathology by adding extensive parts of his existential philosophy to the original work, in particular in the 4th edition of 1942.

The central motive that connects Jaspers' manifold works is the idea of human existence. He conceives it as the foundation of all scientific theories which are based on the human being without being able to grasp it completely. Scientific investigation should therefore be complemented by a permanent reflection on prescientific human experience. This idea remains valid independently of Jaspers' existential philosophical terminology. It may be reformulated as follows: Science is based on the human life-world, i.e., on subjective and intersubjective experience. It starts from this experience and gains its final destination from it. Only in constant dialogue with the life-world is science able to attain relevant knowledge without decoupling itself from human self-understanding. This is true in particular for the sciences, whose subject matter is the suffering human being, i.e., medicine in general, and psychopathology and psychiatry in particular.

When Jaspers published his "General Psychopathology", the field of psychiatry was characterized by a rapid expansion of the neurosciences, above all neuroanatomy and neurophysiology. Jaspers was aware of the risk that psychiatry could lose its anchoring in the patients' subjective experience by indulging in what he called "brain mythologies". In this situation, his main concern was to bring order into the field by meticulous descriptions of subjective phenomena, concise definitions of concepts, and systematic classifications of types of disorders, thus endowing psychiatry with a valid and reliable method.

With his psychiatric *opus magnum*, Jaspers became the uncontested founder of psychopathology as a science with its own object and methodology. This establishment of psychopathology was essentially based on the rejection of scientific reductionism, which claimed that all mental phenomena and disorders could be sufficiently explained by their organic substrates in the brain. We find it to be particularly important in the current situation of academic discourse to remind ourselves of the important contribution of Jaspers in trying to overcome simplistic and reductionist programs in the human sciences and medicine. His work is still an encouragement for us to "save the phenomena" and to connect psychiatry as a science to the life-world of our patients.

It is for this reason that we compiled contributions for this volume which take a close look at Jaspers' method and the possibilities of integrating his key ideas in current debates. The volume emerged from the International Conference "Towards the Centennial of Karl Jaspers' 'General Psychopathology'", which was held at the University of Heidelberg in September 2011. We wish to express our gratitude to Rixta Fambach and the members of the *Section Phenomenology* at the University Clinic for General Psychiatry Heidelberg for their help in organizing the conference. We also thank Lukas Iwer for the editorial work on this volume.

August 2013   Thomas Fuchs
Heidelberg   Thiemo Breyer
                                                                   Christoph Mundt

Contents

Contributors

Matthias Bormuth Institute for Philosophy, University of Oldenburg, Oldenburg, Germany

Carlos Cornaglia University of Neuquén, Neuquén, Argentina

Otto Dörr Faculdad de Medicina, Universidad Diego Portales, Santiago de Chile, Chile

Dept. de Psiquiatria, Facultad de Medicina, Universidad de Chile, Santiago de Chile, Chile

Thomas Fuchs Psychiatric Department, Centre of Psychosocial Medicine, University of Heidelberg, Heidelberg, Germany

Andrés Heerlein Universities of Chile and del Desarrollo, Santiago de Chile, Chile

Sabine C. Herpertz Klinik für Allgemeine Psychiatrie, Zentrum für Psychosoziale Medizin, Universitätsklinikum Heidelberg, Heidelberg, Germany

Alfred Kraus Klinik für Allgemeine Psychiatrie, Zentrum für Psychosoziale Medizin, Universitätsklinikum Heidelberg, Heidelberg, Germany

Christoph Mundt University of Heidelberg, Heidelberg, Germany

Sonja Rinofner-Kreidl Department of Philosophy, Karl-Franzens-University Graz, Graz, Austria

René Rosfort Centre for Subjectivity Research, Copenhagen K, Denmark

Louis A. Sass Rutgers University, Graduate School of Applied and Professional Psychology, Piscataway, NJ, USA

Michael A. Schwartz Texas A&M Health Science Center College of Medicine, Round Rock, TX, USA

Giovanni Stanghellini Faculty of Psychology, Università degli Studi G. d'Annunzio, Chieti, Italy

Samuel Thoma Hermannstraße Berlin, Germany

Osborne P. Wiggins University of Louisville, Louisville, KY, USA

Part I
History and Methodology

Chapter 1
Psychopathology and the Modern Age. Karl Jaspers Reads Hölderlin

Matthias Bormuth

1.1

In the first edition of the *General Psychopathology* in 1913 there is already a hint that Jaspers was preoccupied with the role that Friedrich Hölderlin's medical history played for his poetry. With a study by the Tübingen psychiatrist Wilhelm Lange in mind Jaspers writes: "Pathography is a delicate matter" (Jaspers 1963, p. 729). His scepsis toward psychopathographical thinking was largely prompted by Lange's attempt not only to dismiss Hölderlin's Tower Poems, written after 1806, as "a product of mental illness" but also to pathologize the earlier poems from the period starting in 1800, the so-called late poetry (Lange 1909, p. 100; Oelmann 2002, p. 423).

The Heidelberg philologist Norbert von Hellingrath's view of these poems could not have been more different. Indeed it was with the first edition of this controversial late poetry that he launched the "Hölderlin renaissance" of the time. The first sentence of his foreword is a direct rebuttal of Lange: "This volume contains the heart, core, and pinnacles of Hölderlin's oeuvre, his true legacy" (Hölderlin 1916, p. XI). So it comes as little surprise that with his background in psychiatry, Jaspers opened his study of Hölderlin a decade later with the controversy between Lange and Hellingrath, demonstrating obvious affinity with the philologist and his "foreword" (Jaspers 1926, p. 100).

The focus of this essay is Jaspers' pathographical reading of Hölderlin from 1913/14 onward, and the positive influence that Jaspers felt the poet's psychopathology had on his modernity. The German literary scholar Walter Müller-Seidel had made this point several years beforehand in his interpretation of Hölderlin, making direct reference to Jaspers' topos of the "boundary situation" and emphasizing that the psychiatrist had aligned himself in his anthropology with Dilthey (Müller-Seidel 1995, p. 71).

M. Bormuth (✉)
Institute for Philosophy, University of Oldenburg,
Postfach 2503, 26111 Oldenburg, Germany
e-mail: matthias.bormuth@uni-oldenburg.de

T. Fuchs et al. (eds.), *Karl Jaspers' Philosophy and Psychopathology*,
DOI 10.1007/978-1-4614-8878-1_1, © Springer Science+Business Media New York 2014

In his essay Müller-Seidel posited an "epochal affiliation" between romanticism and modernism on the basis of their shared receptiveness to the idea of illness as "a means of higher synthesis" (Müller-Seidel 1995, p. 42 ff). Müller-Seidel paid tribute to Dilthey for championing the morbid poet in the positivistic interim of the nineteenth century, when good health was glorified: "It is the highest form of pathological interest that so intrigues us about this poet" (Müller-Seidel 1995, p. 59). Even as a young psychiatrist Jaspers impacted upon Müller-Seidel's perspective. So it is not surprising than in his late portrait of the poet, Müller-Seidel alludes directly to Jaspers when he writes: "Hölderlin's mental state, as is often the case in the modern period, is a boundary situation in many respects" (Müller-Seidel 1993, p. 244).

The conceptual nexus of psychopathology and modernity is not only key to Jaspers' study of Hölderlin; it informs his entire pathographical oeuvre, as will become clear by comparing his thoughts on van Gogh, Nietzsche, and Max Weber. Amazingly, this view also surfaces in his *Notizen zu Martin Heidegger* [notes on Martin Heidegger] when Jaspers compares Heidegger's famous interpretation of Hölderlin with the edition published by Hellingrath two decades earlier. Jaspers also read the elegy "Bread and Wine," which was to become so central for Heidegger, with remarkable intensity. No other poem in Jaspers' personal copy of the Hellingrath edition is surrounded by a greater profusion of pencil markings and notes (Hölderlin 1916).

1.2

As part of the inner circle around Max Weber, Jaspers doubtless joined other scholars from the circle at the enthusiastic readings and elucidations on Hölderlin that made Hellingrath legendary in Heidelberg around 1913/14 (Rilke and von Hellingrath 2011, p. 100). As a former psychiatrist who was now influential as a psychologist among philosophers, Jaspers would have made an attractive conversation partner for the young philologist, at a time when the late poetry was still widely regarded as an expression of psychopathological experience. Indeed in a letter dated June 1914 to Gustav Radbruch, an historian of law who belonged to the Weber circle, Jaspers writes: 'Hellingrath has published a Hölderlin volume which brings almost everything together in an entirely new way. I recently looked at some of Hölderlin's manuscripts with him. It was most moving to have his whole life right there before me in his own handwriting. H[ellingrath] had specimens from all phases of his life'. The two men shared a graphological interest that had been kindled by Ludwig Klages in Munich, perhaps at a similar time (Schmidt 1963/64, p. 148).

Whatever the case, the meeting in Heidelberg certainly informed the Hölderlin chapter that Jaspers added in 1921 to *Strindberg and van Gogh. An Attempt of a Pathographic Analysis with Reference to Parallel Cases of Swedenborg and Hölderlin.* Initially he seems keen to intercede in the controversy with Lange, writing: "Both opinions, excluding each other in their evaluation, need not be incompatible in every respect, concerning the facts on which their observations are based. Lange can be correct by declaring the psychosis to be the cause of the changes in the poetry, and so can v. Hellingrath when he detects changes without asking questions in regard to the psychosis" (Jaspers 1977, p. 165). But Jaspers by no means persists in maintaining a diplomatic stance. On the one hand he rejects—in an allusion to Lange—the pathographical application of "crude categories" to such magnificent poetry: "It is quite dangerous to be quick about declaring something 'incomprehensible', therefore 'crazy', to call something void, trivial, farfetched, confused" (Jaspers 1977, p. 135 f). On the other, he reveals his admiration and respect for Hellingrath's philological reading of Hölderlin: "If we ask what experts have said about these changes, we find the answers exceedingly instructive. We wish to refer to the excellent analyses of v. Hellingrath who makes profitable use of the difference between a rough and a smooth construction" (Jaspers 1977, p. 136).

It follows that in his pathographical outline of Lange's thesis, which argued that from 1802 onward the psychotic process had a solely destructive impact, he directly endorses Hellingrath's view. Namely that the late poems represent a "continuous development" which "took place until the complete collapse" and which "from a mental standpoint, is entirely understandable" (Jaspers 1977, p. 136). In Jaspers' personal copy of the Hellingrath edition, the passages in the foreword that draw a distinction between the intelligible development of the poetry until 1806 and everything that followed, are heavily underlined and marked. Here Hellingrath writes: "This development proceeds without leap or jolt: neither the year 1801 nor the stay in France and the outward signs of madness constitute a discernible break of any kind. However, a clear line can be drawn after the final baroque step of this path: that which I have allocated to the sixth volume is no longer the directly logical continuation of the path pursued at the outset (some might call it the path to madness): there is a rupture. These are no longer the works of an artistic will striving clearly onwards (some might call it straying); the creations of effort and strain. It is a relaxed drifting, untethered by the will [...]" (Hölderlin 1916, p. XIX f).

To anyone with a knowledge of psychiatry, it is clear that in differentiating between intelligible development and unintelligible process, Hellingrath is applying the famous category which became the methodological premise of Jaspers' *General Psychopathology*. This is referred to in psychiatric circles today as Jaspers' theorem of unintelligibility. Central to its pathographical relevance for Jaspers is that in "the analysis of incomprehensible causal relationships, e.g. between the onset of mental illness and an artist's creative work" unequivocally genealogical explanations are avoided. Ultimately Jaspers regarded the sick but prodigiously talented artist as a mystery that no science could fully fathom in either psychopathological or existential terms. As he wrote in the foreword to the second edition of the pathography which was published in a series of "Philosophical Studies" in 1926: "Not by supposedly supreme insights, by which we might perhaps discover 'the truth', but by insights which provide the perspective from which the actual problems can be recognized" (Jaspers 1977, p. IX). Even the advanced psychotic process could have a beneficial impact on the innovative quality of the artwork, he believed: "Just as a diseased oyster can cause the growth of pearls, by the same token schizophrenic processes can be the cause of mental creations of singular quality" (Jaspers 1977, p. 134).

It is not clear whether Hellingrath arrived at this opinion in the course of his conversations with Jaspers, through the study of his methodological classic, or whether he developed it quite independently. Even in his appraisal of Hölderlin's "Pindar Translations," he dissociates himself from the right, claimed by Lange, to draw genealogical conclusions between work and illness, "because I must not leave the territory of pure descriptiveness and literary observation" (von Hellingrath 1944, p. 42). Like Jaspers he felt he had no authority to investigate any hidden connections to the process of the illness, his subject being the intellectual relevance of the unusual words and their idiomatic application. Thus in the speech he gave in Munich on "Hölderlin's Madness" in 1915, Hellingrath also talks about the "mysterious" and "incomprehensible" pathology of the artist, which in the minds of many has obviously "overshadowed [...] the miracle of the work." Yet the "madness" constitutes, he suggests, "the signature of the form of his talent," whose intellectual contours cannot be fathomed by "unbidden professional verdicts on his illness" (von Hellingrath 1944, p. 152). Von Hellingrath was undoubtedly alluding to Lange's pathography, which rejected all productive influence of mental illness and only underscored its destructive effects: "Catatonia on the other hand completely diminished or destroyed his abilities; Hölderlin's 'madness' has nothing to do with his genius" (Lange 1909, p. 216 f).

While Lange essentially sought to apply psychiatric categories to apprehend the formally and linguistically unusual nature of Hölderlin's art as an expression of alterity, Jaspers wanted to learn from the philologists. He was inspired not only by Hellingrath but also by Wilhelm Dilthey, whose 1906 collected volume *Poetry and Experience* included an essay on Hölderlin (Dilthey 1916). Jaspers describes this as the "most brilliant" interpretation of Hölderlin he had encountered (Jaspers 1926, p. 102), and shows particular fascination for the way in which Dilthey—like Hellingrath—distinguished between the later poems as the highpoint of productivity and the poetry of the final period, which he describes as a mere expression of the destructive pathology: "It is the fatefulness of Hölderlin's last epoch that his entire poetic development surged toward a complete liberation of the inner emotional rhythm from the restrictive metric form, but that he does not take this last step until he has touched the line of insanity." Jaspers is also delighted that in reference to "Hälfte des Lebens" (The Middle of Life), Dilthey talks of the "strange and eccentric hues" in Hölderlin's richly metaphorical language; it reminds Jaspers of the paintings by van Gogh which, on Max Weber's recommendation, he had so enjoyed seeing in an exhibition at the Cologne Werkbund in 1912 (Jaspers 1926, p. 102).

Jaspers follows the two humanists a considerable way in their hermeneutic attempts to interpret Hölderlin's late poetry as a sublime experience of modernity. Yet he also accentuates the psychiatric understanding that strange-seeming phenomena are the expression of a pathological process. He writes, with obvious ambivalence: "I read in the fourth volume of the v. Hellingrath edition, a different atmosphere in the linguistic and formal expression (except for a number of poems at the outset of the volume, which date back to 1800 or to the end of 1799), but I am not about to objectify this feeling" (Jaspers 1977, p. 138). Jaspers resolves the conflict with a reference to partial ruptures: "It is self-evident that we are not dealing with an absolutely sudden leap. For after all the severe state of his insanity, which undoubtedly actually represents a break, a complete snap in the development came about in the extremely slow transitions. Off and on the early process flickers more strongly, only to disappear almost altogether, until a first heavy attack changes everything almost completely" (Jaspers 1977, p. 138).

One could say that Jaspers regarded Hölderlin as a poetic mystery in whom the psychopathology acted as a productive force which enhanced his modernity, until the point where it shifted to pure destructiveness around 1806. The "understandability boundary," which he had originally applied to otherness in psychopathology is now brought to bear on otherness in modernity. The sick artist thus appears as a doubly distinguished figure of alterity. The prerequisite for this, however, is his personal genius, which Jaspers believed links Hölderlin with van Gogh. As Jaspers wrote about van Gogh and his ability to express the spiritual and psychological destitution of the time: "The shaping and disciplining power is capable of dissolving the shock. Just as his painting serves van Gogh as a lightning rod, so Hölderlin's poetry is his salvation" (Jaspers 1926, p. 112).

1.3

At the beginning of 1888, Nietzsche described the new fashion for discrediting unusual thinking as an expression of illness, exactly a year before he himself was overcome by mental illness in Turin: "But a man is *constantly* paying for holding such an isolated position by an isolation which becomes every day more complete, more icy, and more cutting. […] They are now getting out of the difficulty with such words as 'eccentric', 'pathological', 'psychiatric'" (Nietzsche 1921). Several years earlier in the first essay of his *Untimely Meditations* he had already struck out against the conservative educated classes, positing the huge value of psychopathology over psychological well-being in the quest for deeper knowledge: "For it is a cruel fact that 'the spirit' is accustomed most often to descend upon the 'unhealthy and unprofitable', and on those occasions when he is honest with himself even the philistine is aware that the philosophies his kind produce and bring to market are in many ways spiritless, though they are of course extremely healthy and profitable" (Nietzsche 1983, p. 28). The target of his attacks was the "cultural philistine" of the *Gründerjahre* who had a tendency to try to ignore points of view that he considered uncomfortable and unusual, and to therefore brand them as pathological: "Finally he invents for his habits, modes of thinking, likes and dislikes, the general formula 'healthiness', and dismisses the ever uncomfortable disturber of the peace as being sick or neurotic" (Nietzsche 1983, p. 12). It is no accident that Nietzsche responded by taking a stand for "the memory of the glorious Hölderlin," distinguishing him from the others as a "non-philistine" with the ironic question as to "whether he would have been able to find his way in the present great age" (Nietzsche 1983, p. 12).

Nietzsche's criticism of the *Gründerzeit* ideology of good health contrasts starkly with the psychiatric topos of genius and madness, whose considerable popularity at the time was largely due to Cesare Lombroso's *genio e fillia* of 1887 (Lombroso 1887). The artistic avant-garde, which was pushing vehemently, subversively and provocatively for political, social and economic change, was diagnosed as degenerate, and Lombroso was regarded as its chief enemy (Nordau 1892, p. VIII). The German equivalent of the Italian psychiatrist was, Max Nordau was the leading champion of this pathologizing discourse. His standard work *Degeneration* from 1892 psychiatrized entire social groups which, like the modernist artists and their followers, did not conform to the moral ideals of the ruling middle classes (Nordau 1892, p. 469). "Degenerates are not always criminals, anarchists, and pronounced lunatics; they are often authors and artists" (Nordau 1913, p. VII). In the cultural crisis it is the doctor, he said, who takes on the important task of examining questionable intellectual works, specifically seeking out their pathological genesis, in order to warn against them with the authority of a professional.

This was the very role that Wilhelm Lange was fulfilling with respect to Hölderlin's suspect late work. As he writes at the beginning of his pathography, the aim of his psychiatric study was to "provide the literary historian, the philosopher, the historian with a report which could be used to assess anything that might be considered psychologically abnormal in a person's work" (Lange 1909, p. VII). He also issued a stern warning against the modernistic fashion for regarding the topos of genius and madness in a positive light, and by extension mental illness as source of the particular charisma in Hölderlin's work: "It has fascinated the masses, it has allowed psychosis to be mistaken for genius and has presented Hölderlin's fate as a form of martyrdom" (Lange 1909, p. 217).

Jaspers certainly did not see himself as a coldly objective examiner who wanted to warn against the work of a sick artist. Yet nor did he number himself among those who sweepingly praised the "art of the insane" as an avant-garde achievement (Jaspers 1926, p. 148). But his pathographies are eager to emphasize the destructive effects of pathology whenever he has philosophical difficulties with the intellectual products. The problems that this "subjectivistic inclination" represents for value theory have been amply noted in academic research (Häfner 1963; Janzarik 1974; Schlimme 2010). This inclination is particularly pronounced in the pathography of Strindberg, whose pluralistic modernity Jaspers found fundamentally dubious (Jaspers 1926, p. 84).

Jaspers' pathography of Nietzsche emphasizes both the productive and the destructive effects of psychopathology. It forms part of the 1936 study *Nietzsche: An Introduction to the Understanding of His Philosophical Activity.* Jaspers writes: "The 'sick' factors not only [...] *were of a disturbing nature* but may even have made possible what would otherwise not have eventuated" (Jaspers 1997, p. 107). Accordingly the pathography depicts Nietzsche as a herald and interpreter of the modern "experience of world crisis" (Jaspers 1997, p. 107), who suffered immeasurably as a result, and whose pathologically induced insights took him to unattainable heights and plunged him into absurd depths. Jaspers' assessment correlates with his philosophically ambivalent verdict of Nietzsche's work: "He has a capacity for stirring us deeply, awakening our most essential impulses, intensifying our earnestness, and illuminating our insights; but that does not prevent him from repeatedly giving the impression of failing, of plunging into a void, as it were, of having an oppressive effect through narrowness, immoderation and absurdities" (Jaspers 1997, p. 105).

Jaspers observes the artists van Gogh and Hölderlin primarily and almost exclusively under the productive influence of the psychological process, which continued right up to the point of mental breakdown. He considered them exceptional artists whose psychological abnormality, paired with their talent, was fundamental to their deeply profound work. "Here we have not only a productivity exaggerated through tension, a productivity which also leads to the discovery of new approaches which then tend to enrich the general artistic expression; rather, new forces come into being which gain objective form, forces which, within themselves mental, are neither healthy nor sick but thrive on the soil of illness" (Jaspers 1977, p. 197).

Essentially, Jaspers' openness to considering psychological unusualness as a productive element of intellectual life stemmed directly from his early days in Heidelberg with Max Weber, who remained the point of reference for Jaspers' thinking throughout most of his life (Henrich 1988). Weber called into question the dominant paradigm of degeneration on the grounds that it was based on cultural judgements and not only natural facts (Peukert 1989). Weber himself believed that psychologically and socially marginal figures possessed significant potential for the development of society: "The evidence of ethnology seems rather to show that the most important source of innovation has been the influence of individuals who have experienced certain 'abnormal' states (which are frequently, but not always, regarded by present-day psychiatry as pathological) and hence have been capable of exercising a special influence on others" (Radkau 2005, p. 314; Weber 1978, p. 321).

This was also the perspective from which Jaspers observed Weber's own psychological illness, which consigned him to the margins of academic life. He saw Weber's illness as the productive motor of his creative understanding of the demystified and spiritually disjointed *lebenswelt* of the twentieth century. As he writes in his late notes: "Max Weber's illness, no coincidence? [...] his philosophical understanding has deepened, broadening his view immeasurably. What would he be without the illness?" His notes place the brilliant scientist, who struggled with psychiatric problems for many years and teetered on the brink of suicide a number of times, within the context of sick thinkers and poets who were constitutive for the existential understanding of the modern age. "Is illness a prerequisite for the deepest insights? Kierkegaard, Nietzsche? Hölderlin?" (Jaspers 1981, p. 649).

For Jaspers, in other words, the sick artist and thinker pays a price for his intellectual radicality, which springs from the bedrock of psychological disorder. He is unable to take refuge under the shelter of normality and is condemned to perceive the mental chaos of the time with his senses wide open. This will take him to the limits of his endurance and often far beyond. The normal citizen, on the other hand, is able to hide in the orderliness of his life without becoming sick in the general sense of the word. Yet the price he pays for this is an inability to glimpse reality's more profound rifts and contradictions.

1.4

Against this background Jaspers portrays Hölderlin as a mentally ill artist with "an unstable frame of mind," who seeks protection from the experiences which are destroying him in the orderly lives of his middle-class friends. He cites a letter from 1797 in which Hölderlin describes "well-composed rationalists" as a safe shelter "because they direct you so well when you do not know whether you are in accord with yourself and the world." A few years later the anguished poet feels exposed, vulnerable and stalked by dark forebodings. Jaspers illustrates this agitated state with a letter from 1801: "Once I could shout with joy because of a new truth, because of a better understanding of Him who is above us, now I am afraid that my lot might be like that of old Tantalus, who received more from the gods than he could bear" (Jaspers 1977, p. 148).

The psychological crisis, which redirects Hölderlin's life away from the path of the ordinary and into liminal regions of the mind, is constitutive for his status as an exceptional figure, whose talent for finding enduring forms for his perceptions remains with him right to the point of collapse: "But the experience, caused and aggravated by the illness, offers sense and has depth; it is not indifferent, it can burst forth like a revelation, it can be godlike." Jaspers uses dramatic terms to describe the "vehemence of divine influence" (Jaspers 1977, p. 148), which only has a genuinely negative impact on the poet when his mental disturbance is at its most extreme: "*Prior* to the beginning of his illness he hints at seemingly similar ideas only in a fragment of 'Empedokles' [...] Now it is the poet himself who is in danger, exactly he whose task it is to weave the divine danger into his poetry in such a way that it can be harmlessly passed on to man" (Jaspers 1977, p. 148 ff).

Wider society profits from the self-sacrifice of the artist, whose work transforms the truth from its devastating origins into a form that is bearable yet challenging. Hölderlin saw it this way himself. Jaspers cites from "As on a Holiday": "And hence it is that without danger now/ The sons of Earth drink heavenly fire./ Yet, fellow poets, us it behooves to stand/ Bareheaded beneath God's thunderstorms,/ To grasp the Father's ray no less, with our own two hands/ And, wrapping in song the heavenly gift/ To offer it to the people" (Jaspers 1926, pp. 111; Hamburger 1967, p. 375 f). Jaspers illustrates the destructive impact of the higher truth and the deficiencies of man as its ambassador with two lines from "Bread and Wine": "For not always a frail, a delicate vessel can hold them/ Only at times can our kind bear the full impact of the gods" (Jaspers 1926, p. 112; Hamburger 1967, p. 249).

The postulate of Jaspers' pathography, as substantiated by the cases of van Gogh and Hölderlin, is that in the modern age severe mental illness is a prerequisite for attaining deeper insights into reality: "Such experience, truly genuine, truly dangerous, is only possible among schizophrenics" (Jaspers 1977, p. 152). In *Strindberg and van Gogh* the chapter on "Schizophrenia and Modern Civilization" is devoted to the unique perspective which is opened up by the richly metaphysical art of the mentally ill. Never before, he wrote, had schizophrenic psychosis played such a dominant role within culture, so that "a number of high ranking people of today who became schizophrenic have impressed us with works from their years of illness"

(Jaspers 1977, p. 200). With van Gogh and Hölderlin in mind he writes: "It is as if a last wellhead of life should fleetingly come within sight, as if the hidden 'Whys' of all life had found here an immediate basis on which to resolve themselves. For us this is an emotional trauma which we could not endure for long, to which we would gladly turn our backs. [...] It is a trauma which does not easily lead to the assimilation of what is foreign, but which demands the transposition into a different form, which is acceptable to us. His world is terribly exciting but it is not our world. Questions emanate from it—an appeal to our own existence with the beneficial effect that a change takes place" (Jaspers 1977, p. 202).

It is these experiences of crisis, Jaspers writes, intensified through pathology, that distinguish the sick poets of the emerging modern age from those of the classical era: "Goethe, for instance, could never have had this experience" (Jaspers 1977, p. 152). Jaspers then hones in further on the bourgeois hero Goethe, who had also been superseded by Hölderlin as the principal intellectual figure in the Stefan George circle: "No other works can be compared with them. In contrast, even Goethe can be compared with others and represents, as it were, the highest type of human expression" (Jaspers 1977, p. 153).

Twenty-five years later, in his acceptance speech for the Goethe Prize, Jaspers developed this point of view more explicitly, categorically prioritizing the morbid modern age over the harmony of classicism. The existential philosopher explained its title "Our Future and Goethe" with laconic clarity: "Goethe's world is over." He refused to see the "modern world," Jaspers explained, and in his worldly wisdom blithely ignored all the evidence that even in his day pointed to a "rupture in *Dasein*" (Jaspers 1951, p. 40 ff). Everything that [Goethe] described as "sick," Jaspers regarded as a worthy "exception." Goethe's good health, he believed, his desire "to be a well-rounded individual" had closed him off from a more profound view of things: "Goethe opted for the realization of a full human life; he was not a victim like Kierkegaard or Nietzsche" (Jaspers 1951, p. 50 ff).

For Jaspers, the philosophers Kierkegaard and Nietzsche stand, alongside the artists Hölderlin and van Gogh, for the productive connection between psychopathology and modernity, with Max Weber as their representative from the sciences. At the end of his pathography Jaspers reaffirms the singular importance of illness for the life's work of each of these exceptional figures, starting with Hölderlin: "This uniqueness originates in the fact that a quite extraordinary poet who, while not yet ill, was a poet of the first order, becomes schizophrenic in just this manner. There is no other case of such a combination. The only other case which stands comparison is van Gogh in the field of the graphic arts" (Jaspers 1977, p. 153).

Undoubtedly, the enthusiastic view of the link between genius and madness that appears in Jaspers' pathographies has its origins, in terms of the history of ideas, in the classical genius aesthetic, which celebrated the expression of "the unlearned, the underived, the unlearnable, the underiveable, the profoundly individual, the divine" in defiance of *Regelpoetik,* [the prescriptive poetry of the Baroque] (Schmidt 2003). This is, however, a far cry from the "promethean genius with his self-assured declaration of autonomy" as the young Goethe phrased it. Jaspers' understanding of genius, in keeping with Hölderlin, was bound up with receptivity, "a kindred intimacy with the giver," as the hymn "As on a Holiday…" describes it (Schmidt 2003, p. 135 f). The schizophrenic suffering merely intensifies the receptivity that is already present in the original and individual talent. Thus the intuition of divine unity enters into a charged relationship with the experience of the disjointedness of the time, and finds sublime expression in the philosophical, poetic, and artistic work.

1.5

Astonishingly in Jaspers' *Notizen zu Martin Heidegger*, which he mostly made after 1945, there are also entries which revolve around the topic of "exception" and "illness." Provocatively, he writes: "The great talent which confuses itself with the exceptions of existence." What occasioned this harsh judgment of his former friend, whom Jaspers never personally spoke to again after severing all contact in 1933, aside from a few letters which were exchanged in later years? The annotations show that it was Heidegger's Nietzsche lectures that provoked Jaspers to react so strongly. After reading them Jaspers noted how presumptuous it was of Heidegger to count himself among the "rare few who were called to the path of thought" (Jaspers 1978, p. 206). Jaspers' response is an allusion to the topos of genius and madness: "Confusing the great cost of exceptionality and mental illness with that which is neither exceptional nor illness but a de facto claim to the singularity of grandiloquent whisperings." When Jaspers then inquires into Heidegger's "reaction to van Gogh, Hölderlin, Kierkegaard, Nietzsche," he notes disapprovingly that Heidegger has obviously set himself the task of "'appropriating' the exception" but that this has resulted in a "confusion of greatness, talent, genius and exception." Jaspers sums up with a rhetorical question: "Heidegger touches on something essential, debases it, sheds a false light on it and makes false claims for it. The normality of the healthy mind, which wrongly and in vain adopts the gestures of the exceptional one?" (Jaspers 1978, p. 207).

Jaspers first encountered Heidegger attempting to approach such an exceptional figure in his 1936 lecture "Hölderlin and the Essence of Poetry." A good year before Jaspers received a copy sent with "best regards" from the author, he was informed about its salvation history dimension by Karl Löwith, who had attended the lecture in Rome. A former student of Heidegger's at Marburg who had been forced into exile as a German of Jewish descent, Löwith asked in astonishment why his teacher was now talking about Hölderlin's later poems, that were so ahead of their time while wearing insignia that was so very much of the time: 'His Hölderlin lecture was beautifully and artfully composed—but what the essence of poetry has to do with the swastika he was wearing in his button hole is difficult to fathom.' His solution must be this: "to make a decision is to be guilty one way or another." By the way, he closed with verse 7 of *Bread and Wine*: 'what to say or do in the meantime,/ I don't know, and what use are poets (=philosophers) in such destitute times?'.

Although Jaspers received *Elucidations of Hölderlin's Poetry* for Christmas 1943 from Heidegger, and made a number of markings on "Hölderlin and the Essence of Poetry," he probably did not make any notes on the eschatological dimension of Heidegger's thinking until he received *Off the Beaten Track* with "best wishes" in 1950 (Heidegger 1950). His anger at its portentous salvation history elements shines through in the dry sarcasm of his résumé: "Heidegger's new writing, essentially the preparation for the preparation, is directed at the entire Western world, and at something absolutely new that he 'senses',—thus: anticipating and whispering where it will be seen—[…] and in these texts—from Hölderlin but apparently from others too (e.g. Nietzsche) he finds sentences for which 'we are not yet ready'" (Jaspers 1978, p. 65).

This is not the place to dwell on Heidegger's understanding of Hölderlin in terms of the history of salvation. The point is to look at Jaspers' comparative notes to see the importance he ascribed to mentally ill exceptional figures as pioneers of the modern age, and also how firmly he drew the line at the possibility of approaching them with an eye to disambiguating their unconventional insights. Thus we see how, with Heidegger in mind, Jaspers notes the difficulty, within the context of "creativity […] in the mentally ill" of listening to those who like Hölderlin "without becoming untruthful, bear witness to that which cannot be appropriated and remain unchanged." He counters Heidegger's interpretations with his unintelligibility theorem, raising the exceptional cases of Nietzsche and Hölderlin onto a psychopathological pedestal, so to speak, as prophetic figures of the modern age, in order hermeneutically to afford them their due respect: "The intellectual works of the mentally sick are not sick—they can be understood—but not assimilated like the works of the healthy, but at a distance of reverence before that which is manifesting itself, in the case of Hölderlin or van Gogh, not with every person with this type of mental illness" (Jaspers 1978, p. 232).

Jaspers' pathographical distancing from Heidegger's reading of Hölderlin is yet more pronounced in his late notes on the poet. Unpublished during his lifetime, these constitute the conceptual framework of a chapter that was to address "Philosophers in Poetry" in volume III of *The Great Philosophers*. In the introduction, Jaspers cites Hellingrath's edition as an outstanding example of how to fuse the late poetry into a provisional whole without conclusively pinning down the psychotically accelerated shifting of thought: "There was a mutability in Hölderlin—during the transition period and once delirium had set in—which it is hopeless to try to follow in terms of understanding his seeing and thinking, because this mutability is not one single objective path, but increasingly, when compared against clearly defined intentionality, becomes haphazard inconsistency." Here, too, Jaspers' "understandability boundary" guards against the hermeneutic temptation to appropriate Hölderlin for outside interests (Jaspers 1981, p. 967).

In order to illustrate what might constitute a transgression of that boundary, Jaspers adds a "distant analogy to the fantastical interpretations of pre-Socratic fragments." This is an implicit reference to Heidegger's interpretation of Anaximander, a passage which in Jaspers' personal copy of *Off the Beaten Track* is covered with annotations. His notes on Hölderlin draw a contentious parallel between "the destruction of the texts and the ruination of the fragments in the transcriptions," equating the unavoidable pathologies of the historical process with the biological destruction meted out to Hölderlin by the psychotic process (Jaspers 1981, p. 967).

Jaspers does not directly name Heidegger until just after this, when he accuses him of appropriating the poetic eschatology for his history of being, much in the way that psychiatrists violate the understandability boundary when faced with the alien phenomena of mental illness: "Such outrageous attempts resemble interpretations of schizophrenic delusions—they are grounded in the methodological principles which Heidegger established as a form of 'thinking' against science and without science,—as a 'dialogue' (but the other party does not respond)" (Jaspers 1981, p. 967). Jaspers closes with a verdict which he put forward in a similar form around this time in response to psychoanalytical and psychosomatic interpretations: "[Such attempts] are the ruin of reason, the release of the abominable, of claims to power—fantasies, which people are increasingly ready to be enchanted by, but which resolve nothing" (Jaspers 1981, p. 967).

In his notes on Hölderlin, Jaspers emphasizes the destructive side of psychopathology in order to protect the poet from intrusive interpretations using the postulate of the understandability boundary. He is not, however, implying that the late poems cannot be read in a meaningful way. Jaspers' thoughts seek a third way between the psychopathological Skylla of total incomprehensibility and the philosophical Charybdis of totalizing comprehension. Thus on the one hand, he calls to mind Hellingrath's admirable efforts concerning the late texts, which for so many people—according to Lange's pathography—had seemed like a "confusion" until that point. On the other hand, Jaspers urgently warns against Heidegger's interpretations: "It would be a new error to want to find more in these papers than there is—to want to interpret more into them than is meaningfully possible" (Jaspers 1981, p. 967; Schmidt 1995, p. 111).

1.6

To sum up, one can say that Hellingrath's edition inspired the Stefan George circle to mythically inflate the eschatological context of "Bread and Wine," shifting it, so to speak, into the "unreal distance" (Hoffmann 1995, p. 87). Later, Heidegger philosophically accentuated the salvation history dimension in Hölderlin. Jaspers was more than skeptical of this totalizing interpretation. His disapproval corresponded with his pathographical position that when dealing with Hölderlin, it is essential to recognize an understandability boundary that is both existential and psychopathological.

Finally, if we turn to Jaspers' own engagement with Hölderlin's "Bread and Wine," the numerous annotations suggest that this elegy spoke to him more than any other poem in the Hellingrath edition. His marginal note "Night," the title under which the poem was published separately in 1807 (Frühwald 2012, p. 494 f), shows that he must have been reminded of the romantic enthusiasm for the first stanza.

The connection to the romantics is also evident in the way Jaspers pathographically re-situates their interest in the borderline experience of psychological illness within the context of modernity. Thus his citations from the poem stem primarily from the seventh stanza, in which man is described as a "delicate vessel" that cannot contain the "fullness of the gods." One could also say: exhausted by the suffering he has endured and the knowledge he has received, the afflicted poet can only sit and wait, torn between feelings of emptiness and repletion, which Hölderlin associates with the night in equal measures. Such "hallowed night" is equivocal and is always bound up with man's claustrophobic "frenzied, wandering" (Hölderlin 1916, p. 124).

Yet such a state of emotional turmoil can appear ludicrously ecstatic to the ordinary eye, as Hölderlin describes it: "[…] may jubilant madness laugh at those who deride it,/ When in hallowed Night poets are seized by its power" (Hölderlin 1916, p. 121). His poem revolves around "holy drunkenness and frenzied oblivion" two phenomena that are as much part of the extraordinariness of this night as the "onrushing word, sleepless as lovers," or the "wine-cup more full" or the "life more daring." Ultimately however, the reality of the night for Hölderlin is a boundary experience, and one particularly "sacred" to "all those astray" (Hölderlin 1916, p. 120).

As a possible context for interpretation the night's ecstatic dimension, which is bound up with love and drunkenness and often teeters on madness, is just as valid as the salvation history worldview. Both perspectives undoubtedly have a radiance of their own and coincide, perhaps not coincidentally, in the symbols of bread and wine. In the poetic approach these symbols combine numerous variations on ecstasy and eschatology, Christian, classical, religious, and secular contexts for interpretation. Jaspers' reading shares Hölderlin's desire for a richness of meaning which, in the "destitute times" of the self-contained and self-destructive modern age, arises in people who are receptive by nature. Key for Jaspers, however, is the positive vagueness associated with the image of the night. Exceptional states and insights do not allow themselves simply to be translated into the language of day. The ancient-Christian ambiguity of truth which, as Plato put it, likes to wrap itself in the mask of madness, might be described as an appropriate challenge to an appropriative reading of the poet who regarded Plato's *Phaedrus* dialogue as a key text for his poetology (Kreuzer 2010, p. 27 f).

In this sense Jaspers' pathography of Hölderlin provides a unique interpretation of the productive ambiguity of the metaphysically animated poet, which has underpinnings that are both existential and psychopathological. Like Kant, Hölderlin did not seek the "path to absolute knowing." Yet from an early age his waking life was marked by the religious belief in a totality, which he intuited poetically but could not access philosophically. This apparently anachronistic dilemma of metaphysical "destitution," which Hölderlin happened upon in the context of idealism (Henrich 1992, pp. 767, 770), is what for Jaspers constituted his enduring modernity, particularly at a time when nothing seemed to point to any higher historical order. This awareness of the limits of the speakable reached its unconventional peak in the late poems, and it was not until a hundred years later that it would resonate with the zeitgeist.

Jaspers was a pathographer who came from psychiatry and tested his philosophical thinking with the exceptional figures of Hölderlin, Nietzsche, and van Gogh. In terms of interpretative approach, he showed critical reserve toward the growing temptation in the modern age to intellectually indulge "metaphysical needs" beyond the individual and their conscious life. Like Hölderlin, he owed this hermeneutic caution to Kant's critical philosophy. So it is not surprising that in Jaspers' copy of Hellingrath's edition, alongside "Bread and Wine" the epigram "The Root of All Evil" received the most attention. It reads: "Being at one is god-like and good, but human, too human, the mania/ Which insists there is only the One, one truth, and one way" (Hölderlin 1916, p. 3).

Acknowledgments My thanks to Lucy Powell for her excellent translation. Without footnotes, however, the finer details of her work cannot be properly conveyed.

References

Bormuth, M. (2002a). Lebensführung in der Moderne. Karl Jaspers und die Psychoanalyse. Stuttgart.

Bormuth, M. (2002b). Karl Jaspers als Pathograph. *Fundamenta Psychiatrica, 16*, 154–159.

Bormuth, M. (2006). *Life conduct in modern times. Karl Jaspers and Psychoanalysis.* New York.

Bormuth, M. (2007). Einsicht und Willen. Karl Jaspers als Pathograph Nietzsches. In M. Bormuth, K. Podoll, & C. Spitzer (Eds.), *Kunst und Krankheit. Studien zur Pathographie* (pp. 11–26). Göttingen.

Dilthey, W. (1916). *Das Erlebnis und die Dichtung.* Berlin.

Frühwald, W. (2012). *Gedichte der Romantik.* Stuttgart: Reclam.

Häfner, H. (1963). Prozeß und Entwicklung als Grundbegriffe der Psychopathologie. *Fortschritte der Neurologie und Psychiatrie, 31*, 393–438.

Hamburger, M. (1967). *Friedrich Hölderlin. Poems and Fragments.* Ann Arbor: University of Michigan.

Heidegger, M. (1944). *Erläuterungen zu Hölderlins Dichtung.* Frankfurt am Main: Vittorio Klostermann.

Heidegger, M. (1950). *Holzwege.* Frankfurt am Main. : Vittorio Klostermann

Henrich, D. (1988). Denken im Blick auf Max Weber. In K. Jaspers & M. Weber (Eds.), *Gesammelte Schriften. With an introduction by Dieter Henrich* (pp. 7–31). Munich: Piper Verlag.

Henrich, D. (1992). *Der Grund im Bewußtsein. Untersuchungen zu Hölderlins Denken (1794–1795).* Stuttgart : Klett-Cotta-Verlag.

Hoffmann, P. (1995). Hellingraths dichterische Rezeption Hölderlins. In G. Kurz, et al. (Eds.), *Hölderlin und die Moderne* (pp. 74–104). Tübingen: Attempto Verlag.

Hölderlin, F. (1916). *Sämtliche Werke. Vierter Band. Gedichte 1800–1806*, Ed. Norbert v. Hellingrath. Munich: Georg Müller Verlag.

Janzarik, W. (1974). *Themen und Tendenzen der deutschsprachigen Psychiatrie.* Berlin: Springer-Verlag.

Jaspers, K. (1926). *Strindberg und van Gogh. Versuch einer pathographischen Analyse unter vergleichender Heranziehung von Swedenborg und Hölderlin* (2nd ed.). Berlin: Springer-Verlag.

Jaspers, K. (1951). Unsere Zukunft und Goethe (1947). In K. Jaspers (Ed.), *Rechenschaft und Ausblick* (pp. 30–58). Munich: Piper Verlag.

Jaspers, K. (1963). *General psychopathology* (2 Volumes; trans: J. Hoenig & M. W. Hamilton). Baltimore: Johns Hopkins University Press.

Jaspers, K. (1977). *Strindberg and van Gogh. An attempt of a pathographical analysis with reference to parallel cases of Swedenborg and Hölderlin* (trans: O. Grunow & D. Woloshin). Tucson: University of Arizona Press.

Jaspers, K. (1978). *Notizen zu Martin Heidegger*, Ed. Hans Saner. Munich: Piper Verlag.

Jaspers, K. (1981). *Die großen Philosophen. Nachlaß 1. Darstellungen und Fragmente*, Ed. Hans Saner. Munich: Piper Verlag.

Jaspers, K. (1981). *Die großen Philosophen. Nachlaß 2. Fragmente, Anmerkungen, Inventar*, Ed. Hans Saner. Munich: Piper Verlag.

Jaspers, K. (1997). *Friedrich Nietzsche. An introduction to the understanding of his philosophical activity.* Baltimore: Johns Hopkins University Press.

Kreuzer, J. (2010). Das geistesgeschichtliche Klima in Hölderlins Jugend. In U. Gonther & J. E. Schlimme (Eds.), *Hölderlin und die Psychiatrie* (pp. 18–37). Bonn: Psychiatrie-Verlag.

Lange, W. (1909). *Hölderlin. Eine Pathographie.* Stuttgart: Enke Verlag.

Lombroso, C. (1887). *Genie und Irrsinn: in ihren Beziehungen zum Gesetz, zur Kritik und zur Geschichte.* Leipzig: Reclam Verlag.

Müller-Seidel, W. (1993). Nachwort. In W. Müller-Seidel (Ed.), *Exzentrische Bahnen. Ein Hölderlin-Brevier* (pp. 211–244). Munich: Deutscher Taschenbuch Verlag.

Müller-Seidel, W. (1995). Diltheys Rehabilitierung Hölderlins. In G. Kurz, et al. (Eds.), *Hölderlin und die Moderne* (pp. 41–73.) Tübingen: Attempto Verlag.

Nietzsche, F. (1921). *Selected letters.* Whitefish, MT: Kessinger Publishing.

Nietzsche, F. (1983). *Untimely meditations.* Cambridge: Cambridge University Press.

Nordau, M. (1892). *Entartung* (2 Volumes). Berlin: Duncker.

Nordau, M. (1913). *Degeneration* (2 Volumes). London: heinemann.

Oelmann, U. (2002). Norbert von Hellingrath. In J. Kreuzer (Ed.), *Hölderlin-Handbuch. Leben—Werk—Wirkung* (pp. 422–426). Stuttgart: Metzler.

Peukert, D. (1989). *Max Webers Diagnose der Moderne.* Göttingen: Vandenhoeck & Ruprecht.

Radkau, J. (2005). *Max Weber. Die Leidenschaft des Denkens.* Munich: Carl Hanser Verlag.

Rilke, R. M., & von Hellingrath, N. (2011). *Briefe und Dokumente,* Ed. K. F. Bohnenkamp. Göttingen: Georg Müller Verlag.

Schmidt, J. (1963/64). Der Nachlass Norbert von Hellingraths. *Hölderlin-Jahrbuch, 13,* 147–150.

Schmidt, J. (1995). Hölderlin im 20. Jahrhundert. Rezeption und Edition. In G. Kurz, et al. (Eds.), *Hölderlin und die Moderne* (pp. 105–125). Tübingen: Wallstein Verlag.

Schmidt, J. (2003). Hölderlin: Die idealistische Sublimation des naturhaften Genius zum poetisch-philosophischen Geist. In T. Roberg & F. Hölderlin. *Neue Wege der Forschung* (pp. 115–139). Darmstadt: Wissenschaftliche Buchgesellschaft.

Schlimme, J. (2010) Karl Jaspers. Pathographie zwischen 'genetischem Verstehen' und Existenzerhellung. In U. Gonther & J. E. Schlimme (Eds.), *Hölderlin und die Psychiatrie* (pp. 177–193). Bonn: Psychiatrie-Verlag.

von Hellingrath, N. (1944). *Hölderlin-Vermächtnis,* Ed. Ludwig v. Pigenot. Munich : Bruckmann.

Weber, M. (1978). *Economy and society,* Eds. G. Roth & C. Wittich. California: University of California Press

Chapter 2
Hermeneutical and Dialectical Thinking in Psychiatry and the Contribution of Karl Jaspers

Otto Dörr

2.1 Hermeneutics and Psychiatry

Hermeneutics has been conceived as a method oriented to the understanding and correct interpretation of texts. But according to Gadamer, the hermeneutic problem vastly exceeds the domain of the methodological, since "the understanding and interpretation of texts is not merely a concern of science, but obviously belongs to human experience of the world in general" (2006, p. XX). The founder of hermeneutics in the 19th century, Schleiermacher, states something similar: "the art of understanding is necessary for the interpretation of texts, but also in the interaction with persons" (cit. by Gadamer 1992, p. 293). In the same sense, Gadamer states: "What is to be understood is now not only the exact words and their objective meaning, but also the individuality of the speaker or author" (Gadamer 2006, p. 186). When trying to understand what tradition has meant in any of the fields of human experience, we cannot avoid going beyond the mere understanding of the text we have before us, since this will transmit to us, inevitably, certain viewpoints and/or certain truths. And how can we be sure of the legitimacy or truth value of what is understood? This is precisely the role of hermeneutics: *to constitute the experience of truth*, where natural science appears surpassed, as it occurs with history, art, law, etc. (i.e., in the social sciences). Now, Gadamer himself expresses in another context: 'That art of understanding we call hermeneutics has to do with what is incomprehensible and with the process of grasping the unpredictable aspects of the psycho-spiritual functioning of the human being'. We ask: With hermeneutics so defined, is it possible to find the existence of a more characteristic field for its application than that

O. Dörr (✉)
Faculdad de Medicina, Universidad Diego Portales, Santiago de Chile, Chile
e-mail: odoerrz@gmail.com

Dept. de Psiquiatria, Facultad de Medicina, Universidad de Chile,
Campus Oriente, Av. La Paz 841, Santiago de Chile, Chile

T. Fuchs et al. (eds.), *Karl Jaspers' Philosophy and Psychopathology*,
DOI 10.1007/978-1-4614-8878-1_2, © Springer Science+Business Media New York 2014

of psychopathological phenomena? In what other field dealing with human beings are we going to find these two conditions more obviously united: that something is at the same time incomprehensible and unpredictable? Every experienced psychiatrist will be able to recognize how often psychopathological phenomena surpass the possibilities of natural sciences, e. g. by attempting to "explain" delusion with the energetic theory of psychoanalysis or through measurement of neurotransmitters.

Following Dilthey, Jaspers (1959/1997, p. 250 ff.) recognized early this particularity of the psychopathological world when he separated precisely what is explainable from what is understandable. With the method of explanation we approach clinical reality in the manner in which physicists study matter, and thus we calculate the size of cerebral ventricles, quantify intellectual capacity or measure the concentration of catabolites of neurotransmitters in urine, etc. With the method of understanding, on the other hand, we have access to phenomena that resist our own eagerness to quantify them, such as feelings and emotions, the experience of art in general, the world of interpersonal atmospheres, etc. Or one may say generally, here we are dealing with the whole world of meaning. How one psychic phenomenon arises from another is something very different from the linear causality of the physical world, and the method of understanding intends to do justice to that difference. To be able to understand the biographic sense of a given illness or to interpret a delusion within itself and not from supposed extraconscious causalities are two typical tasks where the psychiatrist has to employ the methods of understanding and hermeneutics in their purest forms. But a warning is in order that, namely, Jaspers' understanding-explanation distinction is no longer fully valid if one looks at it from the perspective of the new paradigm of the natural sciences, also called the paradigm of "complexity." The historical evolution of epistemology in the 20th century has drawn methods of explanation close to those of understanding (Hawking and Mlodinow 2010; Kuhn 2002).

This distinction between the understandable and the explainable has also been discussed by Wiggins and Schwartz (1988). These authors claim that it is very wide, it does not sufficiently clarify the different types of existing connections, and that it is valid only in some cases (i.e., what they call cases "of higher region") (p. 21). There would be a lower level of connections, which corresponds to causal relationships, but also "an 'intermediate region', (where) meanings and causes interweave … and become almost indistinguishable. The concepts of meaningfulness and causality fail to capture adequately what is essential to this teleological region" (p. 21). Besides, "Jaspers fails to tell us why this self-evidence should be found in meaningful connections and not in causal ones" (p. 18). In agreement with these authors, modern epistemology clarifies that unquestionable evidence exists only in spontaneous and naïve everyday life because in science all evidence must be submitted to critique (Bunge 1980). However, one has to recognize that Jaspers puts rather strict limits on the method of understanding, since for him not only the extraconscious elements would remain inaccessible to comprehension, but also existential freedom, and thus, personal decisions would stay outside the field of the understandable. On the other hand, however, he proposed with conviction that meaningful relations are self-evident in the general framework, but that in the particular cases we can only affirm the reality or truth of a relation when objective data exist (Jaspers 1997, pp. 357 f.).

Now, what first interests us in this context is to clarify the relationship between understanding, in the sense of Jaspers, and hermeneutics. They certainly have much in common and in fact the two first "laws" of psychological understanding, according to Jaspers, have also been elaborated in detail by Hans-Georg Gadamer (2006). Jaspers' first "law" says that every understanding is an interpretation, and hermeneutics has been defined for the past two centuries as the art and/or science of interpretation. The second law asserts that understanding occurs "in a hermeneutical circle," and this corresponds almost exactly to Gadamer's "rule of hermeneutics": "The movement of understanding therefore roams so from the whole to the part and again to the whole. The task is to widen in concentric circles the understood unit of meaning ... The confluence of all details in the whole is the criterion for the rightness of understanding" (Gadamer 1992, p. 63). But we must remember that the movement of understanding works in this manner not only in hermeneutic sciences, but also in natural sciences. Nothing is an isolated "in itself": "everything that *is* and *appears* is a local distinction with respect to the field *from where* it appears and *where* it appears" (Pelegrina 2006; to see Luhmann 1998).

In spite of the similitude of these two methods, there are also some differences. First, Jaspers limits his method to the world of meaningful connections of psychic life, particularly the one of psychiatric patients. Thus, he says: "We sink ourselves into the psychic situation (of our patient) and *understand genetically by empathy* how one psychic event emerges from another" (1997, p. 301). Second, the hermeneutical method is wider than Jaspers', because it can be applied not only to the psychic (the subjectivity of the other), but also to texts and to the whole of reality. Thus, Gadamer postulates that the concept of understanding acquires an "almost religious tone" and that "to understand is to participate immediately in life, without any mediation through concepts" (2006, p. 208). Third, while the strict relation existing between hermeneutical and phenomenological method, in Husserl's sense, appears unquestionable, Jaspers resisted taking the step from descriptive to eidetic phenomenology, although we find in many passages in his *General Psychopathology* statements clearly pointing toward this method. So, for example, when he says "sinking oneself into the particular case often teaches us—from the phenomenological point of view—what is general for a multiplicity of cases." This general component, which is captured from the particular case, does not correspond to a mere generalization from determined empirical findings, but evidently to the perception of an *eidos*. By contrast, however, Husserl's call "to the things themselves," or his statement that the method of free variation "allows us to extract the *eidos* as something invariant starting from the diversity of manifestations," show an extraordinary similitude with Gadamer's claim regarding the hermeneutical method: "All correct interpretation must be on guard against arbitrary fancies and the limitations imposed by imperceptible habits of thought, and it must direct its gaze 'on the things themselves'" (Gadamer 2006, p. 269). We will return later to the topic of the relations between phenomenology and hermeneutics.

Even during the first encounter with a psychiatric patient, one is already faced with the need to adopt a hermeneutic attitude. Let us consider Rümke's description of the "Praecox-Gefühl" (feeling of the schizophrenic), which he considers the central element in the diagnosis of this illness (Rümke 1958), and especially heed how it precisely matches the important concept of "prejudice" in Gadamer's thought, that is, "a judgement that is rendered before all the elements that determine a situation have been finally examined" (2006, p. 273). We described something similar with respect to depressive illness (Doerr-Zegers 1979, 1980). There also exists something like a "feeling of the melancholic," which becomes more intense the closer the condition becomes to stupor, the objective side of which is the phenomenon that we called "cadaverization" affecting the depressive body. The strict separation of *true* from *false* prejudgments is seen as one of the major tasks of hermeneutics in the interpretation of both art and history. In psychiatry, on the other hand, it will be an important task for the teacher to perform for his pupil, to teach him to grasp these atmospheric emanations coming from the patient and to distinguish true from false impressions while making the diagnosis.

This first encounter with the patient acquires particular importance in the field of psychoses. In these diseases the hermeneutical task must begin in that moment, apparently somewhat more superficially; this is the atmospheric emanation in the sense set forth by Tellenbach (1968). Gadamer himself was open to the possibility of incorporating the pre-verbal world to the hermeneutical task through the importance he attached to the concept of "taste" or rather of "good taste" (p. 32). For Gadamer "taste, in its essential nature, is not but a social phenomenon of the first order" (2006, p. 32). What is normally called "lack of contact," "flat affectivity," or "distance" in the schizophrenic patient is difficult to define, yet it corresponds to a pre-verbal originary phenomenon as accurate as taste. For Gadamer "good taste is always sure of its judgement" (2006, p. 32). In encounters with the schizophrenic patients, we lack a certain feeling of community, our emanations do not harmonize; they do not have the same tonal quality. Subsequent difficulty in verbal communication through language is almost always preceded by this failed pre-verbal communion.

In the case of depressive patients, it is not harmony that is missing but the sensation that the patient is not completely a subject in his own right. In him there is a lack of that particularity evident in interpersonal encounters by which one is not there for the other as a mere object (in the way of things), but rather as a subject (i.e., as person). The fundamental element in which the other appears directly to me as a subject is, according to Sartre (1966), the look of the other. That look, which, when it objectifies me, allows me to perceive the other as a subject and not as a thing, is weakened in the depressive patient. In a certain way, "it has sunk behind the eyes," as we described in previous papers (Doerr-Zegers 1979, 1980). To know how to correctly interpret the shades of the interpersonal encounter with mental patients in the pre-verbal stage is also a hermeneutical task of great importance for the development of a good doctor-patient relationship.

Still, where hermeneutics reaches its greatest importance for psychiatry is in the *verbal moment* of the relationship with the patient. Here, we will leave aside the transcendental role of hermeneutics in psychotherapy in order to only refer to the diagnostic interview. Language is for Gadamer certainly not only the medium, but also the horizon of every hermeneutic experience: "Language is not just one of man's possessions in the world; rather, on it depends the fact that man has a *world* at all. The world as world exists for man as for no other creature that is in the world. But this world is verbal in nature" (2006, p. 440). On few occasions do we have the opportunity of proving this assertion of Gadamer with greater certainty than when we face a schizophrenic patient? Since the first descriptions of this disease, central importance was given to thought/language disturbances. The so-called loosening of associations by Bleuler (1911), classical incoherence (*Zerfahrenheit*), or neologisms have always been considered among the basic symptoms of schizophrenia. In a previous paper, we tried to demonstrate, within the multiplicity of forms that this disorder can adopt, that its most *substantive phenomenon is perhaps the loss of the "dialogical" character of the word.* And how does this alteration appear in the encounter with the patient? Perhaps the most characteristic feature is the sensation that the doctor has of understanding and of not understanding what the patient is saying at the same time. Let us omit the severe disturbances of language and focus our attention only on the loosening of associations. Here there are no failures in grammar nor in the structure of syntax; neither are there flagrantly abstruse contents, which in themselves confound communication. Nevertheless, we fail to understand what the patient wants to say. Gadamer himself provides the answer when he states: "Not only is the world world insofar as it comes into language, but language, too, has its real being only in the fact that the world is presented in it" (2006, p. 440).[1] In other words, if the world changes, language changes; if the perception of the world is altered, its expression will necessarily be altered. Now, in the failed dialogue with the schizophrenic patient the distance of his world from ours is manifested to us, but at the same time we perceive that the dialogue itself becomes schematic and difficult. What Gadamer underlines as the essentials of a conversation does not occur here: we cannot manage it as we wish; on the contrary, the conversation leads us in unexpected directions. "Thus a genuine conversation is never the one that we wanted to conduct. Rather, it is generally more correct to say that we fall into conversation, or even that we become involved in it" (2006, p. 385). Conversations with the schizophrenic patient occur, inversely, in an awkward way in that they are interrupted at every moment. Or, the investigator feels empty, without ideas, and has to make an effort to pose new questions and becomes more focused on simply avoiding the loss of the dialogue in an uncomfortable silence. In summary, what Gadamer described as the central element of a true conversation, of the hermeneutical dialogue, is missing here.

In the depressive patient the moment of verbal communication also has quite specific peculiarities. The most extreme form of this disturbance is certainly found

---

[1] In this context it is necessary to point out that in the framework of contemporaneous linguistics the idea prevails that linguistic meaning demands (as fundament) an extra-linguistic referent, i.e., embedded in a pre-linguistic ontology. Each being has its own features ("onto") and the differential, communicative correlation constitutes its "logos."

in depressive stupor. No reply comes from the patient; the other is absent. We are faced with something like a lifeless body. The process of "cadaverization" mentioned before is almost complete. In the moderate depressions of everyday practice the communicative disturbance is, naturally, much less severe. It maintains, however, that seal of lifelessness. Every psychiatrist will be able to remember that slow and somewhat forced nature which characterizes dialogues with the depressive patient. Unlike encounters with schizophrenic patients, there is nothing incomprehensible here. At no time are we perplexed, but rather we are annoyed by how slow he is and by the narrowing of his interests, which are limited to his own body or to the other classic themes of poverty and guilt. Even after the depressive episode has been resolved, communication is not very easy. These patients are too laconic to describe their improvement and, in turn, the doctor feels after the dialogue has begun that there is nothing else to talk about. A marked contrast is also observed between, on one hand, numerous complaints and the expression of suffering during the depressive state and, on the other hand, the near oblivion of the illness once the episode is past.

The same analysis can be done with respect to other psychopathological conditions, such as obsessive-compulsive disorder or hysteria. It seems fundamental to us that in each of these disorders a particular style of communication can be found the description and interpretation of which require the development of a hermeneutical attitude in psychiatry.

In summary, hermeneutics and psychiatry appear interrelated prior to all theory and any therapeutic process. In addition to its obvious importance in psychotherapy, hermeneutics plays a basic role in the moment of the first interview and of diagnosis, and also in the initial, wordless moment where the grasping of atmospheric emanations from the other as well as the creation of a concordant and consequently common atmosphere occurs.

2.2   Dialectics and Psychiatry

Dialectics dates back to the beginning of philosophic thinking, appearing in different forms in the two great pre-Socratic philosophers: Parmenides from Elea and Heraclitus from Ephesus. For Parmenides dialectics is a method which allows one to prove the falsehood of appearances that the senses give us and, in this way, to purify the thinking of irrationalities. For Heraclitus, on the contrary, dialectics represents the basic principle which structures and directs all that exists, since reality is ordered in polarities which need one another (see Verneaux 1977):

> Should there be no injustice, even the name of justice would be ignored. (Fragment No. 23)
> Good and evil are one. The physicians cut, burn and torture... making the patients a good that seems an evil. (Fragment No. 58)
> Illness makes health agreeable, hunger makes satiety agreeable, fatigue makes rest agreeable. (Fragment No. 111)

Plato uses dialectics as a method to get to the truth through dialogue and by proving the contradictions inherent in nature as well as in thinking. In Hegel the concept of dialectics reaches its greatest universality: dialectics would be to a certain extent, identical with the perhaps more universal feature of reality, which is its "restlessness." This concept is similar to that of "energeia" in Aristotle (1961). "Energeia" is present in daily life in the form of movement, but is also the motor of history and of all that exists in time. Both reality and knowledge would be one and the same process, but the truth of a process is only reached at the end since every cross section will show its internal contradiction: the contradiction between the bud and the blossom that refutes it will be resolved in the fruit; this is the so-called dialectic moment, when the synthesis overcomes the contradiction between the thesis and its denial, the antithesis.

We find dialectic thinking and/or dialectic interpretation of reality not only among philosophers. The religious historian Mircea Eliade (1967) demonstrated how dialectic thinking is at the foundation of every religion and particularly of the Asian ones. The Christian dogma itself of the "Incarnation of the Word" is a good example of what is radically sacred and what is radically profane. But the dialectic moment also appears frequently in works of great poets. Thus we read in Goethe's Book of Aphorisms:

> We and objects
> light and darkness,
> body and soul,
> spirit and matter,
> God and universe,
> idea and extension,
> what is ideal and what is real,
> sensuality and reason,
> phantasy and understanding,
> being and nostalgia. (Goethe 1966, p. 707)

Also, dialectic interpretation of reality is present today in all the natural sciences. It deals, however, with dialectics of contrary elements that constitute a unity, rather than with dialectics of contradictory elements that nullify themselves (see Jasinowski 1957). Ilya Prigogine (1996) asserts that a lack of "balance is the fundament of all stability."

Karl Jaspers was the first to apply dialectic thinking to psychiatry. For Jaspers, "psychic life and its contents are polarized in opposites. It is through the opposites, however, that everything is once more re-connected. Image calls forth counter image, tendencies call forth counter-tendencies and feelings other feelings in contrast" (1997, p. 340). He distinguishes categorical, biological, psychological and intellectual opposites. These opposites manifest themselves in different ways:

1. They oscillate back and forth through time without consciousness actively causing the transitions, as inspiration changes into expiration, grief into cheerfulness, etc.
2. The opposites fight with each other, the one hurling itself against the other.
3. The self decides between the opposites, excluding one in favor of the other.

"The two latter modes lead to radically different dialectical movements: a synthesis of 'this as well as that', in the other a choice—'either-or'" (p. 342). In the first form, a synthesis is produced between the opposites and a new movement arises, which opens the way to the whole. In the second, dialectics engages to the limits of the decision. Both forms carry a special risk for the psyche. Aiming at the whole, the psyche can lose the ground and "be enticed into pleasing generalities" (p. 242). On the other side, when the psyche endeavors to reach *the sure ground by deciding*, ergo sacrificing one of the opposites, it may become unnaturally and psychically impoverished.

Among Jaspers' many contributions to dialectic perspective, the most interesting is perhaps his attempt to apply it to the understanding of opposites in psychopathology. With schizophrenic patients, for example, the phenomenon of a drastic emancipation of a tendency without its counter-tendency is posited (e.g., automatism in accord with commands, echolalia, or echopraxia). Likewise, there are examples of failures in the union of the opposites, as it is the case with ambivalence. The emancipation of the counter-tendency can also result, which occurs, for example, in negativism. In this framework, Wolfgang Blankenburg (1966) successfully interpreted delusion as the emancipation of a theme with respect to the whole of the psyche. When it comes to neuroses, phenomena are also reported that could be interpreted as a sort of dialectics. One example is exhibited by the inability to make decisions or to arrive at some objective; but the most characteristic is without a doubt, according to Jaspers, the permanent (dialectic) alternation between tension and relaxation suffered by the neurotic, an opposition which can reach even biological levels. Finally, Jaspers describes how opposites have been described in most studies of the character and personality of humans: introversion/extraversion, narcissism/object-cathexis, schizoid character/hyperthymic character, etc. Jaspers warns, however, about the risks of the absolute generalization of the opposites and reminds us that "the deeper we grasp the understandable meaning, the more we are pointed on into the non-understandable, extra-conscious ground of life and the non-understandable, historical absolute of Existence itself" (p. 345).

But it was Wolfgang Blankenburg (1962, 1965, 1974, 1981) who definitely introduced dialectic thinking into psychiatry. Blankenburg's starting point is the hypothesis that certain positivity can be enclosed in what is *negative* (i.e., in the abnormality or illness). The question of the positivity of what is negative is found in many forms in daily life and also in the religious world, e. g. in Christianity: "the last will be the first"; "it is necessary to die in order to be resurrected"; etc. And thus Blankenburg (1965) underlines the positive aspects of schizophrenia, like the depth of the perception these patients have of the world, their nearness to genius, their metaphysical sense, their authenticity, etc. and later the positive aspects of hysteria, as, for example, the lack of rigidity, the easy adaptability, the capacity for entertaining, etc. of hysterical patients (Blankenburg 1974).

Following the line suggested by Blankenburg, we have tried to advance the dialectic perspective of the great psychopathological syndromes. As the initial model, we took the manic–depressive dyad in which the polar and dialectical character is evident: mania is the reverse of depression and vice versa. But at the same time,

Disor-ganized schizo-phrenia	Paranoid schizo-phrenia	Catatonic schizo-phrenia	Schizo-affective psychoses	Delusional mania or depression	Bipolar depression	Unipolar depression
Histrionic personality disorder	Conversion disorder	General-ized anxiety disorder	Panic disorder (ancient phobic neurosis)	Agora-phobia	Obsessive-compulsive disorder	Obsessive personality

Fig. 2.1   Polar structuration of the psychotic and non-psychotic syndromes

each one needs the other emphatically so that in some way the one is contained in the other and vice versa. It is noteworthy how frequently we perceive infinite sorrow behind the joy and hyperactivity of the manic, and, inversely, how we perceive feelings of envy and aggressiveness behind the sorrow and inactivity of the depressive patient, which are almost impossible to intuit from solely considering his weakened and harmless appearance. Additionally, what draws one's attention is the fact that situations triggering the two illnesses seem to be inclined to produce the opposite effect; they are marked by an inverse sign: what would result in joy for any normal person (a move to a better house, the happy marriage of a daughter, the birth of a child who is wanted, promotion at work, etc.) may trigger a depression, while those precipitating mania generally represent intolerable setbacks (e.g., the death of a very loved person, financial bankruptcy, the diagnosis of a serious or mortal illness, situations of great pressure, etc.). In other words, the manic develops his mania *against* depression, while the depressive patient develops his depression *against the* mania. What is manic can be seen as *what is positive* with respect to depression as a defense against that inability, that congealed anguish, that stopping of time. And conversely, what is depressing can be conceived as *what is positive* with respect to mania, as being saved from exhausting hyperactivity, from continuous disrespect for others or from an inability to maintain both thinking and behavior within rational and socially acceptable limits. We also observe a dialectic structure in the polarity established between the "not being able to" (*das Nicht-Können*) of the depressive phase and a total ability and availability in the manic phase.

But all the formerly-called endogenous conditions can also be seen as distributed between the depressive pole and the schizophrenic pole (Fig. 2.1). The extremes would be represented by unipolar depression and so-called disorganized schizophrenia. The schizo-affective psychoses would be equidistant from both poles. From these psychoses in the direction toward the schizophrenic pole, we observe the deployment of the rest of the forms of this illness: catatonic, paranoid and hebephrenic schizophrenia. In the other direction, we find cycloid psychoses, delusional manias, delusional depressions, bipolar forms and finally, unipolar depression. Janzarik (1959) suggested something similar in his description of "dynamic constellations

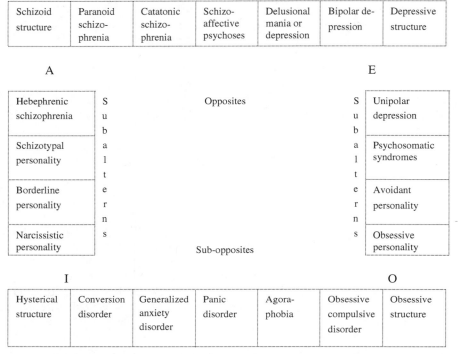

Schizoid structure	Paranoid schizo- phrenia	Catatonic schizo- phrenia	Schizo- affective psychoses	Delusional mania or depression	Bipolar de- pression	Depressive structure

A   E

Hebephrenic schizophrenia	S u b	Opposites	S u b	Unipolar depression
Schizotypal personality	a l t		a l t	Psychosomatic syndromes
Borderline personality	e r n		e r n	Avoidant personality
Narcissistic personality	s	Sub-opposites	s	Obsessive personality

I   O

Hysterical structure	Conversion disorder	Generalized anxiety disorder	Panic disorder	Agora- phobia	Obsessive compulsive disorder	Obsessive structure

Fig. 2.2 Fundamental psychopathological structures and their relation to common psychiatric syndromes (cf. Doerr-Zegers 1987)

in endogenous psychoses." This conceptualization allows a greater fidelity to the clinical fact of the multiple transitions among the different psychopathologic syndromes and resolves the old dispute between the theory of the "unique psychosis" and the one postulating the existence of perfectly different nosological entities (Doerr-Zegers 1987). If we enforce this dialectic conceptualization and widen it to the previously called "neuroses" and to the severe personality disorders, we can order all psychopathological, non-organic syndromes in a rectangle very similar to the one Aristotle employed in the logic of judgment, with contrary, subcontrary, subaltern, and contradictory elements (Figs. 2.2 and 2.3).

Such a resolution deals with a strange case of isomorphism between the logical structure of judgment and the forms through which that psychopathological region of reality is disclosed to us. This scheme allows us to distinguish between contrary (schizophrenic and depressive, hysterical and obsessive) and contradictory (depressive and hysterical, schizophrenic and obsessive) structures. There are transitions between the contraries and not between the contradictions. Regarding the contradictions and excluding the character of hysteria and depression, I refer to the interesting works of Alfred Kraus (1977, 1987) and in reference to another dyad (i.e., schizophrenic versus obsessive structure), to an enlightening work carried out by Hermann Lang (1985).

Fig. 2.3 Aristotle's square of oppositions

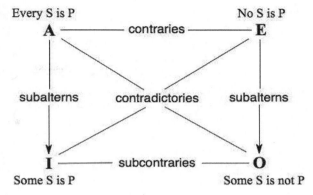

These structures are not simple reifications as is the case for categorical diagnoses, but "ideal" types, in the sense of Jaspers (1997, p. 560). For Jaspers, "dialectics is the form in which a basic aspect of meaningful connections becomes accessible to us" (1997, p. 345) and that is also precisely a structure in the style of the ones we are describing. The ideal types are for Jaspers always self-evident; they do not lead to theories but rather correspond to patterns through which particular events can be measured (1997, p. 357). Hence, Riemann (1975) described these same four structures from the perspective of the different forms of anxiety that characterize them. We, as well, have attempted in other works (Doerr-Zegers 1987) to do something similar, but from the point of view as to how temporality, spatiality and interpersonality are experienced as given to the person (especially as to how he experiences these in a bodily way).

To show what is depressive as polar with respect to what is schizophrenic, or what is obsessive with respect to what is hysterical is more than a semantic game or a mere theoretical digression. By seeing one as the positive side of the other and vice versa, we widen our capacity for understanding, prejudices are eliminated with respect to the supposed negativity of one or the other condition and a privileged way of therapeutic action is opened up to us. In order to avoid a mere adaptation to that non-existent "average" state of being, one must attempt to make the patient aware of the positivity of his supposedly "abnormal" features or symptoms, but in such a way that he begins a journey in the opposite direction toward the opposite pole. By doing so, he can approach the Greek notion of moderation because, as the old wisdom by Heraclitus says:

> (In the end) cold becomes warm, warm becomes cold, humid becomes dry and dry becomes humid. (Fragment No. 126)

2.3 Hermeneutics, Dialectics and Psychiatry

We have outlined some aspects of the relationship between hermeneutics and psychiatry and also between psychiatry and dialectics. We have underlined that hermeneutics already appears essential in the first encounter with the patient, both in its pre-verbal moment and in the verbal one. We have also pointed out the advantages that the dialectic perspective offers in psychiatry and how it is better adapted to the richness and complexity of psychopathological phenomena than other ways of thinking, for example, causal and linear ones.

Now the question arises: which relationship exists between phenomenology, hermeneutics and dialectics, and then between all of them and psychiatry?

Wiehl (1970) states that the relationships between phenomenology, dialectics and hermeneutics can be better understood if one starts from the concepts of theory and method. Thus, phenomenology is undoubtedly more a method than a theory, while dialectics is perhaps both at the same time; it even demands a dynamic (dialectic) unity between theory and method. Hermeneutics, in turn, is neither a theory nor a method, but something like an original understanding, which can allow one to distinguish between and establish the dialectic relationship between theory and method. As Jaspers says, the world as a whole is to a certain extent opened to hermeneutic understanding. We could add that one of the first perceptions resulting from this attitude is the dialectic structuring of reality. The distinction between theory and method appears as one of those dialectic structures. Phenomenology, hermeneutics and dialectics can be distinguished from any other form of theory because of their absolute reference to what is originary and primordial.

What has been developed up to now allows us to understand why phenomenology, hermeneutics and dialectics are so important for psychiatry. The object of our work as psychiatrists is the mentally ill human being, that is to say, the most complex reality in the universe, since what gets ill is precisely that what makes knowledge, culture and finally the human world possible: the mind or spirit. Therefore, it is a great temptation to fall into reductionist interpretations of human phenomena, whether these are of a psychological or a biological type. The complexity of the object of our science and the fact that we must finally objectify ourselves, however, force us to maintain as open an attitude as possible; and nothing is better to achieve this goal than adopting a hermeneutical attitude through which we can discover the dialectic structures of the human being. The phenomenological method will serve us, on the other hand, to deeply explore some particular aspects of this reality, while, last but not least, helping us achieve the right application of the derivative and quantitative methods of natural sciences, which in turn will enable us to manage this same reality.

Plato was the first to see the essential relationship between hermeneutics and dialectics. The "opening" characterizing hermeneutics is materialized in the question. In this context, Gadamer (2006, p. 356) states: "We cannot have experiences without asking questions." Now, certain negativity is inherent to the question. Socrates brought this negativity to its most radical dimension in his famous sentence: "I know that I know nothing." And this negativity of the hermeneutical question is isomorphic with the negativity of dialectic experience. "True experience is always negative," states Gadamer (2006, p. 347) and later adds: "The concept of experience means precisely this, that this kind of unity with oneself is first established. This is the reversal that consciousness undergoes when it recognizes itself in what is alien and different" (2006, p. 349). In his *Aphorisms*, Goethe says: "The experience is always only the half of the experience" (1966, p. 703), and, in the *Conversations with Eckermann*, states, "Experience consists in the fact that, in experiencing, we experience what we would have liked not to experience" (Eckermann 2000, p. 316). In consequence, each experience must pass through failure to reach its true dimension. To question, thereby starting from an attitude of the widest "opening," and to make manifest the experience of negativity are both substantive elements of everyday psychiatric practice. It is impossible to exercise the vocation of psychiatry without knowing how to question, how to fail and how to dialectically rescue some knowledge from this failure.

References

Aristotle. (1961). *Metaphysik*. Paderborn: Ferdinand Schöningh.
Blankenburg, W. (1962). Aus dem phänomenologischen Erkrankungsfeld innerhalb der Psychiatrie (unter Berücksichtigung methodologischer Fragen). *Schweizer Archiv für Neurologie und Psychiatrie, 90*(2), 412–421.
Blankenburg, W. (1965). Zur Differentialphänomenologie der Wahnwahrnehmung. *Der Nervenarzt, 36*(7), 285–298.
Blankenburg, W. (1966). Die Verselbständigung eines Themas zum Wahn. *Jahrbuch für Psychologie, Psychotherapie und medizinische Anthropologie13* (pp. 137–164). Freiburg: Karl Alber.
Blankenburg, W. (1974). Hysterie in anthropologischer Sicht. *Praxis der Psychotherapie, 19*, 262–273.
Blankenburg, W. (1981). Wie weit reicht die dialektische Betrachtungsweise in der Psychiatrie? *Zeitschrift für Klinische Psychologie und Psychotherapie, 1*(29), 45–66.
Bleuler, E. (1911). Dementia Praecox oder die Gruppe der Schizophrenien. In G. Aschaffenburg (Ed.), *Handbuch der Psychiatrie (Vol. IV, 1)*. Vienna: Deuticke.
Bunge, M. (1980). *Epistemología*. Barcelona: Ariel.
Doerr-Zegers, O. (1979). Análisis fenomenológico de la depresividad en la melancolía y en la epilepsia. *Actas Luso-Españolas de Neurología y Psiquiatría, 7*(2), 291–304.
Doerr-Zegers, O. (1980). Differentialphänomenologie des depressiven Syndroms (with H. Tellenbach). *Nervenarzt, 51*, 113–118.
Doerr-Zegers, O. (1987a). Fenomenología del lenguaje y esquizofrenia. In D. Barcia (Ed.), *Psiquiatría Antropológica* (pp. 129–154). Murcia: Secretariado de Publicaciones de la Universidad.
Doerr-Zegers, O. (1987b). Pensamiento dialéctico y estructuras de personalidad. *Rev Psiquiatría, 4*, 21–30.
Eckermann, J. P. (2000). *Conversaciones con Goethe*. Barcelona: MM Océano Grupo Editorial S. A.
Eliade, M. (1967). *Lo sagrado y lo profano*. Barcelona: Editorial labor.
Gadamer, H.-G. (1992). *Verdad y método II*. Salamanca: Ediciones Sígueme.
Gadamer, H.-G. (2006). *Truth and method*. New York: Continuum International Publishing Group.
Goethe, J. W. (1966). Aphorismen. In *Naturwissenschaftliche Schriften II*. Zurich: Artemis Verlag.
Hawking, S., & Mlodinow, L. (2010). *El gran diseño*. Barcelona: Crítica, S. K.
Janzarik, W. (1959). *Dynamische Grundkonstellationen in endogenen Psychosen*. Berlin: Springer Verlag.
Jasinowski, B. (1957). *Saber y dialéctica*. Santiago: Ediciones Universidad de Chile.
Jaspers, K. (1959). *Allgemeine Psychopathologie, 7*. unveränderte Auflage. Berlin: Springer.
Jaspers, K. (1997). *General psychopathology* (trans: Hoenig, J. and Hamilton, M. W.). Baltimore: Johns Hopkins University Press.
Kraus, A. (1977). *Sozialverhalten und Psychose Manisch-Depressiver. Eine existenz- und rollenanalytische Untersuchung*. Stuttgart: Ferdinand Enke.

Kraus, A. (1987). Fenomenología diferencial de la histeria y la melancolía. In D. Barcia (Ed.), *Psiquiatría Antropológica*. Murcia: Secretariado de Publicaciones de la Universidad.

Kuhn, T. (2002). *El camino desde la estructura*. Barcelona: Paidós.

Lang, H. (1985). Reflexiones antropológicas sobre el fenómeno de la obsesión. *Revista Chilena de Neuro-Psiquiatría, 23*(1), 3–9.

Luhmann, N. (1998). *Complejidad y Modernidad*. Madrid: Trotta.

Pelegrina, H. (2006). *Fundamentos Antropológicos de la Psicopatología*. Madrid: Ediciones Polifemo.

Prigogine, I. (1996). *El fin de las certidumbres*. Santiago: Editorial Andrés Bello.

Riemann, F. (1975). *Grundformen der Angst*. Munich: Reinhardt.

Rümke, H. (1958). Die klinische Differenzierung innerhalb der Gruppe der Schizophrenien. *Nervenarzt, 29,* 49–53.

Sartre, J. P. (1966). *El ser y la nada*. Buenos Aires: Losada.

Tellenbach, H. (1968). *Geschmack und Atmosphäre*. Salzburg: Otto Müller Verlag.

Verneaux, R. (1977). *Textos de los grandes filósofos. Edad Antigua*. Barcelona: Herder.

Wiehl, R. (1970). Begriffsbestimmung und Begriffsgeschichte. In R. Bubner et al. (Eds.), *Hermeneutik und Dialektik* (pp. 167–213). Tübingen: Mohr.

Wiggins, O. P., & Schwartz, M. A. (1988). Karl Jaspers' psychopathology and the problem of meaning. *Theory & Psychology, 8*(1), 16–27.

Chapter 3
Phenomenological Intuitionism and Its Psychiatric Impact

Sonja Rinofner-Kreidl

> *The fact is that the beginner in phenomenology finds it difficult to acquire a reflective mastery of the different focusings of consciousness with their different objective correlates.*
>
> Husserl 1983, p. 141

3.1 Introduction

The complexity of human beings and human behavior comes distinctly to light on occasion of psychic impairments and mental disorders. In order to understand complex modes of behavior we need complex methodologies. This is presumably the most basic and far-reaching insight we owe to Karl Jaspers' methodological considerations in his *General Psychopathology*. Accordingly, he demands for combining methods of explanation and methods of understanding.[1] As far as the latter is concerned, Jaspers claims to bring together hermeneutics as known from Wilhelm Dilthey's historically stamped "Lebensphilosophie" and Edmund Husserl's

---

[1]Relevant comments are spread throughout Jaspers's texts (1997a, cf. e.g. pp. 45–46, 303–305, 1997b, cf. e.g. pp. 451–462). Among others, the following passage draws on explanation and understanding as complementary methods: "The investigation of the meaningful aspects will always find both its limitation and its complementation in the causal findings while causal enquiry itself can penetrate into those fields where meaningful units provide elements for the posing of causal problems (as for instance the problem of the connection between certain personality-types, certain psychoses and certain types of creativity). If psychopathology is confined to one or other of these two lines of enquiry it is always in danger of becoming either an unreal fantasy or pure physiology denuded of the psyche." (Jaspers 1997b, p. 712, 1973, p. 596)

S. Rinofner-Kreidl (✉)
Department of Philosophy, Karl-Franzens-University Graz,
Heinrichstrasse 26/5, 8010 Graz, Austria
e-mail: sonja.rinofner@uni-graz.at

T. Fuchs et al. (eds.), *Karl Jaspers' Philosophy and Psychopathology*,
DOI 10.1007/978-1-4614-8878-1_3, © Springer Science+Business Media New York 2014

phenomenological explorations of human consciousness. At first glance, this looks like a daring eclecticism since Husserl's so-called pure and transcendental phenomenology seems incompatible with Dilthey's or Heidegger's hermeneutic projects. Jaspers' approach, however, makes sense when we take into account that the young psychiatrist Jaspers, when he sought an investigative method for psychopathology, focused on Husserl's early, pre-transcendental period and "reworked" Husserl's phenomenological procedures "so that they incorporated the hermeneutic insights of Dilthey [...], Simmel [...] and Weber [...]" (Schwartz and Wiggins 2004, p. 356). Correspondingly, it follows to conceive of complex methodologies as mixed methodologies composed of heterogeneous components. Indeed, it is a common notion that Jaspers bridges the gap between psychiatry and philosophy, on the one hand, and different philosophical traditions, on the other hand. This mixed methodological approach has gained recognition as an outstanding and paradigmatic project even though it fails (and always has done so) in representing mainstream psychiatric research.

The personal and philosophical relation between Jaspers and Husserl has been analyzed from different points of view.[2] Yet some aspects still await clarification. What is still missing, among others, is a reevaluation that takes into account the immanent hermeneutic potential of Husserl's *transcendental* phenomenology, which has remained widely unacknowledged. Therefore, the focus can avoid thoroughly discussed issues like horizontal intentionality, association, original time-constitution and other forms of passivity that have already been dealt with via genetic-phenomenological investigations. *Genetic phenomenology* is the project Husserl follows in his last working period comprising roughly the 1920s and 1930s. As is well known, Jaspers' interest in Husserl's phenomenology does not address this period. It rather refers to Husserl's early *descriptive psychology* as introduced in his two-volume masterpiece entitled *Logical Investigations*, which was published in 1900 and 1901. The influence exerted by the *Logical Investigations* on Jaspers' psychopathological work has been extensively and controversially discussed. Jaspers scholars seem to agree tacitly that referring to Husserl's transcendental philosophy cannot deliver any worthwhile findings given Jaspers' specific and restricted concern for phenomenology. Admittedly, Jaspers did not know the first volume of Husserl's *Ideas,* published in 1913, which was the breakthrough of transcendental phenomenology in his published works. Moreover, he explicitly rejects Husserl's conception of eidetic knowledge, which is an indispensable part of transcendental phenomenology. Husserl considers his transcendental turn an attempt to introduce his phenomenological method in a more explicit and more sophisticated manner than he did in the *Logical Investigations*. The latter, according to Husserl's retrospective self-criticism, was deficient insofar that it could not reliably ward off psychologism in the domains of logic and epistemology as long as the basic forms

---

[2] Cf. Walker (1994a); Walker (1994b); Walker (1995a); Walker (1995b); Wiggins et al. (1992); Wiggins and Schwartz (1997); Rinofner-Kreidl (1997); Schwartz and Wiggins (2004); Luft (2008); Rinofner-Kreidl (2008); Wiltsche (2008).

of human understanding remained conceived within the methodological framework of descriptive psychology.

In relation to the above-sketched methodological issues, the present paper aims at unfolding and supporting three theses. First, we contend that:

> **T1**) Husserl's transcendental phenomenology fosters arguments with substantial hermeneutic implications.[3] These arguments do not (primarily) build on well-known hermeneutic determinations of understanding, bringing into play the hermeneutic circle and similar issues of that ilk. They rather refer to the basic concepts underlying and guiding Husserl's intentional analysis (e.g., *intentional object, intentional act, intuition, attitude*).

Though this certainly strikes one as unusual—if one considers Dilthey's individualized biographical and historical brand of knowledge—"hermeneutics," in the present context, indicates the mode of understanding and intuitively explicating those mental contents that are given in pure consciousness. As a result, we do not have a stake in concrete tokens of individual consciousness. Human consciousness, rather, is considered exclusively as a manifestation of a specific form, namely a nexus of intentional structures. The relevant structures are actually realized in a particular consciousness even though they might be realized in every other individual consciousness as well. For the sake of clarity, we therefore associate Husserl's transcendental phenomenology with the project of *rational hermeneutics* in contrast to the more conventional *individualizing and historicizing hermeneutics*. Correspondingly, the notion of *personal intuition*, as we shall see later, does occur in Husserl's investigations, but only in a very specific context and in a thoroughly subordinate meaning, whereas it is of crucial importance in Jaspers' *Psychopathology* (cf. Jaspers 1997a, p. 313, 1973, p. 260). Presumably, there will be Husserl scholars who argue that emphasizing Husserl's rational hermeneutics amounts to reading his work against the grain. To be sure, Husserl's philosophy as a whole cannot be labeled as hermeneutic. It does not embody and, indeed, is incompatible with a full-blooded conception of hermeneutic philosophy. This is obvious if we, for instance, consider his quest for ultimate foundations and his goal of establishing a philosophical method in the form of rigorous science. Husserl himself is inclined to stick to traditional divisions when it comes to comparing such projects as hermeneutics and transcendental philosophy. However, in the course of several decades of research, Husserl became increasingly alert to the hermeneutic and aporetic aspects inherent to his project of intentional analysis. This inherent tendency typically appears when he considers the limits of phenomenological description, especially with respect to the original constitution of inner-time consciousness.[4] In the following we shall not

---

[3] For a more detailed account of how hermeneutics and transcendental phenomenology are related to each other see Rinofner-Kreidl (2002) and (2003).

[4] Cf. Husserl (1991); Rinofner-Kreidl (2000, pp. 431–436).

raise the special issue of an ineffable ultimate origin of consciousness. Rather, we shall be concerned with the general dynamics of a phenomenological description that comes into play due to its methodological framing. We contend that tracing out the hermeneutic aspects of transcendental phenomenology allows for gaining a more profound understanding of how to make use of an intuitive method to inquire into the multifarious manifestations of human consciousness. In particular, Husserl's phenomenology offers refined notions of intuition and subjectivity that are suited to improve our understanding of what goes on in certain areas of psychological and psychiatric research without succumbing to subjectivism and dogmatism. Our second thesis runs as follows:

> **T2)** Husserl's intuition-based transcendental phenomenology steers clear of subjectivism and dogmatism owing to its crucial interest in our ability to freely choose and change attitudes. The relating thesis will be labeled "AID," thus referring to the fact that, according to the methodological framework of transcendental phenomenology, the notions of *a*ttitude, *i*ntuition and *d*escription are inextricably interrelated.

In terms of T1) and T2), we will devote our most extensive considerations to offer a plausible interpretation as to how phenomenology and hermeneutics interact. In doing so, we shall pave the way for a new defense of a phenomenological intuitionism.[5] Throughout our reasoning, we will not dwell on a detailed discussion of Jaspers' methodology in his *General Psychopathology* though, occasionally, we will indicate some of its crucial points. In this respect, the main thrust of our considerations can be summarized in the following thesis:

> **T3)** As far as Husserl's early phenomenology ("descriptive psychology") is concerned we must indeed admit "that there is no real convergence between Jaspers' phenomenology and that of Husserl" (Walker 1994a, p. 132). Yet, it is shortsighted to refer exclusively to Husserl's *Logical Investigations* and ignore his later work. Earlier incongruities notwithstanding, it does promote our understanding of Jaspers' *Psychopathology* to explore the AID-thesis.

---

[5] For an instructive discussion of the general epistemological meaning of intuitive givens and intuitionism respectively see Pust (2000) and Bealer (1998). One of the most prominent critiques of ethical intuitionism, which is also relevant to epistemological intuitionism, was launched by Mackie (1977).

3.2 Intuitive Givenness and Methodological Framing

The idea that an entire philosophical theory could be grounded by accurately describing what is present to the mind is among the most fascinating and prolific projects of modern philosophy. In respect to method, this exciting project, which received a fresh impetus at the turn of the 19th to the 20th century, revolves around the notions of description and intuition. The phenomenological movement gathered momentum when Husserl, following the footsteps of his admired academic teacher Franz Brentano, called for cleaning the desk and gaining a new start by ignoring the sweeping (idealistic) philosophical systems of his age in favor of focusing on the immediately given contents of consciousness. Since then, turning one's attention to the immediately given contents of consciousness has been called "phenomenology," thereby indicating that one feels committed to *go back to the things themselves, that is, to the phenomena.*[6] Phenomena, spelled out in a phenomenological fashion, represent modes of appearances (of something) and modes of givenness, respectively.

According to Husserl, being able to justify one's beliefs with regards to structures and contents of the reality in which we find ourselves immersed, regardless of whether it is natural, social or spiritual, ultimately requires the ability to grasp the given phenomena intuitively and to describe their intentional content adequately. Therefore, the precise nature of the intuitive evidence at issue varies in dependence on the respective types of objects or states of affairs that the relating acts are directed toward.

> Genuine science and its own genuine freedom from prejudice require, as the foundation of all proofs, immediately valid judgments which derive their validity from originally presentive intuitions. The latter, however, are of such a character as prescribed by the sense of the judgments, or correlatively by the proper essence of the predicatively formed judgment-complex. (Husserl 1983, p. 36)

The quantity and nature of fundamental regions of objects that are discernible and the pertaining types of presentive intuitions, according to Husserl, cannot be postulated in advance or gained by way of deduction. One can only, as he maintains, "ascertain them by insight," meaning that one has to disclose them by originally presentive intuitions and fix them by judgments "which are faithfully fitted to what is given in such intuition" (Husserl 1983, p. 36). Proceeding like this, we cannot forestall that delusions, erroneous reports and inadequate linguistic representations of intuitive givenness occur.[7] Hence, ultimately relying on presentive intuitions does not exclude misinterpretations and conflicts that may occasionally arise (cf.

---

[6]Cf. "But to judge rationally or scientifically about things signifies to conform to the things themselves or to go from words and opinions back to the things themselves, to consult them in their self-givenness and to set aside all prejudices alien to them." (Husserl 1983, p. 35)

[7]Cf. "How many of the results of the analyses undertaken here are definitive, only the future can tell. Certainly much of what we have described will have to be described otherwise sub specie aeterni. But one thing we may and must strive for: that at each step we faithfully describe what we, from our point of view and after the most serious study, actually see." (Husserl 1983, p. 235)

Husserl 1983, p. 37). Given that we bear in mind these qualifications, we can state the basic commitment of a phenomenological intuitionism as follows:

> Immediate 'seeing', not merely sensuous, experiential seeing, but seeing in the universal sense as an originally presentive consciousness of any kind whatever, is the ultimate legitimizing source of all rational assertions. (Husserl 1983, p. 36)

As we shall explain in the next section, this phenomenological intuitionism requires further qualification. Still, it is clear that for Husserlian-style phenomenologists it is vital to acknowledge different types of intuitions according to different types of objects referred to. Therefore, our talk about "intuitions" remains ambiguous and misleading unless we specify the beliefs (and judgments) at issue and the relating types of legitimizing intuitive evidence. For instance, "intuition" may refer to sensuous intuition, that is, perceptual givenness, or to acts of clear and distinct imagination. Equally, it may be the case that we seize specific concepts by means of rational insight. In this connection, we may be faced with pieces of a priori knowledge that cannot be warranted unless we intuitively grasp necessary relations between contents that either are of a purely formal character (e.g., relations of transitivity) or are materially determined. In the latter case we, for instance, contend that it is necessarily true that no spatially existing object can simultaneously be red and green all over. Whatever examples we have in mind, it should be clear that phenomenologists address *a concrete manifold of different modes of intuitive givenness*. This being so, a new understanding of "complex methodology" emerges. The relating complexity need not, without exception, result from bringing together fundamentally different methodological approaches such as statistical methods, on the one hand, and introspection, on the other hand. Methodological complexity may also arise due to different types of intuition that are involved in certain fields of research. If Husserl's considerations are on the right track, we do not need to consider the interplay of different types of intuition as a merely contingent fact. Rather, we need only to direct our attention to the constitution of the objects at issue. Methodical issues cannot be detached from the concrete nature of the objects investigated. Clarifying our methodological tools and coming to know the peculiar nature of the objects at hand are two aspects of the very same process. In this vein, a phenomenological intuitionism in terms of the above-sketched *multiple intuition approach* can be of use to psychiatrists too, even if they do not share Husserl's specific philosophical interest in eidetic knowledge.

Phenomenology, for many decades, has been acknowledged as a prominent and vigorous branch of philosophical theorizing. Yet it has met an equally permanent critical appraisal. The relevant critiques do not dwell on marginal and minor issues. They straightforwardly challenge the ideas of description and intuition which, according to the understanding of Husserl and other phenomenologists, constitute the very core of a phenomenological philosophy. In the present context, we need not enter into those detailed debates on methodological, epistemological and ontological issues that originate from and demonstrate the splitting up into different brands of phenomenological philosophies. Among others, these different brands are represented by Brentano, Husserl, Heidegger, Scheler, Sartre, Lévinas, and many others. However, it is important to note that, in addition and parallel to this *philosophical* variety of doing phenomenology, there is variety in another respect. For scientists who are affiliated to different empirical disciplines it is quite common to refer to (merely) descriptive tasks. Scientists are familiar with the experience that, while seeking out a proper evidential basis, the relevant phenomena, *on certain conditions*, can be given in an intuitive way. However, scientific utilizations of descriptive methods typically refer to limited parts of an overall research work and theory construction. Therefore, they should not be confused with the idea of description as a basic methodological principle of phenomenological philosophy. In scientific contexts, descriptions (and intuitions) function in a preparatory and ancillary way as part of an overall research activity that is meant to ultimately approach full-blown explanatory projects.[8] As far as scientists are committed to the tasks of explanation and prediction, they do not subscribe to the idea that descriptions and intuitions actually warrant (or ever could warrant) the expected results, the basic principles or the main purpose of their work. From this brief description of the philosophical and non-philosophical varieties concerning the *phenomenologically given* it should be clear that any well-founded judgment of a phenomenological method requires adequately specifying the notions of description and intuition according to varying theoretical and practical contexts (cf. Rinofner-Kreidl 2004). It is both these specifications and the relative importance phenomenologists attach to the ideas of description and intuition that give rise to critical objections.

When Husserl reconsidered his project of describing the human mind in the first decade of the 20th century, his predominant endeavor was to distinguish sharply between phenomenological from non-phenomenological philosophical projects on the one hand, as well as philosophical-phenomenological analyses from scientific utilizations of descriptive methods, on the other hand. The appropriate methodological device to meet this requirement, according to Husserl, is the so-called *phenomenological reduction.*

3.3 Attitude, Intuition, Description (AID): How the Phenomenological Reduction Radically Changes the Picture

The phenomenological reduction appears in Husserl's research manuscripts a few years after he published his *Logical Investigations*. The first public reference can be found in his lectures on *The Idea of Phenomenology* (1907). What does the phenomenological reduction achieve? Why should we consider it indispensable for a phenomenological analysis? The reduction demands that when doing phenomenology one restricts oneself to describing intentional relations to objects and states of affairs and, thereby, ignore all those existential beliefs that normally, in our everyday

---

[8] Cf. Jaspers (1997a, p. 9 f, 25–31, 302–303). After all, we should keep in mind Jaspers's remarkable comment about his General Psychopathology: "It is wrong to call this book ‚the principal text of phenomenology. The phenomenological attitude is one point of view and one chapter has been devoted to it in some detail as the viewpoint is a new one. But the whole book is directed to showing that it is only one point of view among many and holds a subordinate position at that." (Jaspers 1997a, p. 48, 1973, p. 42)

practice, are associated with the relevant relations. While ignoring all existential claims that are constitutive of our *natural attitude*, we do not deny that these objects truly exist beyond and independent of the intuitively or symbolically given mental representations of them as intentional objects. Asserting as well as denying the real existence of intentional objects is a metaphysical claim and hence has to be "bracketed," as Husserl maintains. Doing so, we only talk about what is given in pure, that is, phenomenologically reduced consciousness. We do not judge about things themselves, that is to say, things that are thought to be mind-independent on principle. We rather judge how things appear and how they are meant to be according to the intentional content of the relating acts. Any description following this methodological rule is called a *phenomenological description*.[9] Ideally, phenomenological descriptions report those and only those contents of our experience that correspond to a purified intuition. The purification of intuition occurs via a deliberate correlation of it with the *phenomenological attitude*; or put another way, the phenomenological reduction must itself be manifested in the *subject's* attitude (cf. Rinofner-Kreidl 2000, pp. 179–183). In § 24 of the first volume of his *Ideas*, Husserl introduces the phenomenological principle of intuition ("the principle of all principles") by stating

> that every originary presentive intuition is a legitimizing source of cognition, that everything originarily (so to speak, in its 'personal' actuality) offered to us in 'intuition' is to be accepted simply as what it is presented as being, but also only within the limits in which it is presented there. (Husserl 1983, p. 44)

Introducing this basic principle, Husserl does not literally refer to the phenomenological reduction or the phenomenological attitude, respectively. Nonetheless, the latter is part of the above-stated principle. It is included (or hidden) in the closing phrase "only within the limits in which it is presented there." Although it may be tempting to ignore this clause or to reduce it to an unspecified request for accuracy and prudence in doing our descriptive work, it actually urges us to understand the principle of intuition as qualified by the phenomenological reduction or any other attitude that defines the relevant scope of experience.

Astonishingly, it is in connection with a seemingly restrictive methodological operation that Husserl embraces a universally relevant insight and methodological technique whose impact goes far beyond the specific theoretical interests of transcendental phenomenology. The relevant insight is: What is given intuitively co-varies, in an explicable and a priori determined manner, with changing attitudes that are adopted and abandoned according to the requirements of varying situations. These requirements, at least partially, are defined by the theoretical or practical interests of the epistemic agent (cf. Husserl 1973, §§ 13–14). Husserl's transcendental phenomenology explores this insight by inquiring into and describing possible forms of experience. Correspondingly, it redefines the task of a philosophical analysis in terms of an *attitude concerned with attitudes and their pertaining possibilities*

---

[9] The phenomenological reduction is a more rigorous version of the principle of physical, psychical and metaphysical presuppositionlessness which Husserl formulated in § 7 of his introduction to volume II of his Logical Investigations. Cf. Husserl (1970a, pp. 177–79).

of givenness.[10] It is from this meta-theoretical and transcendental point of view that Husserl throws light on the peculiar character and implications of different attitudes which amount to (mostly unconsciously practiced) techniques of veiling and unveiling certain aspects of reality. For instance, it is a distinctive feature of the so-called *natural attitude* that it does not dwell on its own techniques of grasping objects from a general point of view, thereby transcending its present interest. This holds good both for our life-world practice and the intellectual activities devoted to the positive (empirical and formal) sciences. It is part of our natural attitude that, in acting according to this attitude, we normally do not realize doing so. If this is true, the importance should be evident of a philosophical treatment of human understanding that yields a release from our daily tasks and commitments. It is due to this release that a phenomenological analysis of intentional experience is apt to bring to light the usually unchallenged conditions, that is, ontological interpretations and assumptions, lying beneath our everyday normal as well as pathological intentional life.

In connection with this, we should bear in mind that Husserl distinguishes between the *phenomenological reduction* that opens up the field of pure subjectivity, that is, the field of phenomenological description comprising all possible forms of intentional experience, on the one hand, and so-called *thematic reductions*, on the other hand (cf. Husserl 1983, §§ 56–61). The latter refer to all possible objects of description we can direct our attention to within the framework of pure phenomenology. Clearly, there is a great variety of description-projects we can embark on. For instance, we can inquire into the relation holding between presentation and judgment or the passive meaning-constitution processes that must have taken place whenever a judgment occurs in consciousness. Equally, we can analyze the mode of givenness of valuable objects ("goods") and how it is related to value-perceptions. Or we can investigate the intentional structure of memory and phantasy. According to Husserl, all these projects require that we, first, perform the phenomenological reduction and, second, selectively explore the field of pure subjectivity. Observational guidance in terms of fixing a specific directedness and mode of turning toward possible objects of description is due to what Husserl calls "thematic reduction." The research activity of non-philosophical sciences can also be analyzed in terms of specific thematic reductions that constitute the relating research fields (cf. Husserl 1989a, pp. 27–29, 189–194).

Philosophy, in a Husserlian vein, is characterized by a specific form of detachment. It calls for going beyond the particular purposes, tasks, and intellectual projects that render invisible all those parts of reality that do not seem fit from the point of view of our daily interests. While philosophizing, we abandon our usual modes of being immersed in everyday concerns. A transcendental phenomenologist does not deal with, for instance, the concrete contents and epistemological quality of the experiences a schizophrenic patient undergoes. Digging into such concrete empirical concerns is not in the philosopher's province. From a transcendental point of view (according to Husserl's brand of transcendentalism), our main concern is neither how specific forms of intuition could be utilized in order to gain suitable and workable categorizations of mental illness nor how "seeing" precisely informs

---

[10] Cf. Husserl (1989a, p. 183 f, 189 f); Rinofner-Kreidl (2000, p. 162 f).

the processes of analyzing, interpreting and commenting on case studies. (Jaspers whose phenomenology operates at a descriptive-psychological level has a clear stake in both these issues.) Our main concern, as philosophers, is to understand what we do when we embark on these very activities. What are the tacit presuppositions of describing human behavior? We are interested in specifying how different types of attitudes, different types of intentional experience and different kinds of objects and states of affairs, respectively, are correlated with each other. Within this field of "pure" intentional analysis we then discover that we need hermeneutic abilities since our intuitions do not occur as a succession of isolated impressions. Intuitive givenness is the result of a process of exploration that, step by step, lays bare different aspects and meaning-layers of intentional experiences.[11]

As long as one adheres to the phenomenological attitude one "seeks to *understand* the 'how' [of person perception, SR] by illuminating the constitutive perceptual framework (*Einstellung*) of the perceiver." (Churchill 1998, p. 181) This wording is correct and instructive for the following reasons. First, it emphasizes the demand for understanding intentional experience as distinguished from explaining why certain experiences occur at certain instants of time or within certain periods. Secondly, it recognizes that a phenomenological investigation does not dwell on the varying material contents of the diverse types of experience but, instead, deals with formal qualities in terms of the intentional structure of the relevant experiences. Thirdly, the correlation holding between noetic and noematic aspects, that is, between the specific type of act performed and the specific way an object or state of affair is referred to, is implicitly acknowledged. Accordingly, it is evident that in order to inquire into the "how" of perception, judgment, remembrance, imagination and so on, one must notice the subject's overall attitude taken while performing the respective acts.

---

[11] In his Berlin lecture on Phenomenology and Anthropology (1931), Husserl remarks: "Was uns naiv als Eines und eventuell als völlig unverhändert Verharrendes gegeben ist, wird zum transzendentalen Leitfaden für das systematisch reflektive Studium der wesensmäßig zugehörigen Bewußtseinsmannigfaltigkeiten. So für jedes Seiende, so für jedes einzelne Reale und auch für die Welt als Totalphänomen. [...] Die Möglichkeit [...] dieser Forschungen hängt an der Auffindung der Methode der Korrelationsforschung, der Methode, von der intentionalen Gegenständlichkeit konkret enthüllend zurückzufragen. Echte Bewußtseinsanalyse ist sozusagen Hermeneutik des Bewußtseinslebens als eines immerzu Seiendes (Identisches) Vermeinendes. Seiendes in sich in wesenszugehörigen Bewußtseinsmannigfaltigkeiten intentional Konstituierenden." (Husserl 1989b, p. 177, Translation: "This thing that is naively given to us as one thing, and possibly as something permanent and completely unaltered, becomes the transcendental clue that leads us to the systematic reflective study of manifolds in consciousness that essentially pertain to any one thing. This is the case for every entity, for every individual reality, and also for the world as a total phenomenon. [...] The possibility of carrying out [...] these investigations depends on discovering the method of correlation-research, the method for questioning back behind intentional objectivity [intentionale Gegenständlichkeit]. Genuine analysis of consciousness is, so to say, the hermeneutic of conscious life, where the latter is taken as that which continuously intends entities (identities), and constitutes them within its own self in manifolds of consciousness that pertain to those entities in essential ways.") The so-called zig-zag course of investigation, which Husserl occasionally mentions, points to methodological difficulties that adhere to his hermeneutic of conscious life. Cf. Husserl 1969, p. 125 and Husserl 1970a, p. 175 (annotation to the second edition, 1913).

Attitudes are responsible for the specific way we approach situations in order to grasp phenomena (cf. Churchill 1998, p. 181 f). This includes two important insights going beyond what we normally expect from intuitive methods. On the one hand, the relevant intuitive grasping cannot simply "depict" an omnipresent und unproblematic reality without our having taken a specific attitude beforehand. On the other hand, the evidential presence of the phenomenon does not occur in an accidental way since it is the researcher who willingly and actively gives rise to the object's appearance by taking an appropriate attitude. Of course, giving rise to the *appearance* of an object (or, allowing the phenomenon to come into view) must not be confused with giving rise to the *existence* of the appearing object.[12] If it is correct that we channel appearances by using the methodological tool of (different types of) reductions, we must acknowledge that our intuition-based phenomenological analysis, to some extent, harbors constructive as well as hermeneutic ingredients. The phenomenological notion of intuition, therefore, qualifies as a complex notion. Due to its methodological underpinning, it does not represent a naively posited claim for immediacy. Rather, we should argue that whenever someone takes for granted having given intuitively some object, state of affairs or person, that it must then be possible to specify those purposes and thematic interests that have been brought to bear. Nothing can be intuitively given without there also being, at the same time, some effective purpose or interest (whether the agent is actually aware of it or not).[13]

Attitudes can be spelled out in different ways. Husserl did not put much emphasis on this requirement. However, applying his idea of a phenomenological analysis to empirical projects of investigating consciousness, it seems appropriate to offer a more explicit and sophisticated conception of attitude. For instance, we may draw on dispositions, habitual ways of comportment, elements of tacit knowledge and passivity including, among others, specific modes of bodily vulnerability that strongly form our daily experiential life as constitutive parts of specific attitudes.[14] Scientific as well as philosophical attitudes are typically and predominantly composed of *explicit* moments that are accessible to *processes of deliberation and rational choice*. Scientific and philosophical attitudes are not brought to bear in a mute, obvious, and matter-of-

---

[12] Doing phenomenology in a Husserlian vein we do not (and actually cannot) commit ourselves to metaphysical idealism. The latter clearly goes beyond the legitimate domain of a phenomenological description.

[13] Cf. "Whenever we apperceive, we have already brought into the situation that which renders apperception possible and gives it form. If what we bring falsifies our view we call it 'prejudice' but if on the contrary our apperception has been enabled and enhanced, we speak of 'presupposition'." (Jaspers 1997a, p. 16, 1973, p. 13 f) "We can only know what questions to ask if we have a fund of general knowledge. The conceptual schemata and the structure of our conceptual knowledge are the real sense-organs of our questioning." (Jaspers 1997b, p. 825, 1973, p. 687)

[14] As far as mental disorders are concerned, it is vital to carefully note the specific impairments of bodily abilities and the specific modes of bodily vulnerability or irritability that typically accompany the relevant psychic disturbances. According to a phenomenological approach, these bodily phenomena must not be reduced to static and isolated objects of observation. They represent enabling functions that determine peculiar modes of approaching the (social) world, that is, peculiar modes of "I can" (cf. Husserl 1989a, p. 159 f) which either enhance or impede the agent's (expression of her) cognitive, affective and volitional intentions.

fact way. Rather, they are utilized in a problematic and fluid manner by accommodating changing interests and tasks of research work. It is only with regard to these reflexive modes of attitudes that we can literally say that someone consciously adopts a specific attitude in order to grasp specific types of objects or states of affairs.[15]

According to Husserl's investigation in the *Crisis* (1936) (cf. Husserl 1970b), scientists tend to rule out time-consuming processes of comprehension, which elude exact measuring, by replacing them with purely symbolic representations. The latter, if possible, refer to research material that is made available in terms of quantification. To the extent that such a replacement of intuitive givenness by symbolic representation takes place not only sporadically but also in a systematic manner, scientists are inclined to interpret ontologically that which is nothing but a well-established and approved methodological approach. This process, according to Husserl, thus combines a considerable loss of intuitive evidence with a misidentification of methodology and ontology. Yet it would be misguided to consider this interpretation as a merely psychological failure or individual inability to adequately perform acts of cognizance. On the one hand, following this procedure does not hinder successful scientific explanations and, therefore, should not be considered from an exclusively critical point of view. On the other hand, the modern conception of science is based on the ideas of technically supported observation, quantification, and efficient calculation. Hence, it is biased in favor of symbolic representations. Accordingly, it gives rise to an idea of objectivity that is not impaired by individually varying abilities of perception and the like. Objectivity, therefore, requires abandoning all those elements that seem to falsify the expected results due to their subject-dependence, the latter referring to varying qualifications for intuition, remembrance, cognition, and so on. This being the case, our scientific projects flourish on condition that they restrain subjectivity or, as Husserl maintains, that they are accompanied by *self-forgetfulness*.[16] Scientists are caught up in a state of self-forgetfulness, which renders their scientific attitude invisible (this, of course, varies according to the scientific discipline in question). It is only due to our philosophical efforts that we are capable of seeing through these processes involved in our scientific activities. Philosophy aims at discovering and querying variable ways of relating to the world on different levels of human experience. Although Jaspers'

---

[15] See e.g.: "[…] the psychologist tries to guard against distractions of any kind, whether they be personal concerns, extraneous interferences, or even the psychologist's own curiosity. In general, distractions are the correlates of an intending gaze that, for the moment, is not motivated by psychodiagnostic interests. It is the self-monitoring alertness of the psychologist that redirects the psychologist's attention to the task-related interests […]" (Churchill 1998, p. 198).

[16] In our daily life self-forgetfulness is indispensable for smoothly feeling, perceiving, moving, and acting. It is only due to the retrospective philosophical gaze that we raise the issue of how our pre-reflective comportment is interrelated with its subsequent "objectification." "The perceiving body does not successively occupy different points of view beneath the gaze of some unlocated consciousness which is thinking about them. For it is reflection which objectifies points of view of perspectives, whereas when I perceive, I belong, through my point of view, to the world as a whole, nor am I even aware of the limits of my visual field. The variety of points of view is hinted at only by an imperceptible shift, a certain 'blurred' effect in the appearance" (Merleau-Ponty 1958, p. 384). For very similar reasons, Husserl argues that attitude is a transcendental notion. While living and acting in conformity with the natural attitude we cannot grasp its very nature as an attitude.

notion of philosophy does not correlate with Husserl's, they both stress the intrinsic tendency of science to be ignorant of its own limits. Therefore, scientists, by taking their respective methodological approaches as absolute, are inclined to render invisible the diversity of possible modes of relatedness to the world.

> [...] the sciences also tend to obscure Being itself by the knowable facts and keep us tied to preliminaries without end. They tend to make absolutes of our limited insights and convert them into a supposed knowledge of Being itself. They tend to make us forget the essential and restrict our free view of phenomena, narrow down our experiences, images and ideas to rational definitions and paralyze our psychic activity with rigid concepts that follow from too much learning and knowing. But it is a mistake to complain that we know too much, that knowledge is a tyrant, that there is nothing more to know and that knowledge paralyses life. There is no need for this to be so and it only arises from a misunderstanding departure from true learning. (Jaspers 1997b, p. 771, 1973, p. 644)

The philosopher's challenge is to offer assistance for gaining a more lucid and encompassing understanding of those aspects of experience and meaning-constitution that permanently elude our attention as long as we are caught up in the natural attitude (as Husserl says). As soon as we abandon the phenomenological attitude and return to the natural attitude, that is, to our daily business as parents, lovers, lawyers, taxpayers, entrepreneurs, or psychiatrists we can still profit from our philosophical activities in an indirect way. By doing phenomenology, according to the above delineation, we come to realize that even the most empathetic understanding, which leads toward total identification with another person or living being in general, can take place within a framework that ensures some kind of methodological detachment. From a practical point of view, this should not surprise anyone engaged in therapeutic work. Doing this work efficiently requires being able to imaginatively transpose oneself into the position of the patient and, nonetheless, keep one's distance insofar as a mere empathetic "doubling" of the patient's experience would undermine the therapeutic aim. Keeping track of this aim necessitates that, to some extent and in some specifiable way, the therapist maintains her autonomy and self-control.

3.4 Applying AID to Jaspers' Psychopathology

How can we make use of our phenomenologically informed notions of intuition and subjectivity in connection with psychiatry? Why should a psychiatrist expect to benefit from philosophical reflection about her conceptual tools? Raising this issue in connection with our general methodological considerations, I do not have in mind systems of nosological classification or other intricate conceptual issues that are addressed in debates on mental and physical health, theories of illness, and similar topics. Rather, I shall restrict myself to the phenomenological notions of intuition and subjectivity. Is there anything we may gain from philosophy at this abstract level? I would like to mention two fundamental insights. First, by wrestling with phenomenological ideas of intuition and subjectivity, which draw on a specific project of intentional analysis, we realize that the way we introduce our basic notions in theoretical contexts always endorses tacitly specific methods of research. Hence, referring to intuitions is never neutral or innocent in terms of methodological commitments.[17] Along with this, such notions like intuition and subjectivity, secondly, acquire an equivocal meaning that must not be ignored. Whenever we realize that theorizing in some specific domain of scientific research can hardly be elaborated and pushed ahead without, at some point, using these concepts (as holds good, for instance, with regard to psychiatry), we must explicitly introduce and define them. Doing so includes specifying the achievements of intuitive givenness in terms of those peculiar attitudes that are constitutive of the relevant object-domain.

At this point, it is worth remembering that Jaspers' *General Psychopathology* (1st edition, 1913), in the course of its several editions, shows an increasing amount of philosophical content. This tendency to enrich the philosophical content particularly manifests itself in a comprehensive part (Part VI: *The Human Being as a Whole*), which Jaspers included in the 4th edition (1946) (cf. Jaspers 1997b, pp. 747–822, 1973, pp. 624–686). It discusses the existential impact of living as a human being, especially the problem of how one might, within a psychiatric framework, adequately consider the peculiar striving for totality (*Ganzseinwollen*) that is characteristic of man from the point of view of existential philosophy. It is crucial that this whole or totality, which is said to elude scientific explanation, is not only represented by thoughts. According to Jaspers, it is rather in some sense intuitively present. Strictly speaking, a totality cannot be given—if givenness were considered in terms of "ordinary," perception-like modes of intuition. The relevant totality can only be grasped like a Kantian idea (cf. Jaspers 1997b, pp. 560–561, 1973, p. 468 f). Yet, it is of the utmost importance because it is through reference to ideas that psychiatrists succeed in making accessible relevant spheres of phenomena.

> Anticipatory intuitions of a whole open up fresh areas for observation and at the same time create new organs of apperception but later it is just the theorizing urge that curtails fruitfulness because it thinks its detailed designs fully comprehend the real essence of all that underlies existence. It is the basic deceptiveness of theory-building that however much it starts from a first glimpse of the whole it ends by losing itself in the trappings of a rational construction. The initial enthusiasm of feeling in contact with reality turns into a fanaticism of knowing which is falsified as it grows into a developed dogma. The deceptive crisis lies in the transition from the conquest of fresh facts to the presumed knowledge of them and with that a new blindness in the pigeonholing and classifying of them. (Jaspers 1997b, p. 548, 1973, p. 460)

Referring to ideas fulfills a twofold task in Jaspers' *Psychopathology*. First, it safeguards the multifaceted variety of reality against the reductionist tendency of theoretical representations. Secondly, it reminds the psychiatrist of his double role as a researcher who must adhere to the standards of scientific practice, on the one hand, and as a fellow-being who is able to sympathetically grasp the meaning of existence.

> Only a psychopathology which takes its starting-point from an indomitable interest in the infinite variety of reality, in the richness of the subjective approach and the objective facts, the multiplicity of methods and the uniqueness of each, does justice to its task as a scientific discipline. [...] It wants to protect its freedom against the theoretical world of technical and supposedly known Being and withdraw from it to fully present reality (it wants to protect the man in the scientist, so that he does not lose his accessibility to Existence itself and therefore

---

[17] We might even find out that it isn't neutral or innocent in terms of metaphysical commitments. In the present context we cannot dwell on this problem. Cf. Bonjour (1998, pp. 153–186).

to the problem of the limits of psychopathology rather than of its subject matter, through being led away by the pseudo-knowledge of some theory. (Jaspers 1997b, p. 549, 1973, p. 460)

According to Jaspers, there is a dialectical tension between those theory-driven background assumptions, which scientists commonly make use of, on the one hand, and large-scale intuitions addressing *ideas*, on the other hand. The latter touch on the *encompassing* (das *Umgreifende*) without allowing for rational recognition. Relating to this, it is important to note that Jaspers' intuitive grasping of ideas can by no means be identified with Husserl's eidetic intuition although both lay claim to a higher-level intuition (cf. Husserl 1983, pp. 5–32). When talking about the encompassing, Jaspers responds to an actual metaphysical reality that in some way can be experienced despite its being beyond the reach of human knowledge. Contrary to this, Husserl's eidetic intuition refers to essences in terms of *pure possibilities of experience* that can be known by means of a higher-level intuition. Recognizing *eidé* neither involves my personal, singular ego nor does it maintain that the essences in question are actually realized or that we could predict or should promote their future realization (cf. Rinofner-Kreidl 2000, pp. 131–159). Eidetic intuition, according to Husserl, is a necessary component of transcendental phenomenology. However, it can also be part of specialized scientific research (e.g., mathematics) because of its applicability to different domains of objects. Acknowledging these different notions and functions of intuition, it comes as no surprise that in Husserl's philosophy we do not find an equivalent to Jaspers' distinction between *understanding psychology* (*verstehende Psychologie*) and *illuminating existence* (*Existenzerhellung*). Accordingly, Husserl does not endorse Jaspers' connected view of how psychopathology depends on philosophy without being either affirmed or refuted by philosophical reasoning (cf. Jaspers 1997b, pp. 768–770, 775–778). Furthermore, Husserl's phenomenological reduction introduces a sharp distinction between transcendental phenomenology and positive science (e.g., psychology). The former, however, does not establish an existential philosophy. As mentioned above, Jaspers does not accept Husserl's demand for philosophy as rigorous science. He seems to repudiate Husserl's transcendental phenomenology because he identifies it with eidetics and does not take notice of Husserl's otherwise complex notion of intuition (see AID). It is our opinion, however, that this complexity is exactly that, which renders the phenomenological notion of intuition attractive and efficient for psychiatric purposes.

The differences mentioned above notwithstanding, Husserl and Jaspers agree with regard to the following assertions (though their respective explanations do not coincide):

- Fixing concepts is unavoidable although problematic. If we want to gain access to ever-new phenomena ("the conquest of fresh facts," Jaspers 1997b, p. 548; "Erobern neuer Sichtbarkeiten," Jaspers 1973, p. 460) we must go beyond traditional philosophical and scientific terminologies.
- The sciences tend to suffer from an altogether missing or insufficient self-delimitation due to the fact that they do not draw on the intrinsic relations between attitude, intuition and description in a systematic way.

- There is an intrinsic methodological as well as psychological (motivational) connection between intuition and attitude which undermines the so-called myth of the given. In general, it is our deliberate, sensible and reflexive use of methodological tools that enables us to turn toward the relevant phenomena in a careful and attentive manner.
- Phenomenology does not mainly focus on subjective moments in terms of concrete contents of (some person's) consciousness. It rather refers to the form or mode of their (psychic) experience.

Until now, we have not discussed the third point. To do this, it is helpful to refer to one of Jaspers' statements in order to clarify the relating affinity *and* difference between Husserl and Jaspers.

> To reach a phenomenological clarity we have to direct the patients, so far as they can manage it, to give us the form of their psychic experience and observe themselves so that we can learn something of the subjective mode of their experience and not merely its content. (Jaspers 1997b, p. 827, 1973, p. 689)

According to Husserl's view, it is the phenomenological reduction that enables us to reliably focus our attention on the form of experience instead of being absorbed in its content. Yet, in general, we cannot expect psychiatric patients to be able to adopt a methodological attitude, which in philosophical contexts is often (though problematically) connected with the idea of an *impartial observer.* Certainly, this would be overdemanding even if there might be, now and then, exceptions to the rule. Occasionally, it has been argued that suffering from mental disorders under certain conditions can make it easier to approach the phenomenological reduction. For instance, there seems to be a certain similarity between schizophrenia and the phenomenological attitude as far as the reflexive distance to the world of our everyday practice is concerned (cf. Depraz 2003). This being so, the schizophrenic nonetheless does not share the specific theoretical interest which, in Husserl's case, refers to subjectivity in terms of pure intention relations. When Jaspers calls on us to learn from the subjective mode of the patient's experience, he dwells on a "thick" notion of subjectivity that is essentially informed by the patient's self-description of her experience and denies "purification" in terms of Husserl's reduction.

Despite the obvious differences, we take the methodological considerations referring to Husserl's transcendental phenomenology as vital for understanding Jaspers' *General Psychopathology.* Yet, with respect to the present psychiatric context, the importance of these considerations cannot be drawn from their respective understanding of phenomenology. The concomitant differences primarily hinge on the notions of subjectivity and intuition and their methodological status, respectively. Jaspers' view is strongly determined by his conception of *phenomenology* as *empathic understanding of other persons' mental states.* Only present mental states, accordingly, are said to be intuitively given, although these states, as lived-through by another person, are experienced in a merely indirect mode, that is, by means of displacing oneself ("Hineinversetzen") in the other person's mind. This view obviously responds to the theoretical and practical needs of a psychopathological (research) work. As indicated above, Husserl's interests are quite different. Consequently, his notion of intuition strongly reflects the requirements of *rational understanding*, thereby *focusing on intentional contents and their interrelatedness* instead of communicating about and interpreting concrete experiences or empathically approaching those persons who actually undergo these experiences. Correspondingly, what it means to be interested in formal aspects of human consciousness leads to different questions, depending on whether we embark from the idea of empathic understanding or from the idea of rational understanding. Within a psychopathological horizon, forms of experience, for instance, comprise depressive modes of behavior, suicidal dispositions, delusional ideas (*Wahnideen*), affective disorders, which are due to schizophrenic states, and many other issues of this kind. Husserl's "forms of experience" represent much more basic types of intentional directedness, the functioning of which must also be involved in psychiatrically classified forms of experience. Otherwise, the latter could not be described in a differentiated way. The psychiatric meaning of relevant (self-) descriptions requires that we understand fundamentally the different ways of how persons, in general, can relate to an appearing reality. For instance, if a patient's self-description gives rise to the assumption that, given her overall mental state or mood, perceptions and imaginations are not any more distinguishable for her, we will certainly interpret this as part of a specific mental disorder. Hence, the forms of experience that Husserl and Jaspers are interested in are of different kind. This being the case, we should not assume that the relating types of formal issues could be efficiently treated with the same methodological tools, while also being based on the same understanding of perception and cognition. We cannot exclude the possibility that different types of problems require different types of phenomenology.[18]

In spite of their profoundly different notions of intuition and their different approaches in their respective types of analysis, Jaspers and Husserl share a minimal yet fundamental *methodological* agreement: They both assert that it would be naïve to assume a) that any object whatever could be grasped and determined by any method whatever, and b) that we could succeed in capturing the richness and variety

---

[18] It is a serious deficiency of Chris Walker's otherwise convincing correction of a persistent misinterpretation of Jaspers's relation to Husserl that he is largely ignorant of the requirements and achievements of transcendental phenomenology. Walker rightly concludes that Jaspers was deceived by the early designation of Husserl's phenomenology as "descriptive psychology." Consequently, he erroneously compared his conception of empathic ("subjective") understanding to Husserl's Logical Investigations, thereby failing to notice that the latter were devoted to the idea of a non-empirical (eidetic) science of pure consciousness. Stressing that Jaspers fundamentally mistook Husserl's intentions, the author clears up important differences between Husserl's and Jaspers's ideas of phenomenology (cf. Walker 1994b; Walker 1995a; Walker 1995b, p. 250 ff). It is indeed worth contemplating whether "Jaspers is not a Husserlian but rather a Kantian phenomenologist" (Walker 1995b, p. 265). However, despite rectifying false views of how Husserl's and Jaspers's phenomenology are (not) related to each other, Walker himself falls prey to farreaching misunderstandings. These include the following: that "the concept of form [...] is [...] fundamental to Jaspers' phenomenology, but not to be found in Husserl" (Walker 1995a, p. 79); that the notions of appearance, representations and content are "completely absent from Husserl's phenomenology" (Walker 1995a, p. 65); that "Husserl is a protobehaviorist who denies the possibility of access to the other person's subjective experience" (Walker 1995b, p. 254); that "[e]mpathy, for Husserl, is a person's awareness of his or her own inner state of consciousness" (Walker 1995b, p. 254); that "empathy and understanding have no role at all in Husserl's phenomenology" (Walker 1995b, p. 255); and that for Husserl "all knowledge would be reducible to [...] absolute and necessary essence" (Walker 1995a, p. 72).

of reality as a whole by means of one single method only (whatever it may be).[19] Consenting to b), we are ready to acknowledge a plurality of methods. The latter suggests itself as soon as we go beyond those restrictively defined notions of reality that correspond to scientism.[20] Statement a) can be rephrased in a positive way by arguing that there is a non-causal correlation between our most basic ideas concerning the structure and diversity of the world as we experience it, on the one hand, and the methodological tools meant to render these ideas applicable, on the other hand. If this is correct, we must assume that any attempt to exclude feasible and available methods by arguing that they do not comply with currently dominating models of science seriously risks losing touch with substantial parts of reality.[21] Any such self-restriction is premature as long as we have not yet tried, in fact, to utilize the respective method and have not yet discovered its infeasibility or poor results.

According to a still widespread view, having recourse to intuitions amounts to putting an end dogmatically to processes of reasoning, regardless of whether the decision to do so roots in an individual or collective intention. Correspondingly, intuitions are frequently said to be static, immediately present and all-in-one grasped mental contents that do not allow for doubts and wavering beliefs. What is given in an intuitive way, according to this view, is absolutely certain. It is this view, that, for decades, has been attacked under the heading "myth of the given." Yet, according to the above, there are good reasons to deny the poor and static picture of intuition that lies beneath the myth of the given. We suggest that these reasons are directly relevant to Jaspers' explanations in his *General Psychopathology*.

3.5 Dynamic Intuitionism: How AID Rules Out the Myth of the Given

As argued above, AID asserts that intuitive givenness is by necessity functionally intertwined with varying attitudes which, for the most part, are hidden ("tacit") though constitutive ingredients of the relevant givenness. If this is correct, we must consider the

---

[19] For a detailed discussion of b) under the heading of "methodological particularism" see Rinofner-Kreidl (2008). Cf. "There is no complete set of facts, ready-made, which are being considered merely from diverse points of view. Through the application of each method, something becomes apparent that belongs only to it, as well as something rather vaguely defined which does not belong. Similarly, the totality that becomes apparent through all our methods is not any consistent total reality nor is there any one universal method which will reveal everything that is. All we can do is to try and apprehend individual realities clearly and unequivocally with the help of individual methods." (Jaspers 1997a, p. 48, 1973, p. 41) Cf. Jaspers 1997a, pp. 47, 312–313.

[20] Cf. Jaspers (1997a, pp. 31–38); Rinofner-Kreidl (2008). "Object and scientific meaning change according to the method used. We make a mistake if we play the one against the other and expect from the one what only the other can provide. The scientific attitude is ready to adopt any method and asks only for those universal scientific criteria: general validity, convincing insights (which can be proved), clarity of method and the possibility for a meaningful discussion. [...] it would narrow psychopathology down too much if the scientific approach were confined to any one particular kind of testability." (Jaspers 1997b, p. 768 f, 1973, p. 642)

[21] See Michael Huemer's lucid explanation of why intuitionism has been mostly unpopular in 20th century philosophy. Cf. Huemer (2005, pp. 240–248).

dynamic aspects of intuition to be much stronger than commonly acknowledged. As far as the development of Husserl's phenomenology is concerned, it is worth noting that the relevant dynamic interpretation of intuition, which comes to the fore in a second-order analysis of what takes place in phenomenological inquiries, cannot be extracted from Husserl's *Logical Investigations*. This is not to deny that Husserl, in the *Logical Investigations*, correctly captures the dynamic aspects in terms of his first-order analysis, that is, by means of describing relations between signitive meanings, on the one hand, and intuitive fulfillments, on the other hand (see especially the sixth investigation of the second volume). The crucial point is that it is not until we take the transcendental turn into account that we gain a plausible and systematic view on what it means *to bring something to intuitive givenness* (*evidence*) in the course of a process of exploration. This process gradually unveils the perceiver's own presuppositions, tacit knowledge, emotionally induced biases, dispositions, and so on when facing this or that situation and phenomenon. Husserl's project of transcendental phenomenology promotes a profoundly dynamic notion of intuition. This dynamic intuitionism may even be suited to approach those dialectical and hermeneutic moments in psychiatric research and therapy that are strongly present in Jaspers' *General Psychopathology,* especially in its later editions. In particular, it is Husserl's later and methodologically enriched dynamic notion of intuition that enables us to truly understand what Jaspers means when he distinguishes our everyday practice of *sensuous seeing* from the much more complex *understanding seeing* that psychiatrists should be able to practice and, moreover, should be able to invoke in others who are confronted with their subtle descriptions of mental states:

> A histologist will provide an exhaustive description of particular morphological elements, but he will do it in such a way as to make it easier for others to see these elements for themselves, and he has to presume, or else induce, this 'seeing for oneself' in those who really want to understand him. In the same way the phenomenologist can indicate features and characteristics, and show how they can be distinguished and confusion avoided, all with a view to describing the qualitatively separate psychic data. But he must make sure that those to whom he addresses himself do not simply think along with him, but that they see along with him in contact and conversation with patients and through their own observations. This 'seeing' is not done through the senses, but through the understanding. This is something quite special, irreducible and ultimate; and if we are to take even one single step forward in phenomenology we have to train ourselves in it and master it—including such things as 'representing data to oneself', 'understanding', 'grasping' or 'actualizing'. Only so do we acquire a fruitful critical faculty which will set itself against the framing of theoretical constructions as much as against the barren deadly denial of any possibility of progress. Whoever has no eyes to see cannot practise histology; whoever is unwilling or incapable of actualizing psychic events and representing them vividly cannot acquire an understanding of phenomenology. (Jaspers 1968, p. 1316 f, 1990, p. 318)

In the original German text, the final clause reads as follows: "sich Seelisches zu vergegenwärtigen und lebendig zu schauen" ("actualizing psychic events and representing them vividly"). Since it is certainly part of a fine-grained phenomenological description to be attentive to linguistic differences, it may be useful to mention that in German there is a relevant distinction between "sehen" (to see) and "schauen" (to watch). Although it is not easy to accurately represent it, it roughly can be explained as follows. The term "sehen" immediately directs our attention to some particular object or state of affair. The task is to adequately grasp and (mentally or linguistically) represent what obviously presents itself under our eyes' witness. Seeing something,

I am keenly interested in *what it is* that I see (or seem to see) at this moment. By seeing something, I am on the edge of analyzing it. Contrary to this, the term "schauen" suggests a less selective and less focused approach. It indicates that watching the other's state or taking note of it, including the other person's overall mood (or humor), is a time-consuming movement that is concerned with a quite complex condition. To watch someone, in this way, requires one to explore step by step the other's expressions and to make sense of them on different levels. How does, for instance, the other person's bodily behavior coincide to her linguistic expressions? Do they mutually affirm and increase their effects? Or is there any (more or less distinctly felt) discrepancy or inconsistency? As long as we are absorbed in looking at the other person, we normally do not judge these issues. We rather gain a complex impression of the other person's most salient modes of efficacy. In this process, we are not concerned with the details of her appearance but instead with her overall presence. The latter can be described in terms of mood, authenticity, passion, vivacity, sensitivity, intellectual grasp and similar "synthetic" features. Whereas while seeing something, I straightforwardly refer to a specific object or state of affairs that attracts my attention out of my concern to accurately grasp it, the situation is different in the other case. Watching an "object" leaves room for a more passive or responsive attitude. It may even be the case that, while circling my object, I occasionally "lose myself" in its overall appearance. In this case, I literally forget about my exploratory intention in favor of enjoying the presence of what visually surrounds me. Watching something or someone, in this sense, typically proceeds at a slower pace and a lower level of accuracy than perceiving specific features or states. It means to attentively note different shades of (possibly ambiguous) expressions and to aim at integration and synthesis by embracing the ostensible as well as the local, social and temporal backgrounds.[22] On a bodily level, watching something ("schauen") is of a distinctly kinaesthetic and synaesthetic quality. Correspondingly, it is strongly determined by one's own bodily presence. Whereas we see with our eyes, we cannot seriously watch something or someone unless our whole body is involved in this process. "To represent the other's psychic events vividly" ("die seelischen Zustände oder Erlebnisse des Anderen *lebendig schauen*") draws on the imaginative and bodily aspects of the relevant "understanding seeing" as well as its personal and existential involvement, that is, its reference to my actual ability to sympathize with some other person's experiences (e.g., "how does it feel to be depressed?", "how does the world look like for someone who feels exalted?", etc.).

The issue of how a peculiar "understanding seeing" can be exercised in the field of psychology and psychiatry by means of controlling specific attitudes toward the objects of investigation is elaborated in an instructive way, among others, by Scott Churchill. While Jaspers uses the term "understanding seeing," Churchill prefers to designate the relevant ability "active seeing." (As will be clear in the following, "*active* seeing" implies what we just referred to as "schauen.") In order to gain a clear impression of how

---

[22] Since "schauen," therefore, occasionally bears resemblance to a hovering state of waiting it is much nearer to a therapeutically interested listening and interpreting than acts of seeing.

this notion of active seeing, which the author ties to the psychologist's "illuminating presence," is applied, we must direct our attention to the following remarks:

> Psychodiagnostic seeing is not just a recording or considering of information given by the client; it is an active seeing that is at the same time a grasping that looks up, that seeks, that constitutes precisely what about the client's self-givenness is to be considered information in the first place. The self-givenness of the client does not become 'information' for the psychologist unless he understands it in such a way that it is relevant to his psychodiagnostic interests. (Churchill 1998, p. 194)

> The psychologist is not content to merely observe what is apparently self-evident about the client's self-presentation, but seeks to 'see through' [dia-gnosis] the apparent to the psychological phenomena [psycho-diagnosis] that lie waiting to be brought to the surface by a more penetrating gaze. This 'looking for' is at once an act of knowing [gnosis]. [...] Thus, psychodiagnostic seeing is not only a question of simple observation (i.e., the reception of the simple self-presentation of the client in his or her altering modes of appearance) but also, and essentially, a question of constituting and deciphering a relation of signifier to signified, or a relation of the visible to a hidden level of visibility that is 'in-visible'. (Churchill 1998, p. 196)

> This signification is not entirely self-evident; otherwise, anyone present to the client would observe his psychological depths. A psychodiagnostician is called in on the case precisely because of his special powers of perception. This power does not consist of any magic, but rather refers to the psychologist's constitutive presence as an instrument of diagnosis. (Churchill 1998, p. 196)

Churchill calls attention to the relation between intuitive givenness and attitude,[23] thereby assuming that attitudes are indispensable in terms of selective awareness and appropriate application of expert knowledge. He, moreover, maintains that psychiatric seeing allows for considerable individual differences regarding the psychiatrist's empathy and analytic talent, as well as her education and training. Indeed, it is hard to deny these differences if we are, on principle, ready to acknowledge specific modifications of intuition related to variable competing professional types of analysis as they are realized, for instance, in psychiatry and in philosophy. At this point, we may recall Husserl's distinction between different types of intuition corresponding to different types of objects, on the one hand, and different types of epistemic projects (scientific or philosophical), on the other hand (see above, section 2). Accommodating Churchill's question about the specific philosophical interests at issue we may ask: Does the phenomenologist's constitutive presence act as an instrument of intentional analysis? In what precise sense is this true (if ever)? Therefore, we assume that the "presence" at hand refers to specific epistemic

---

[23] Cf. "The striving toward fulfilment of interests during the course of psychodiagnostic seeing reveals something essential about this mode of seeing. [...] there is always a striving toward the contemplation of the 'self' of the client, a striving that seeks to remain focused on the client as a thematic object. Thus, psychodiagnostic seeking involves an active turning away from other possible thematic objects. [...] the psychodiagnostic gaze [...] is a reflective gaze, a seeing of meanings that hover around one central perceptual object, rather than an intense scanning of the surface of an ever-changing perceptual field. [...] These two characteristics of the attentive regard of the psychodiagnostician are distinctive and essential: It is a turning toward one perceptual object and, most important, it is an interest in the explication of 'psychological' profiles or aspects or meanings of this object." (Churchill 1998, p. 197)

virtues, along with cognitive abilities or susceptibilities that, altogether, mark an individual person's "responsiveness" to a given reality. Given that we adhere to Husserl's project of inquiring into the eidetic structures of consciousness, which involves what we call rational hermeneutics, it does not come as a surprise that Husserl's first and foremost interest does not lie in understanding the *individual* mind (with a view to its pathological impairments). In this vein, the phenomenologist's personal intuition, which alleviates and supports this kind of understanding, does not obtain a relative importance comparable to the above-mentioned diagnostic value of the psychologist's "presence." To be sure, personal intuition does come into play in a phenomenological investigation. It is required, for instance, whenever a phenomenologist tries to understand motivational relations that evidently appear in another person's behavior. However, even in this case the phenomenologist does not pretend to switch over to the psychologist's professional role. Accordingly, she is concerned not with the concrete achievements of such a truly individualized understanding, rather with the typical functioning of personal intuitions regarding a general theory of motivation (as part of a general theory of intentionality). In this sense, Husserl acknowledges that my personal intuition is heuristically indispensable for analyzing motivational processes that go far beyond the present contents of someone's consciousness. In order to distinctly grasp the relating differences between the phenomenological analysis of the human mind and the psychological or psychopathological understanding sketched above, we should take notice of Husserl's following consideration:

> [...] I do learn to peer into the interior of the other and to come to know inwardly the person himself, the motivational subject, which is precisely what bursts into view when I represent the other Ego in the way it is motivated.
>
> What is happening when the character-type of a person suddenly lights up for us through someone or other of his glances, positions, or expressions; when we, so to say, "gaze into an abyss"; when we "fathom wondrous depths"; etc.? What sort of "understanding" is that? The answer is certainly the following:
>
> First of all, it would be going too far to claim that empirical understanding is the equivalent of achieving full intuition of the nexuses of experience. Even nexuses of external nature light up very suddenly, before the relations there are analyzed properly, i.e., plainly and clearly in intuition. That only comes afterwards. Similarly, historical nexuses, which may light up in a flash, or even logical nexuses, all manifest themselves prior to explication, prior to the actual subsequent establishment of the nexuses. One speaks here of intuitive "flair," a term which very often signifies just the opposite of intuition, i.e., insight, and is instead a presentiment, a pre-seeing without seeing, an obscure, specifically symbolic, often ungraspably empty, premonition.[24] The actual nexus is then but a goal grasped in anticipation, an empty intention, one which is so determined, however, that we follow the tendency, with its determinate direction, and in the fulfillment of it can acquire a chain of actual intuitions (straightforward experiential intuitions or logical evidence, etc.) To see a man does not mean to already know him. To see a man is [...] different from seeing a material thing. Each thing is of a certain kind. If one knows the kind, the rest can be dispensed with. A man, however, has an individual kind, and each man has a different one. According to the universal, he is a man, but his kind as his character, his person, is a unity, constituted in his course

---

[24] The German original uses "Intuition" instead of "intuitive flair" and "wirkliche Anschauung" instead of "actual intuition." In German the term "Intuition" has a much more ambiguous and problematic tinge than it has in English. We may indicate the difference by stating that the German word "Intuition" is much nearer to "hunch" or "premonition" than to "seeing," "looking at" or "insight." Husserl prefers to talk about "Anschauung."

of life, as a subject of position-takings, i.e., a unity of multifarious motivations based upon multifarious presuppositions. And insofar as one knows from experience analogous traits in different people, one can grasp "with intuitive flair" the particular and peculiar complex in question here and the unity constituted, and therein one can have a guiding line for fulfilling the intentions in insightful intuition, by means of an analysis of the actual nexuses. So, in my opinion, this "intuition" as premonition ought not to be confused with actual intuition. What we have here is the success of a more precisely determining apperception, which, like any apperception, offers a guiding line for the confirmation, in the course of experience, of the intentional nexuses, often extremely complex. (Husserl 1989a, pp. 286–287)

Endorsing a multiple intuition approach and a dynamic notion of intuition along the lines sketched above considerably strengthens intuitionism in terms of its functional adequacy and feasibility. According to the dynamic turn of the notion of intuition, which takes place in the course of Husserl's abandoning descriptive psychology in favor of transcendental phenomenology, it is promising to relieve phenomenological intuitionism from the burden of so-called dogmatism. The functional intertwinement of intuition and attitude that is brought to evidence in connection with the phenomenological reduction allows for a fresh attempt to deny this widespread objection. It might well be that a naïve conception of intuition, following a monolithic and static picture of intuition, falls prey to dogmatism *if* dogmatism means that there is nothing we could elucidate and explain in case that someone challenged our statement that x is immediately given to us. In such situations, a dogmatic intuitionist inevitably falls back to simply repeating his former statement and, presumably, trying to find other and more convincing literal or metaphorical ways to describe what is presently given to her. By contrast, a phenomenologist maintains that it makes sense to quarrel about intuitions. For obvious reasons, this parallels well with an emphasis of more or less subtle and adequate linguistic representations of the intentional contents of one's intuitive givenness. Yet, presently, our primary focus is not linguistic representation. Instead, we refer to the phenomenological task of unfolding those implicitly acknowledged conditions and methodological decisions without which the relating phenomena could not have been traced out and could not have been intuitively given in the very peculiar way they were.[25] We typically become alert to this explicating activity in cases of disagreement.

Disagreement occurs whenever two or more persons perceive or otherwise grasp the (meaning of the) same objects while differing with regard to the intuitive givenness, which they both feel to be reporting honestly. If rival phenomenological descriptions occur, then the explicating activity is, so to speak, methodologically induced owing to the plurality of reductions that presumably lie beneath the descriptions at issue.[26] Correspondingly, explicating how one arrived at certain instances of intuitive evidence and stating the pertaining scope of validity, that is, true givenness, is a methodological

---

[25] Of course, "dogmatism" could be used in a quite different way, referring to the idea that every chain of reasoning that proceeds by means of inference or logical deduction, at every distinguishable "logical" stage, is necessarily based on sensuously graspable elements, concepts, or other moments that either are intuitively given or stand in need of intuitive givenness. In any case, this holds good as long as the whole process is oriented around the idea of truth. Following this idea, "dogmatism" and "foundationalism" are equivalent. In this vein, Husserl clearly endorses dogmatism.

[26] See above on Husserl's notion of phenomenological reduction and thematic reduction. Whereas the latter allows for and requires a plurality of reductions, the former does not.

obligation that a phenomenologist must be ready to meet. This obligation is generally binding. It does not depend on and does not mark out intuitions of a specific epistemic quality. This implies, according to our phenomenological defense of intuitionism, that it is false that sensible explications of intuitions could only be rendered in relation to (allegedly rare) cases of infallible intuition. Let us assume, for the sake of the argument, that anti-intuitionists mostly identify intuitionism with infallibilism. How could a transcendental phenomenologist respond? In the first place, she might insist on acknowledging the variety of different types of intuitions according to different types of objects referred to. Even if we are ready to recognize that there are *some* infallible intuitions, this does not, by any means, rule out fallibilism on a large scale. Given that intuitionists follow Husserl's proposal and commit themselves to a principle of intuition that requires being faithful with regard to a variety of phenomena and different modes of givenness, they do not have any good reason to identify intuitionism with infallibilism. Moreover, we should bear in mind, as Husserl occasionally notes, that while striving to describe phenomena accurately, we should nonetheless "preserve the habit of inner freedom even with respect to our own descriptions" (Husserl 1983, p. 235).[27] Secondly, transcendental phenomenologists agree that every single instance of intuitive givenness that we take notice of is, by necessity, relative to a specifiable set of methodological decisions. These decisions as well as the entire framework of our phenomenological description can be explained— and must be explained if it is true that phenomenologists do not only produce descriptions but, in doing so, know about their procedure and are capable of controlling it. Therefore, we should say that the phenomenological notion of an intuition-based description draws on the idea that true knowledge is reflexively achieved knowledge, while remembering its requirement of making its own conditions and limitations explicit.[28]

For psychological reasons, it appears more promising to understand and eliminate disagreements if intuitionism admits of fallibility. Yet there is no a priori reason why it should be impossible to equally explain failures of recognition with regard to types of objects that, in general, allow for infallible givenness. Disagreement abounds regarding all types of intuitive givenness, including intuition-based a priori knowledge, which also cannot be realized unless certain empirical conditions are met (e.g., the epistemic agent's ability to properly grasp conceptual contents).[29] In general, the most frequent reasons for disagreement are the following[30]:

---

[27] We take it that not only phenomenologists struggle against the "infallibilistic caricature of intuitionism that probably does not correspond to any actual intuitionist's views" (Huemer 2005, p. 237). Currently, fallibilistic brands of intuitionism are advocated by Robert Audi and Michael Huemer among others. Cf. Audi (1997); Huemer (2005).

[28] Relating to this, Jaspers's and Husserl's style of doing philosophy is more akin than either of them is ready to admit.

[29] Of course, it is important to clearly distinguish empirical conditions, whose fulfillment is necessary in order to actually achieve the relevant rational insights, from the intuitive evidence that warrants the validity of, for instance, the judgment "if $a > b$ and $b > c$ then $a > c$." Paying attention to this distinction, it is evidently not the philosopher's task to become absorbed in detailed investigations in the field of cognitive psychology and other empirical disciplines in order to defend the possibility of a priori knowledge. Here, as ever, the philosopher is concerned with analyzing structures, epistemic foundations, conceptual relations, and the like.

[30] For a more detailed explanation of why disagreement occurs with regard to intuitive givenness see Huemer (2005, pp. 128–154, 236–239).

1. One person or more may be, to some degree, impaired with regard to their ability to grasp conceptual or perceptual contents. In particular, the bodily functions involved in perceiving colors, shapes, sounds, tastes, movements, spatial relations, and so on may be hampered. Or the agent may be drunken, sick, totally overwrought, or mentally disabled. Equally, persons may, some to a more or lesser degree, lack the ability to adequately understand other persons' mental states. They may be unable to represent imaginatively these states in a proper way. For various reasons, their ability to sympathize with others may be underdeveloped. Or, they may be unsusceptible to the motivational force of values, due to emotional deficiencies or other reasons.

2. It can be the case that the persons involved (unbeknownst to them) do not talk about the same qualities, objects, or states of affairs. Since reference to objects, according to phenomenological approaches, is a structural component of intentional relations, referential opacity cannot be ruled out, on principle.

3. Intuition-based descriptions may diverge owing to deviant linguistic practices. Even if the persons involved share the same language, they may nonetheless use and interpret the relevant linguistic signs in different ways. Moreover, there is considerable variation with regard to a person's individual talent for languages, level of linguistic performance, and mastery of vocabulary.

4. The former experiences of the persons involved may differ widely with respect to scope and richness. For instance, someone who has never studied early Dutch paintings or does not feel attracted to paintings in general, will have difficulty picking up on the subtly discriminating visual impression of Jan von Eyck's amazing *Arnolfini Portrait* (1434). The same holds true with regard to persons that have never met individuals suffering from schizophrenia, dementia, or Tourette syndrome. In such cases, it makes little sense to conclude that persons unacquainted with these very specific types of behavior are unable to correctly interpret and describe what is intuitively given to them. Rather, they do not "see" the same "things" or states of affairs. This is due to the fact that they do not possess relevant experiences as well as appropriate concepts and stocks of knowledge, which could properly direct their attention and help them form correct and total impressions relating to truth-conducive states of belief.

Why is it worth mentioning that deviating perceptual or higher-order intuitive givenness can be occasioned in rather different ways? Philosophical theories focused on the notion of intuition are confronted with the very common objection that intuitions are merely subjective mental contents, that is, imponderable, unreliable, arbitrary, and inaccessible to processes of verification that warrant intersubjective validity. However, as demonstrated above, there is much we can do to either confirm or deny someone's report on her intuitive givenness in a particular situation. The required process of clarification and explanation will bring to light the above-listed (as well as further) reasons for possible disagreement by exploring the intentional horizon of the relevant intuitions: Phenomenologically put, contextualizing intuitions means to make explicit the constitutive horizons of acts of intuitive givenness.[31] In this vein, phenomenologists hold that it does make sense to quarrel about intuitions and that

---

[31] Cf. Rinofner-Kreidl (1997, p. 92 f); Rinofner-Kreidl (2005). According to the above, contextualizing phenomenological intuitions does not allow for any kind of social reductionism. Yet ruling out

we are able to refine and improve our relating capabilities.[32] Phenomenological intuitionists defy dogmatism by admitting that we cannot utilize intuitive givenness without taking into account its theoretical and practical embeddedness, including its occurrence as part of an individual history of experience.

If our line of reasoning is right, the AID-thesis shows how to challenge a simplified picture of intuition by explaining what it means and what it implies to rely on intuitions. In particular, AID takes into account the difference between *naïve intuitions* and *reflected ("refined") intuitions* because it leaves room for considering reasons why an individual instance of evidence can be false, incomplete, or otherwise imperfect. It shows that intuition, albeit operating as a fundamental principle, is nonetheless relative to varying frameworks constituted by more or less complex attitudes whose appropriateness both depends on the relevant domains of objects and the interests of the epistemic agent. Framework-relativity, in this sense, must be recognized as a universal feature of intuition. Arguing that framework-relativity is a regularly occurring corollary of single episodes of intuition misses the point. Rather, the specific "alertness," which we designated as "attitude," guides our commonly shared view of what counts as intuitive givenness in the relevant field of concern.[33] According to the AID-thesis, intuition is essentially *subject-related* in a structural sense, referring to intentional relations. It is not *subject-dependent*, that is, it is not reducible to *mere* subjectivity in terms of allegedly "private" mental contents. Subject-relatedness and subject-dependence must be carefully distinguished (cf. Husserl 1983, § 65). Advancing this distinction, a phenomenological intuitionism rules out the common objection that, inquiring into consciousness, naturalizing subjectivity (e.g., in terms of brain-physiological explanations of human behavior) would be the only promising way to meet the demand for objective knowledge.[34]

reductionism, it would be instructive to compare the above-sketched phenomenological-intentional contextualization with the ideas advanced by social epistemologists und virtue epistemologists.

[32] Recently, there has been much debate on diverse brands of intuitionism. Pro- and con-arguments especially flare up between "experimental philosophers" and "armchair philosophers," the former denying and the latter demanding the autonomy of philosophy as well as genuinely philosophical uses of intuition.

[33] Taking into account cases of disagreement we should, more appropriately, refer to a commonly shareable view of what counts as intuitive givenness in the respective field.

[34] For valuable comments I would like to thank the participants of the Graz-Chicago Summer-school on Phenomenology and Psychiatry (Graz, August, 2–5, 2011) and the international conference on 100 Years of Karl Jaspers's 'General Psychopathology' (Heidelberg, September 15–16, 2011). Working on this paper, I have especially profited from Thiemo Breyer's comments. I would also like to thank Alexander Englert for his very careful and accurate linguistic corrections.

References

Audi, R. (1997). Intuitionism, pluralism, and the foundations of ethics. In R. Audi (Ed.), *Moral knowledge and ethical character* (pp. 32–45). Oxford: Oxford University Press.

Bealer, G. (1998). Intuition and the Autonomy of Philosophy. In M. DePaul & W. Ramsey (Eds.), *Rethinking intuition. The psychology of intuition and its role in philosophical inquiry* (pp. 201–239). Lanham: Rowman & Littlefield.

Bonjour, L. (1998). *In defense of pure reason: A rationalist account of a priori justification*. Cambridge: Cambridge University Press.

Churchill, S. D. (1998). The intentionality of psychodiagnostic seeing. A phenomenological investigation of clinical impression formation. In R. Valle (Ed.), *Phenomenological inquiry in psychology. Existential and transpersonal dimensions* (pp. 175–207). New York: Plenum.

Depraz, N. (2003). Putting the époché into practice: Schizophrenic experience as illustrating the phenomenological exploration of consciousness. In B. Fulford, K. Morris & J. Sadler (Eds.), *Nature and narrative: An introduction to the new philosophy of psychiatry* (pp. 187–197). Oxford: Oxford University Press.

Huemer, M. (2005). *Ethical intuitionism*. Houndmills: Basingstoke & New York: Palgrave Macmillan.

Husserl, E. (1969). *Formal and transcendental logic* (trans: D. Cairns). The Hague: Martinus Nijhoff.

Husserl, E. (1970a). *Logical Investigations (Vol. 1)* (trans: J. N. Findlay from the Second German edition of Logische Untersuchungen. With a new preface by M. Dummett and edited with a new introduction by D. Moran). London: Routledge.

Husserl, E. (1970b). *The crisis of european sciences and transcendental phenomenology. An introduction to phenomenological philosophy* (trans: with an Introduction, D. Carr.) Evanston:Northwestern.

Husserl, E. (1973). *Experience and judgment. Investigations in a genealogy of logic*. (Revised and ed. by L. Landgrebe. Translated by J. S. Churchill & K. Ameriks. Introduction by J. S. Churchill. Afterword by L. Eley). Evanston: Northwestern University Press.

Husserl, E. (1983). *Ideas pertaining to a pure phenomenology and to a phenomenological philosophy. First book: General introduction to a pure phenomenology (trans: F. Kersten)*. The Hague: Martinus Nijhoff.

Husserl, E. (1989a). *Ideas pertaining to a pure phenomenology and to a phenomenological philosophy. Second book: Studies in the phenomenology of constitution (trans: R. Rojcewicz & A. Schuwer)*. Dordrecht: Kluwer Academic.

Husserl, E. (1989b). *Aufsätze und Vorträge (1922–1937). Mit ergänzenden Texten*. In T. Nenon & H. R. Sepp (Eds.). Dordrecht: Kluwer Academic. English edition: Husserl E. (1931). *Phenomenology and anthropology* (trans: T. Sheehan & R. E. Palmer). http://www.stanford.edu/dept/relstud/faculty/sheehan/EHtrans/g-phenan.pdf. Accessed 11 July 2012.

Husserl, E. (1991). *On the phenomenology of the consciousness of internal time (1893–1917) (trans: J. B. Brough)*. Dordrecht: Kluwer.

Jaspers, K. (1968). The phenomenological approach in psychopathology (translated anonymously). *British Journal of Psychiatry, 114,* 1313–1323.

Jaspers, K. (1973). *Allgemeine Psychopathologie* (9th ed.). Berlin: Springer.

Jaspers, K. (1990). *Gesammelte Schriften zur Psychopathologie*. Berlin: Springer.

Jaspers, K. (1997a). *General Psychopathology (Vol. 1)* (trans: From the German by J. Hoenig & M. W. Hamilton. With a new foreword by P. R. McHugh). Baltimore: The Johns Hopkins University Press.

Jaspers, K. (1997b). *General Psychopathology (Vol. 2)* (trans: From the German by J. Hoenig & M. W. Hamilton. With a new foreword by P. R. McHugh). Baltimore: The Johns Hopkins University Press.

Luft, S. (2008). Zur phänomenologischen Methode in Karl Jaspers' Allgemeiner Psychopathologie. In S. Rinofner-Kreidl & H. A. Wiltsche (Eds.), *Karl Jaspers' Allgemeine Psychopathologie zwischen Wissenschaft, Philosophie und Praxis* (pp. 31–51). Würzburg: Königshausen & Neumann.

Mackie, J. L. (1977). *Ethics. Inventing right and wrong*. Harmondsworth: Penguin.

Merleau-Ponty, M. (1958). *Phenomenology of perception* (trans: C. Smith). London: Routledge

Pust, J. (2000). *Intuition as evidence*. New York: Garland.

Rinofner-Kreidl, S. (1997). *Lebendiges Denken. Zu Idee und Wirklichkeitsgehalt einer dialektischen Phänomenologie*. Karl Jaspers' Psychologie der Weltanschauungen. Jahrbuch der Österreichischen Karl Jaspers Gesellschaft 10, 91–125.

Rinofner-Kreidl, S. (2000). *Edmund Husserl. Zeitlichkeit und Intentionalität*. Freiburg: Alber.

Rinofner-Kreidl, S. (2002). Praxis der Subjektivität. Zum Verhältnis von Transzendentalphänomenologie und Hermeneutik. In D. Carr & C. Lotz (Eds.), *Subjektivität—Verantwortung—Wahrheit. Neue Aspekte der Phänomenologie Edmund Husserls* (pp. 37–56). Frankfurt a. M.: Peter Lang.

Rinofner-Kreidl, S. (2003). Transzendentale oder hermeneutische Phänomenologie der Lebenswelt? Über Chancen und Gefahren einer reflexiven Analyse. In H. Vetter (Ed.), *Lebenswelten. Ludwig Landgrebe—Eugen Fink—Jan Patocka. Wiener Tagungen zur Phänomenologie 2002* (pp. 115–137). Frankfurt a. M.: Peter Lang.

Rinofner-Kreidl, S. (2004). Beschreibung. In H. Vetter (Ed.), *Wörterbuch der phänomenologischen Begriffe* (pp. 71–75). Hamburg: Felix Meiner.

Rinofner-Kreidl, S. (2005). Exploding the myth of the given. On phenomenology's basic discord with empiricism. In. J. C. Marek & M. E. Reicher (Eds.), *Erfahrung und Analyse. Beiträge des 27. Internationalen Wittgenstein-Symposions (8.–14. August 2004)* (pp. 309–311). Kirchberg a. W.

Rinofner-Kreidl, S. (2008). Zur Idee des Methodenpartikularismus in Jaspers' Allgemeiner Psychopathologie. In S. Rinofner-Kreidl & H. A. Wiltsche (Eds.), *Karl Jaspers' Allgemeine Psychopathologie zwischen Wissenschaft, Philosophie und Praxis* (pp. 75–93). Würzburg: Königshausen & Neumann.

Schwartz, M. A., & Wiggins, O. P. (2004). Phenomenological and hermeneutic models. In J. Radden (Ed.), *The philosophy of psychiatry. A companion* (pp. 351–363). Oxford: Oxford University Press.

Walker, C. (1994a). Karl Jaspers and Edmund Husserl, I: The perceived convergence. *Philosophy, Psychiatry & Psychology, 1*(4), 117–134.

Walker, C. (1994b). Karl Jaspers and Edmund Husserl, II: The divergence. *Philosophy, Psychiatry & Psychology, 1*(4), 245–265.

Walker, C. (1995a). Karl Jaspers and Edmund Husserl, III: Jaspers as a Kantian Phenomenologist. *Philosophy, Psychiatry & Psychology, 2*(1), 65–82.

Walker, C. (1995b). Karl Jaspers and Edmund Husserl, IV: Phenomenology and empathic understanding. *Philosophy, Psychiatry & Psychology, 2*(3), 247–266.

Wiggins, O. P., & Schwartz, M. A. (1997). Edmund Husserl's influence on Karl Jaspers's Phenomenology. *Philosophy, Psychiatry, and Psychology, 4*(1), 15–36.

Wiggins, O. P., Schwartz, M. A., & Spitzer, M. (1992). Phenomenological/descriptive psychiatry: The methods of Edmund Husserl and Karl Jaspers. In M. Spitzer, F. Uehlein, M. A. Schwartz & C. Mundt (Eds.), *Phenomenology, language and schizophrenia* (pp. 46–59). New York: Springer.

Wiltsche, H. A. (2008). Überlegungen zum wissenschaftsphilosophischen Subtext' in Karl Jaspers' Allgemeiner Psychopathologie. In S. Rinofner-Kreidl & H. A. Wiltsche (Eds.), *Karl Jaspers' Allgemeine Psychopathologie zwischen Wissenschaft, Philosophie und Praxis* (pp. 53–74). Würzburg: Königshausen & Neumann.

Chapter 4
The Reception of Jaspers' General Psychopathology Outside of Europe

Andrés Heerlein and Carlos Cornaglia

4.1 Introduction

Karl Jaspers began his academic career working as a psychiatrist at the University Clinic of Heidelberg. After a period of transition, he switched to philosophy in the early 1920s. In Europe, Jaspers obtained his widest recognition not only through his publications on philosophical and ethical issues, but also for the different editions of his *General Psychopathology* (GP). Despite the positive reception of his psychiatric and philosophical contributions in the German-speaking world, some authors suggest that outside of Germany Jaspers is a forgotten psychopathologist. However, in current scientific publications in the field of psychiatry and diagnostic classification, Jaspers is often mentioned as having made important contributions to the development of psychopathology and taxonomy, not only in Germany and France but also in other European and Latin American countries. A hundred years since the publication of GP, some authors like Huber (2002), Bolton (2004), or Ghaemi (2009) have suggested that almost every edition played a seminal role in the development of psychiatry in the last century, being one of the most important attempts to introduce scientific order into psychopathology. Central to GP was Jaspers' attempt to create a new psychopathological methodology, providing key elements for a better comprehension of the main problems in clinical psychiatry. Jaspers introduced the concept of "comprehensive facts" (sinnhafte Tatbestände), while utilizing denominations like "understandable relations" (verständliche Zusammenhänge) and "objective connections" (objektive Verknüpfung), which suggested that clinical psychiatry should be considered a practical aspect of medical praxis, while psychopathology should be considered an independent, theoretical discipline.

A. Heerlein (✉)
Universities of Chile and del Desarrollo, Santiago de Chile, Chile
e-mail: aheerlein@vtr.net

C. Cornaglia
University of Neuquén, Neuquén, Argentina
e-mail: sicarloscornaglia@yahoo.com.ar

T. Fuchs et al. (eds.), *Karl Jaspers' Philosophy and Psychopathology*,
DOI 10.1007/978-1-4614-8878-1_4, © Springer Science+Business Media New York 2014

In Germany, GP was first published in 1913, having a great impact and a significant influence on the way in which psychiatrists defined symptoms, facts *(Tatbestände)*, subjective experience, objective manifestation, nosology and diagnosis. The psychopathological model that Jaspers introduced for clinical psychiatry focused mainly on subjective experience, aiming more at the elucidation of the patient's own inner experiences than at the observation of symptoms or behaviors.

Although Max Weber was the first decisive personal influence and Kant the first philosophical influence on Jaspers work, many authors have suggested that Husserl and Dilthey played just as important a role in influencing his development as a psychopathologist. However, there is little agreement on the extent of Husserl's influence on Jaspers' GP. Some evidence supports the notion of a certain influence from Husserl on Jaspers' ideas. Writing about phenomenology, Jaspers mentions Husserl in his *Phenomenological Approach in Psychopathology*. In a few passages of the first edition of GP, in Jaspers' analysis of the disorders of perception, there is also some evidence that suggests that Husserl was very important for the development of his ideas. However, as Berrios (1993) and Figueroa (2008) have pointed out, there are significant differences between Husserl's concept of phenomenology and Jaspers' proposal of a "specific method of phenomenological analysis." Husserl preferred to use the term "phenomenology" in the sense of the "appearance of things" or *Wesensschau*, which differs from the concept proposed by Jaspers in GP of an "empirical method of inquiry." It is clear that Jaspers wanted to retain the philosophical concept of "phenomenology," but not in the Husserlian way. According to Berrios (1993) and Figueroa (2008), Husserl's phenomenology had no influence on the origins and the development of GP. Since then, several discussions about Jaspers' and Husserl's concepts of phenomenology have been published in specialized journals. We ought to mention also that the debates about Jaspers and the influence of Husserl went far beyond the borders of Europe, and that the differences between them may have contributed toward generating the unfortunate confusion of current psychiatry regarding the concepts of nosology, phenomenology and psychopathology.

In the early 1920s, Jaspers made the acquaintance of Martin Heidegger, which played a decisive role in Jaspers' formation as a philosopher. Despite their differences and, at times, difficult relationship, Heidegger and Jaspers were usually associated with each other as the two founding fathers of existential philosophy in Germany.

4.2   International Reception of GP

International recognition of Jaspers' GP started with great enthusiasm in France in the late 1920s with the first publication of his work in a foreign language (Jaspers 1923/1928). Jacques Lacan's thesis "De la psychose paranoique dans ses rapports avec la personnalité" is an example of the excellent reception of GP in France at that time. After the completion of the French translation and during the third and fourth decade of the 20th century, the first edition of his textbook was translated into the

Japanese. After the Second World War, the fourth edition of GP was concluded and a few years later translated into Spanish. This difficult translation task was successfully concluded in 1950 in Buenos Aires, Argentina, while the English translation was published many years later, in 1963 in Manchester (Jaspers 1959/1963). As a result of this atypical evolution of Jaspers dissemination in the western world, the international consideration of his GP started first in France, then in Japan and in Latin America, and only two decades later in the English-speaking world.

4.3   GP in the United States of America

The American Psychopathological Association was founded in 1910 and is one of the oldest research organizations in North America. Its primary goal has always been "to stimulate on specific topics relevant to research in psychopathology". Unfortunately, the initial reception of GP in the U.S. was poor and poorly timed. From the first edition on, acceptance of this new psychopathological approach proposed by Jaspers faced many difficulties in Great Britain and in North America. As a consequence, the first translation of GP into English was completed and published by Hoeing and Anderson in 1963 in Manchester (Jaspers 1959/1963), 50 years after its publication in Germany (Hoeing 2004). According to Havens (1967), Jaspers writings on psychopathology, largely unknown in the U.S., represent the most detailed rationale for eclecticism in psychiatry.

It is interesting to note that in the U.S. Jaspers was successfully introduced by Hannah Arendt in the field of philosophy in the early 1930s, and that after the Second World War his main ideas as a philosopher received progressively more attention and recognition. In 1980, Leonard and Edith Ehrlich founded the Karl Jaspers Society of North America in Boston. Since then, many publications have been associated with Karl Jaspers as a philosopher, but very few have focused on his psychopathological contributions. In fact, Jaspers' psychiatric work remained ignored for decades in most places in the U.S. Only a few authors from the East Coast, like Leston Havens, Paul McHugh and Philip Slavney, have paid attention to his ideas. The majority of the U.S. psychiatrists, however, showed no interest in Jaspers' GP. Havens published in 1967 an interesting article in the American Journal of Psychiatry about Karl Jaspers and American psychiatry (Havens 1967). In his paper, Havens agrees that Jaspers greatly influenced the development of phenomenology, the concept of process and existential analysis. The author reviews the growth of Jaspers' thought out of Emil Kraepelin's and its relation to the psychiatry of content, ego psychology and various psychotherapies. Paul McHugh and Phillip Slavney (1998), from Johns Hopkins, published in 1983 *The Perspectives of Psychiatry*, an excellent textbook for psychiatrists during their time of residency. In 1997, McHugh included his own foreword to the English edition of GP. According to McHugh (2006) Jaspers' "phenomenological method hinges on the human capacity for self-expression—a means of communicating one's experiences to another. This capacity makes it possible for patients to describe the content of their minds and for psychiatrists listening to these descriptions to enter the mental life of such patients." For over three decades, McHugh's and Slavney's textbook was used to teach Johns Hopkins medical students and residents how to formulate and treat patients with psychiatric disorders. However, most of the academic centers of the U.S. showed little or no interest for the proposals of McHugh and Slavney with regard to Jaspers' GP. For instance, the fourth edition of the U.S.'s mainly used textbook, the *Comprehensive Textbook of Psychiatry*, edited by Kaplan and Sadock (1985), does not mention GP at all. The poor reception of the English translation of GP in the U.S. was probably due to different factors, including its late publication in comparison with the French and Spanish translations of 1934 and 1950. What other factors may explain this lackluster reception?

Some authors have tried to explain this poor reception by referencing historical, religious and cultural reasons, including the factor of *ressentiment* against Germany following the Second World War. Despite their differences, Jaspers was very often associated with Heidegger, creating an unwarranted prejudice against him. However, these prejudices are totally unfounded due to the fact that Jaspers was a victim of the National Socialist Regime rather than a supporter, and due to his well-known anti-fascist political ideas before, during and after the war. Other authors believe that the far more limited reception of GP in the U.S. may be associated to the relatively ambivalent position of the famous psychiatrist Adolf Meyer-Gross, who, belonging to the Heidelberg School, introduced GP in the English-speaking countries. According to these authors, Meyer-Gross not only supported Jaspers' ideas, but also criticized them occasionally (e.g., by pointing out that the concept of "psychological comprehension was too flexible, leading to infinite extensions and to the contention that all psychopathological manifestations might be psychogenic").

The minimal interest shown by psychiatrists from North America could also be explained via historical-ideological reasons. For more than four decades, nearly all the major leaders in the U.S. field of psychiatry embraced psychodynamic principles, and used them to shape psychiatric education and training. Psychoanalysis tried to explain the majority of psychiatric disturbances, leaving no space for psychopathology. In 1980, the introduction of DSM III and DSM IV shifted psychiatry into a descriptive-operational dimension with a different philosophical background. First psychoanalysis, then the new paradigm of operational and statistical diagnosis, and, finally, the strong influence of the new "bio-psycho-social paradigm" contributed to reduce the complex problem of human psychopathology into a simple list of symptom aggregates or, recalling the words of Kendell, into a "label of arbitrary groupings of clinical phenomena" (Kendell 1984).

According to the former editor of the American Journal of Psychiatry, Nancy Andreasen (2007), this was the end of phenomenology in the U.S. In 2007, Nancy Andreasen writes:

> Since the publication of DSM-III in 1980, there has been a steady decline in the teaching of careful clinical evaluation that is targeted to the individual person's problems and social context and that is enriched by a good general knowledge of psychopathology. Students are taught to memorize DSM rather than to learn complexities from the great psychopathologists of the past. By 2005, the decline has become so severe that it could be referred to as 'the death of phenomenology in the United States.'

Today we know that, fortunately, psychopathology has not passed away. In the U.S., Michael Schwartz and Osborne Wiggins belong to a growing list of academic psychiatrist's interested in a renewal of psychopathology and diagnosis. In 1987, Schwartz and Wiggins published an article about "Diagnosis and Ideal Types," trying to discover new insights for the problem of psychiatric classification. Based on Weber's concepts, the authors analyze his "ideal types" with the concepts used in modern psychiatric diagnosis. Schwartz and Wiggins propose that, at the outset of the examination, "Weberian ideal types" should be considered in order to provide a better orientation and a reliable method for clinical diagnosis. As a result of this examination method, the psychiatrist should arrive eventually at particular convictions regarding the nature of the patient's problem. In recent years, Nassir Ghaemi (from the U.S.) has published a list of interesting articles about the work of Karl Jaspers, stressing the need for reintroducing the concepts of "pluralism," "transcendence," and "limit situations" as important keys for a better understanding of the psychiatric practice (Ghaemi 2007). In 2009, Ghaemi published an article about DSM and the Jaspers critique of Kraepelin's taxonomy (Ghaemi 2009). According to this author, in the early 20th century, Karl Jaspers provided unique insights into Kraepelin's work, introducing the concept of "ideal types" in a different way (Ghaemi 2009).

4.4   The GP in Latin America

In 1950, Saubidet and Santillán published the first translation of GP into Spanish in Buenos Aires. The focus of the translators concentrated on the methodological dimension of the text, considering it essential for psychiatric practice. The history of the Spanish translation starts in 1946, after the publication in Germany of the fourth edition of the "*GP*." In Europe, this new and refreshing edition had been received with great enthusiasm and was strongly supported by Schneider, López-Ibor, Berner, and Huber, among many other leaders of the European psychiatry.

Outside of Europe, the impact of the fourth edition varied greatly. While the English-speaking world showed little interest for the fourth edition of the "GP," it was in Latin America where Jaspers found excellent reception and early recognition. At that time, Schneider and López-Ibor had a strong influence on Latin American psychiatry. In 1947, the Peruvian psychiatrist H. Delgado (1947) published in Lima a remarkable article about Jaspers and the new edition of his GP. According to Delgado, the first edition of Jaspers book was intended to introduce order, clearness and critiques into the domain of psychopathology. However, Delgado made clear that he found the fourth edition to be an extraordinary revision of the original book, where the role and the importance of the psychiatric method is emphasized, the differentiation between meanings (i.e., senses) and causes is clearly explained and the scientific status of the facts or evidences that contribute toward psychiatric diagnosis is discussed (Delgado 1947). According to Delgado, the main goal in Jaspers GP is the introduction of a new psychopathological method that attempts to find a reliable way to comprehend internal experiences. Jaspers' original introduction of the method of "*sich Einfühlen*," defined here as "understanding through empathy," Delgado considered to be one of the key elements of modern psychopathology (Delgado 1947).

In 1947, only 1 year after the publication of the fourth edition of GP in Germany, the Peruvian Society of Psychiatry accepted it and predicted fruitful consequences for the development of psychiatry not only in Peru but also in many other southern countries of Latin America. As a matter of fact, Saubidet and Santillán started the first translation into Spanish the same year; they completed and published it in 1950 in Buenos Aires.

Five years later in Spain, Martin L. Santos published *Dilthey, Jaspers and the comprehension of the mentally ill* (1955), initiating a productive phase of interesting discussions about Jaspers and the role of psychopathology in the Spanish-speaking world. This book and the strong support it won from different influential Latin American psychiatrists contributed to disseminate GP in Peru, Chile, Brazil, Honduras, and Argentina. Jaspers came to counterbalance the growing influence and the fast dissemination of psychoanalysis in Latin America, mainly in the academic circles of Argentina, Chile, and Peru. Among the Peruvians, a small, brilliant group of Honorio Delgado followers, like Mariátegui and Alarcon, contributed significantly to spreading Jaspers' ideas throughout Latin America. Mariátegui tried to combine some passages of GP with new ideas coming from the psychodynamic school. Alarcón tried to combine some of Jaspers's main ideas with specific cultural topics in social psychiatry.

4.4.1   Chile

In Chile since 1960, different authors like Dörr (1979), Roa (1994), and Figueroa (2000, 2008) have contributed to the spreading of Jaspers's psychiatric ideas, not only at the University of Chile and the Catholic University but also at the University of Valparaíso. The close relationship between some Chilean psychiatrists, who completed postgraduate training at the Psychiatric Clinic of the University of Heidelberg (Germany), also contributed to the spreading of his ideas at the main academic centers of the country. Gustavo Figueroa, professor of psychiatry from Valparaíso, published interesting articles about the relationship between GP and Jaspers's philosophical background. Figueroa suggests that there are significant differences between the phenomenological approach proposed by Husserl and the scientific method proposed by Jaspers in GP. In 2008, Figueroa has raised new and interesting questions about Husserl's role in the development of the method that Jaspers originally called "phenomenological." For Figueroa, Jaspers's phenomenology is an empirical science of the subjective manifestations of psychic-pathological experiences, while for Husserl it's a primary science or "the absolute philosophy of consciousness" (Figueroa 2008).

In Santiago de Chile, Roa introduced with great enthusiasm Jaspers's GP into the general curricula of psychiatry and psychopathology training at the University of

Chile and the Catholic University. Roa was convinced that Jaspers was the first and most important author introducing phenomenology into psychiatry, pointing out that the dichotomy between understanding and explaining is a key element in psychopathology. Psychological events and psychopathological phenomena are eventually understandable, whereas physical causality is not understandable but only explainable in scientific terms. For Roa, GP is a fundamental tool for the adequate comprehension of psychosis, paranoia or delusional disorders (Roa 1994). He also tried to explain how these concepts can be used in the diagnostic differentiation between a schizophrenic process and delusional developments.

By the end of the 60s and after a long period of postgraduate training at the University Clinic in Heidelberg, Otto Dörr started an academic career as a professor of psychiatry in Concepción, Chile. Afterwards, Dörr published several articles and books about phenomenology and anthropological psychiatry. In the last four decades, his contributions to the development of phenomenology and anthropological psychiatry have proven remarkable, as well as his discussions about some specific aspects of GP and his role in clinical psychiatry. Dörr prefers to talk about Jaspers in the context of his philosophy and his concept of "limit situations" (Grenzsituationen). These are situations that were mentioned briefly by Jaspers in his GP but more extensively in his writings on existential philosophy. According to Jaspers, the limit situations are characterized by guilt feelings or acute anxiety, in which the human mind confronts the restrictions and pathological narrowness of its existing forms. According to Dörr the concept of "limit situation" is relevant not only for psychotherapy but also for psychiatric practice in general.

In the last three decades, a new generation of Chilean authors interested in the original ideas of Jaspers and Heidegger has tried to emphasize the role of phenomenology and philosophy in psychiatry. Holzapfel (2003) has published interesting reflections about the concept of "Death and suicide" in Jaspers' work, suggesting that "the existential elucidation of suicide remains a mystery, as a radically incomprehensible act; however, its authenticity lies in as much as does not involve a mere escape," Holzapfel concludes. Existential philosophy, based on the works of Jaspers and of Heidegger, has been integrated by psychotherapists in Chile in order to improve the possibilities of understanding the contents of what many depressive and suicidal patients are trying to express.

In the last two decades in Brazil and in Chile, a more objective method for the evaluation of psychopathological phenomena was introduced: the AMDP-System for the objective evaluation of psychopathological phenomena. The AMDP-System was developed in Europe in the 1960s by the Association for Methodology and Documentation in Psychiatry and has been used in the last three decades for the clinical documentation of psychiatric files, for the documentation of findings in forensic psychiatry and for the measurement of changes in clinical trials. The AMDP-System has been used regularly in the French-speaking and the German-speaking countries by clinical and forensic psychiatrists. This system is not equivalent with Jaspers' methodology described in GP. According, however, to our personal conviction and to one of the founding fathers of this system, Jules Angst, many authors of the AMDP were influenced by Jaspers' GP (Angst 2012). The AMDP-System consists of three anamnestic forms and of two comprehensive rating scales on present psychopathological issues and somatic complaints. It has been translated from German into French, Spanish, English, Italian and Portuguese. In Latin America the AMDP-System has been regularly used in Chile and in Brazil. It was in Brazil where Braz da Silva (1994) used this system in clinical practice and as a research instrument for postgraduate training. In Chile, Heerlein and others introduced it in 1993 for clinical research and for regular pre- and postgraduate education (Heerlein and Santander 1993). The characteristics of the structure and the clearness of the definitions of the AMDP-System are remarkable, and may contribute to a better learning process in psychiatric training, improving the comprehension of difficult psychopathological tasks. Therefore, Heerlein and Téllez have used the AMDP manual regularly in pre- and postgraduate education in Chile (Heerlein and Santander 1993; Téllez 2012).

It is interesting to note that despite of the strong influence of the American Psychiatric Association and DSM III and IV Manuals throughout Latin America that in Chile the leading psychiatric journals are still interested in publishing articles about Jaspers' GP. For instance, some years ago the psychiatric journal, *Revista de Neuropsiquiatría*, published a special edition dedicated exclusively to Karl Jaspers and his GP. Another Chilean journal, *Gaceta Universitaria*, has published several articles about Jaspers' psychiatric and philosophical work. These articles concentrate on the problems of consciousness and delusions in GP, on the biography of Jaspers as well as on the differences between his concept of phenomenology and the concept provided by Husserl. More recently, the parallels between Jaspers and Heidegger, in the field of existential philosophy, have also been analyzed. Every year, the Chilean Society for the Development of Psychiatry (SODEPSY) organizes two postgraduate seminars for young psychiatrists, one about Jaspers' GP and the other about the relationship between Jaspers and Heidegger in the field of psychiatry and philosophy.

Finally, in Chile, Germany and in other countries of Latin America and Europe, Jaspers had a great influence not only in clinical but also in forensic psychiatry. Since the publication of the fourth edition of GP, many forensic psychiatrists have included these methods in their analyses and their reports related to the explanation of criminal behavior (Téllez 2012). Scientific reports from Germany, Chile and Argentina come to the conclusion that in many forensic cases but also in difficult situations with diagnostic doubts, the use of the methodology proposed by Jaspers has been very helpful in order to bring clearness, comprehension and reliability into the forensic reports. For many Chilean forensic psychiatrists, GP is still a valid and a useful tool for the better understanding of psychopathological phenomena eventually related to criminal behavior and legal disputes (Téllez 2012).

4.4.2   Argentina

Karl Jaspers also had a considerable influence on Argentina. Since the publication of the first Spanish translation of GP in Buenos Aires in 1951, an important number of authors and experts have discussed Jaspers' main ideas in the field of psychiatry. However, the majority of those Argentinian authors who have made reference to GP did not take into account the central methodological foundation of the text and the way the text necessarily requires to be read (Cornaglia 1983). Most of the textbooks related to psychopathology and published after the first translation of GP in Argentina are characterized by showing a tendency to associate specific concepts of Jaspers with some psychoanalytic movements, or with so-called descriptive psychopathology. These authors forget to take into account Jaspers' core concepts, the need of a specific methodological awareness before entering the text and the necessity of an intratextual contextualization. Jaspers considered these aspects to be essential before starting any kind of analysis or discussion of his work. According to Bleger (1972) and Paz (1984), most Argentinian authors misunderstood the main aspects of the book in the last decades, by providing only basic references to some general methods (e.g., "understanding" or "explaining"), while failing to consider any of the special methods that are normally required before entering into the logical organization of GP. Only a few authors have analyzed in detail some key concepts such as "process" and "development," namely, Pichon-Rivière (1948/1983) and Paz (1984), or "limit situation," Saurí (1989). Some others, like Feldman (1990), have analyzed the concepts of "delusion," "reaction," "clinical units," "nosology," and "nosography," but most of them have failed to contextualize it methodologically within the whole text. In Argentina, some authors have presented Jaspers' text as "being a part of phenomenology or existential philosophy," disregarding the methodology and the main philosophical roots introduced by Jaspers in his psychopathology. Only a few authors and research groups have tried to investigate more carefully the methodological structure and the contents that underlie GP.

Two different groups of Argentinian authors have analyzed more seriously the methodological character of GP. Isaac, from the National University and from the University of Córdoba, and Nuñez, from the University of Salvador, Buenos Aires, have both delivered important contributions to the study of Jaspers' work. Nuñez noted in 1982 that: "It is a paradox that this extraordinary psychopathological investigation chronologically dated in 1913 and that has dismissively been considered as being "old" is currently on the front line of psychopathology for his methodological pretension in an epistemological attitude." Saal and Cornaglia introduced Jaspers' methodology at conferences and in lectures about special psychopathology and clinical psychology in Córdoba and in other universities of Argentina, thereby continuing the work initiated by Isaac (Cornaglia 1983). Unlike other authors who have only considered one of the concepts included in GP, the works of Nuñez and Isaac and of Cornaglia and Saal are characterized by a tendency to locate each object of knowledge (conceptual or clinical) in the framework of each of the methods proposed by GP, and not only in a general descriptive or phenomenological perspective, as tends to be the case when Jaspers' work is discussed. Nuñez and Cornaglia have presented numerous case examples showing how it is possible to investigate clinical cases according to the possibilities and limits of each one of the methods of GP, avoiding prejudices that are frequent in the dogmatic field of many schools of psychopathology or psychiatry. Cornaglia comes to the conclusion that to understand the substance of the text, and for investigating its reception, we need to know its characterization by the same Jaspers. The task of GP is "to configure the whole." His main task is to introduce clarification, order and education. Jaspers' GP has been designed by its author as being a methodological system, that is, a system of conscious methods that requires methodological order. This is the reason why the principle, which structures the configuration of each part and the whole of the text, is the proper methodological order. In conclusion, the text is a critical methodological and a methodical critique (Cornaglia 2010).

Jaspers' GP has also been relevant for the development of psychiatry in other Latin American countries like Brazil and Honduras. According to D. Espinazo (1980), the publication of the first edition of GP had some influence in Honduras, and the translation of the fourth edition by Saubidet contributed to fruitful discussions about the role of psychopathology in that country.

In 1979, Samuel Pena Reis translated GP into Portuguese with a technical review of Paulo Costa Rzezinski in Brazil (Jaspers 1979). Since 1985, the Brazilian psychiatrist Braz da Silva applied in combination with the *A.M.D.P Manual* the methodology of GP as a heuristic research tool in the postgraduate training of psychiatry residents (Braz da Silva 1994). For Braz da Silva, GP should not be classified as a textbook in a strict sense. On the contrary, it should be considered an intellectual map or a guide for a series of separate but related areas of knowledge. Braz da Silva started a research program with psychiatry students completing residency from the school of medicine at the Pontifical University of Campinas. In this project the residents tried to coordinate each chapter and method of GP with the corresponding chapter of the psychopathological examination method of the AMDP-System, and its application to the analysis of cases filled out and investigated by residents (Braz da Silva 1994). Braz da Silva came to the conclusion that the combination of GP and the AMDP-System is an excellent tool for psychiatric training and for the quantitative evaluation of psychopathological phenomena.

4.5   Discussion

Jaspers founded the Heidelberg School of Psychopathology by collating the psychiatric knowledge of his time with a methodological and structured approach. By doing so, he laid the foundations for modern psychopathology. In Germany, the "Heidelberg School" started with a fruitful activity provided by Gruhle, Mayer-Gross, Homburger, and Beringer (teachers and or colleagues of Jaspers when Nissl was the head of the Heidelberg Clinic), and was continued then by Schneider, von Bayer, Tellenbach, Janzarik, Mundt, Kraus and Fuchs. Outside of Europe the "Heidelberg School" had an interesting evolution in countries like Chile, Argentina, Peru, Brazil, Honduras, the U.S., and Japan. However, in many countries of the world, GP has been ill understood.

How can it be explained that GP is seldom mentioned by the current international psychopathological literature? In our view, most of the recent textbooks about psychopathology are characterized by building up specific theories associated with different psychoanalytic schools, or with the so-called descriptive psychopathology, which does not consider Jaspers' core concepts, his methodological awareness and his emphasis on the required intratextual contextualization. Most of these "new" perspectives incorporate concepts described by Jaspers, such as "understanding" or "explaining," but fail to consider any of the special methods and the logical organization proposed by the author. Only a few authors interested in psychopathology have considered concepts such as *"process," "development," "phase," "reaction," "attack,"* or *"limit situation,"* but they rarely contextualize the concepts in relation to the whole text. In other cases, the text is considered just as an interpretation of existential philosophy. Only a few authors and research groups have devoted themselves to the investigation of the methodological structure and all the contents included in GP. The study of GP requires the consideration of its systematic and its methodological nature, as well as its contents. A typical example that ignores these two aspects, making logical and methodological mistakes that could have been avoided, is the construction of DSM manuals. Some authors postulate that DSM has missed the opportunity to join together all the methods included in GP and to create a central methodological guide in order to organize logically the diagnostic process (Kraus 2008; Ghaemi 2009).

For different reasons, in most parts of the world the influence of DSM and ICD in psychiatric diagnosis has been strong but also controversial. After three decades of research, the validity of DSM criteria and its diagnostic categories has not been confirmed. Now, DSM V is expected to change most of the criteria and categorizations adopted in the past. The British psychiatrist, Kendell, while evaluating the achievements of DSM III, suggested that "DSM diagnostic terms are no more than convenient labels of arbitrary groupings of clinical phenomena" (Kendell 1984). More recently, Ghaemi (2009) suggested that in the U.S., the rise of the neo-Kraepelinian nosology of DSM III resuscitated Kraepelin's work, especially his overtly biological ontology. However, this neo-Kraepelinian system—Ghaemi says—has led to concerns regarding overdiagnosis of psychiatric syndromes ("nosologomania") and perhaps scientifically ill-founded psychopharmacological treatment for presumed neo-Kraepelinian syndromes (Ghaemi 2009).

Many authors talk nowadays of a "crisis of our current diagnostic systems" (Kendel 1984; Kraus 2008; Jäger et al. 2008; Ghaemi 2009). This may be due to the fact that operational diagnostic systems in psychiatry are characterized only by a descriptive and statistical approach. In this context, psychopathological symptoms are interpreted as elementary entities, which can be combined into artificial diagnostic categories. Some critics point out that DSM manuals have more or less "manipulated" the classic psychopathology, depriving it from its rich philosophical content. Many authors agree that ICD-10 and DSM IV categories should not be considered as logical entities, because they do not reflect a specific model of psychiatric disease. For Kraus from Heidelberg, the so-called disorders of DSM are only "aggregates of symptoms" and not logical categories. "Aggregates" are part of the groupings and collections of a pre-logical level, as demonstrated by Piaget (Kraus 2008). Kraus asserts that diagnostic categories configuring DSM manuals are only a collection of "aggregates". We would like to mention that many years before DSM III was introduced into psychiatry, Jaspers, Mayer-Gross and Conrad had already criticized this atomizing procedure. For Portela and Ramos (2005), the abolition of psychopathology on behalf of a nonsatisfactory empiricism and a diagnostic reductionism has pushed psychiatry into sterile paralysis. These authors question operational diagnosis, and find in Jaspers the methodological solution to the present dilemma. Philosophical thinking used to be embedded in psychiatry. This was self-evident since psychiatry and philosophy shared interests in the same matters—*reality, freedom, personal identity, social reality, perception, free will, thought,* and *affec*t. As Jaspers used to say, "in clinical psychiatry everybody inclined to disregard philosophy will be overwhelmed by philosophy in an unperceived way."

Unfortunately, the world's mainstream psychiatrists do not support Jaspers's psychopathological approach. Some authors argue that psychiatry may have lost its essence. Based on the main ideas of the authors of the Heidelberg School and some recent developments in psychiatry outside of Europe, we would like to conclude that Jaspers' psychopathology is far from being obsolete, remaining relevant not only for clinical and forensic purposes but also for biological research and diagnostic classification. Psychopathology should lead all the other psychiatric sub-disciplines, including clinical and basic sciences. Psychiatry needs psychopathology for diagnostics, for therapy and for primary and secondary prevention of mental disorders, but also for biological research. Jaspers' approach cannot offer a definite solution to our diagnostic dilemma, but it leaves room for new developments by completing, correcting and changing many aspects of classical and present psychiatric concepts. Starting from the latest editions of GP the development of new methods and techniques of research are needed, as well as a new configuration of the methodological organization proposed by Jaspers. He was absolutely aware of this need, but he also knew that this task went far beyond the production of texts belonging exclusively to current diagnostic conventions.

Perhaps the worst consequence of the omission of Jaspers from the current psychiatric discourse and practice has been the installation of a worldwide confusion about the different meanings of the concept of "psychopathology". The word "psychopathology" is currently used in a trivial sense, instead of referring to the discipline "that studies the phenomena of mental disorders." This confusion may have contributed to inhibit the development of clinical, biological and forensic psychiatry. We would like to conclude with a statement of E. W. Anderson in the foreword to the first English translation of GP in 1963:

> As long as psychiatric diagnosis and treatment rest on psychopathological investigation, the continuing improvement and sharpening of this tool of investigation must remain a prime concern to psychiatrists. This book is a guide to that technique; still irreplaceable, much of it is still as fresh as the day it was written and still a lively stimulus to others yet to come.

References

Andreasen, N. (2007). DSM and the death of phenomenology in America: An example of unintended consequences. *Schizophrenia Bulletin, 33*(1), 108–112.
Angst, J. (2012). Personal communication.

Berrios, G. E. (1993). Phenomenology and psychopathology: Was there ever a relationship? *Comprehensive Psychiatry, 34*(4), 213–220.

Bleger, J. (1972). *Psicología de la conducta*. Buenos Aires: Centro Editor de América Latina

Bolton, D. (2004). Shifts in the philosophical foundations of psychiatry since Jaspers: Implications for psychopathology and psychotherapy. *International Review of Psychiatry, 16*(3), 184–189.

Braz da Silva, D. (1994). Psicopatologia Geral de Karl Jaspers: Metodología de Estudo. *Jornal Brasileiro de Psiquia, 43*(2), 79–90.

Cornaglia, C. (1983). *Citar la psicopatología General de Karl Jaspers*. Córdoba: Escuela de Psicología, Universidad Nacional de Córdoba.

Cornaglia, C. (2010). *Fundamentos de la Psicopatología. Métodos*. Santa Rosa: La Pampa: Fundación IPSA.

Delgado, H. (1947). Acerca de la Psicopatología General de Jaspers. *Revista de Neuropsiquiatría, 10*(4).

Dörr, O. (1979). Der Einfluss der Heidelberger Psychiatrie auf den spanisch-sprechende Raum. In W. Janzarik (Ed.), *Psychopathologie als Grundlagenwissenschaft*. Stuttgart: Enke.

Espinazo, D. (1980). Reseña Histórica de la Psiquiatría en Honduras. *Revista Medica Hondurena, 48*, 104–108.

Feldman, N. (1990). *Nosología y Nosografía Psiquiátrica. Psicosis: Nosografía y Clínica*. Los espacios del Delirio. IV Congreso Argentino de Psiquiatría. Rosario. Asociación de Psiquiatras Argentinos y Asociación de Psiquiatría de Rosario

Figueroa, G. (2000). La Psicopatología General de K. Jaspers en la actualidad: Fenomenología, comprensión y los fundamentos del conocimiento Psiquiátrico. *Revista Chilena Neuro-Psiquiatria, 38*, 167–186.

Figueroa, G. (2008). La psicología fenomenológica de Husserl y la psicopatología. *Revista Chilena Neuro-Psiquiatria, 46*, 224–237.

Ghaemi, S. N. (2007). Existence and pluralism: The rediscovery of Karl Jaspers. *Psychopathology, 40*(2), 75–82.

Ghaemi, S. N. (2009). Nosologomania: DSM & Karl Jaspers' Critique of Kraepelin. *Philosophy, Ethics, and Humanities in Medicine, 4*, 10. doi:10.1186/1747–5341-4-10..

Havens, L. (1967). Karl Jaspers and American Psychiatry. *The American Journal of Psychiatry, 124*, 66–70.

Heerlein, A., & Santander, J. (1993). El sistema A.M.D.P. en la evaluación psicopatológica. *Revista Chilena Neuro-Psiquiatria, 31*(1), 37–41.

Hoeing, J. (2004). Karl Jaspers' general psychopathology: The history of the English translation. *History of Psychiatry, 15*, 233–236.

Holzapfel, C. (2003). Muerte y suicidio en Jaspers. *Revista Philosófica, 26*, 1–9.

Huber, G. (2002). The psychopathology of K. Jaspers and K. Schneider as a fundamental method for psychiatry. *The World Journal of Biological Psychiatry, 3*(1), 50–57.

Jäger, M., Frasch, K., & Becker, T. (2008). Die Krise der operationales Diagnostik in der Psychiatrie. *Nervenarzt, 79*, 288–294.

Jaspers, K. (1923/1928). *Allgemeine Psychopathologie* (3rd ed.). Berlin: Springer. French edition: Jaspers, K. (1928). *Psychopathologie générale* (trans: A. Kastler, & J. Mendousse). Paris: Alcan.

Jaspers, K. (1959/1963). *Allgemeine Psychopathologie*, 7.unveränderte Auflage. Berlin: Springer. English edition: Jaspers, K. (1963). General Psychopathology (trans: J. Hoenig & H. W. Hamilton). Chicago: University of Chicago Press.

Jaspers, K. (1979). *Psicopatologia Geral* (trans: S. P. Reis). Rio de Janeiro: Atheneu.

Kaplan, B., & Sadock, V. (Eds.) (1985). *Comprehensive textbook of psychiatry*. Baltimore: Williams & Wilkins.

Kendell, R. E. (1984). Reflections on psychiatric classification: For the architects of DSM-IV and ICD 10. *Integrative Psychiatry, 2*, 43–57.

Kraus, A. (2008). Die moderne Diagnostik und Therapie (ICD und DSM) im Lichte der Allgemeinen Psychopathologie. In K. Eming & T. Fuchs (Eds.), *Karl Jaspers-Philosophie und Psychopathologie*. Heidelberg: Winter.

McHugh, P. (2006). *The mind has mountains. Reflections on society and psychiatry*. Baltimore: Johns Hopkins University Press.
McHugh, P. R., & Slavney, P. R. (1998). *The perspectives of psychiatry*. Baltimore: Johns Hopkins University Press.
Paz, J. R. (1984) Psicopatología. Sus fundamentos dinámicos. Buenos Aires. Nueva Visión.
Pichon-Rivière, E. (1948/1983). Historia de la Psicosis maníacodepresiva. In E. Pichon-Rivière (Ed.) (1983), Psiquiatría una nueva problemática. Del Psicoanálisis a la Psicología Social (pp. 177–201). Buenos Aires: Nueva Visión.
Portela, M., & Ramos, P. (2005). Un momento crucial de la psicopatología: La revisión de Heidegger de la Psicología de las concepciones del mundo de Jaspers. Actas españolas de psiquiatría, 33(1), 46–54.
Roa, A. (1994). De la Demencia Precoz a la Esquizofrenia. Criterios conceptuales y síntomas patognomónicos. Revista de Psiquiatría Clínica, 31, 1–24
Santos, M. L. (1955). *Dilthey, Jaspers y la comprensión del enfermo mental*. Madrid: Paz Montalvo.
Saurí, J. (1989). Persona y Personalización. Lohlé: Buenos Aires
Téllez, C. (2012). Personal communication;

Chapter 5
Brain Mythologies

Jaspers' Critique of Reductionism from a Current Perspective

Thomas Fuchs

5.1 Introduction

Karl Jaspers is considered the uncontested founder of psychopathology as a science with its own object and methodology.[1] This establishment of psychopathology was based essentially on the rejection of natural scientific reductionism, which attempted to trace back mental phenomena and occurrences of mental disorders to their source in the organic substrate (i.e., in the brain). Indeed, this reductionism corresponds to the scientific longing for explanations, but it prioritizes the question of *why* over the question of *what* and thus neglects the careful describing and understanding of pathological variations of psychic life. Psychopathology as a science by contrast is based for Jaspers on the assumption that even mental abnormalities have gestalt-like and meaningful characteristics and therefore cannot be explained exhaustively by the listing of symptoms, which would be considered reflections of neurobiological disturbances. In contrast to neurology, which correlates single deficiencies with localized physical lesions, psychopathology begins there where both the holistic *structure of the mental* and, as a result, the *constitution* of experiencing world and self as a whole suffers from a disturbance. This modified or disturbed constitution cannot be described any longer by reference to individual symptoms, but rather requires a phenomenological presentation of the whole structure of the experienced world. Only if this task is accomplished and the mental illness is understood as a modification of the world-constitution can the search commence for

---

Translated by Alexander T. Englert from Fuchs (2008).

---

[1] "Not in regards to the name, rather as a science with its own object of research, own methodology, and own critical consciousness of method was psychopathology directly founded by Karl Jaspers before the First World War" (Janzarik 1974, p. 32f., my translation).

T. Fuchs (✉)
Psychiatric Department, Centre of Psychosocial Medicine, University of Heidelberg,
Voss-Str. 4, 69115 Heidelberg, Germany
e-mail: thomas_fuchs@med.uni-heidelberg.de

T. Fuchs et al. (eds.), *Karl Jaspers' Philosophy and Psychopathology,*
DOI 10.1007/978-1-4614-8878-1_5, © Springer Science+Business Media New York 2014

disturbances' causes, whether they are of a physical, a life-historical, or other sort—namely, by working out from a methodologically secured foundation.

Psychopathology in the 19th Century, by which Jaspers felt confronted, was marked by a dispute between those advocating a "psychic approach" ("*Psychiker*") and those advocating a "somatic approach" ("*Somatiker*"). The former, above all J. C. A. Heinroth and K. Ideler, sought the causes of mental illnesses in an "aberration" ("*Verirrung*") of the psyche itself; often this aberration was interpreted according to moral or even religious perspectives. The latter, on the other hand, amongst them M. Jacobi, F. Nasse, and J. B. Friedreich, denied the possibility that the psyche or the mind itself could fall ill, and they attributed mental illness to physical effects.[2] Thus, both schools of thought failed to conceive of the state of being mentally ill in direct accordance with its own structures—namely, through trying to realize the patient's experience or behavior. Instead, they viewed it solely as a symptom of mental or somatic causes. By doing so, both groups overlooked equally the phenomenological dimension.

Already in the introduction to *General Psychopathology*,[3] Jaspers takes a stance against the "somatic approach" of his time, namely, against reducing everything to the brain's physiology: "The principle of this book is to present a psychopathology which, in its concept-building, its methods of investigation and general outlook, is not enslaved to neurology and medicine on the dogmatic grounds that 'psychic disorder is cerebral disorder'" (GP, p. 4). This dogma, which Wilhelm Griesinger (1861) formulated in 1861, leads psychiatrists to the conclusion that, "if only we had an exact knowledge of the brain, we would then know the psychic life and its disturbances. This has led psychiatrists to abandon psychopathological studies as unscientific" (GP, p. 459). All validity is attributed "solely to cerebral processes, constitution, physiology and the experiments of objective psychology since these [are] purely physiological, and as far as possible excluded from psychic life" (GP, p. 712).

At the same time, Jaspers' critique developed just as severe a criticism of the "psychic approach," namely, of Freudian psychoanalysis in which he perceived a speculative, ideological tendency at work, which went in the direction of unmasking conscious mental experiences as illusions and self-deceptions (cf. GP, pp. 537 ff., 772 ff.). Albeit misjudging the hermeneutic dimension of psychoanalysis and overlooking the possibilities of extended understanding opened up by it, his critique arose from the same impulse, namely, to assert psychopathology and the primary experiencing of the mentally ill as an independent field of phenomenological knowledge. It also arose from the impulse to defend this field against biological as well as psychological reductionism: "We confine description solely to the things that are present to the patients' consciousness," in that we "are not concerned at this stage with (…) any subsidiary speculations, fundamental theory or basic postulates"

---

[2] Cf. regarding this point K. Jaspers, *General Psychopathology* (1997, p. 850f., in the following cited as "GP"), as well as Schneider (1926, p. 383f.).

[3] All translations are taken from: Karl Jaspers, *General Psychopathology* (1997), translated by J. Hoenig and Marian W. Hamilton.

(GP, p. 56). "The psychopathologist, if he is to keep this space free and gain ground for his activities, must set his face against every attempt to create an absolute and to claim that particular methods of research are the only valid, single objectivities, the only true Being as such. He must also take sides on behalf of meaningful understanding in the face of biologism, mechanism, and technics" (GP, p. 770). In Husserl's sense of "To the things themselves!", Jaspers asserts that psychopathology must "withdraw" from the secondary, theoretical world of a purportedly recognized true Being and return "to fully present reality" (GP, p. 549).

In accordance with the dominant psychiatric paradigms of his time, Jaspers' main critique was aimed at biological reductionism. In the following, this confrontation will be examined in more depth; then, its actuality for contemporary psychiatry and neuroscience will be explored.

5.2   Jaspers' Critique of Biological Reductionism

5.2.1   The "Somatic Bias"

At the end of the 19th Century, psychiatry conformed to the natural scientific paradigm that had reigned triumphant in the whole field of medicine since 1850. It concentrated on the search for somatic causes of mental illnesses. To do so, research was promoted above all in the areas of neuroanatomy, neurohistology, neurophysiology, and neuropathology.[4] Most importantly, one believed it possible to have an effect on mental disturbances via somatic therapies. The majority of psychiatrists considered the psyche and psychology as things that had been supplanted by physiology. In fact, T. Meynert, one of Griesinger's pupils, rejected the expression of "mental illnesses" completely and spoke from then on only of a "clinic for illnesses of the forebrain" (Meynert 1884).

Around 1900, however, the preliminary euphoria of the somatic approach began to waver. Many results, which were being enthusiastically awaited, had failed to appear; the discovery of lues as the cause for progressive paralysis could not be adopted for other psychoses. The somatic paradigm neither offered a satisfactory explanation for the majority of mental disturbances nor provided effective forms of treatment. Amongst psychiatrists, Jaspers reminisced later that "consciousness of a stagnation in scientific research" was spreading along with pessimism about therapeutic methods.[5] Jaspers found himself confronted with this situation as he began working on his new system for psychopathology in Heidelberg.

In the introduction of GP, Jaspers refers to the "somatic bias" as threatening psychiatry. This bias presupposes implicitly, that "the actual reality of human ex-

---

[4] Seen, for example, in the work of Meynert, Wernicke, Westphal, Nissl, Alzheimer, Vogt, and Spiermeyer.

[5] Jaspers (1984, p. 21); cf. also Seidler (1976).

istence is a somatic event. Man is only comprehensible when he is understood in somatic terms; should the psyche be mentioned, this is in the nature of a theoretical stop-gap of no real scientific value" (GP, p. 18). This attitude leads to an overhasty identification of morphological or physiological facts with mental experiences and, in the process, arrives at adventurous constructs, which Jaspers refers to as "Brain Mythologies" (GP, p. 18). Natural scientific facts are then offhandedly reformulated into statements about "the psyche," "the person," or "mental illnesses"—an improper stretching of the physical world's domain of validity. This somatic-pathological perspective overlooks, according to Jaspers, the independence of the mental domain, which reveals itself solely through a humanities-oriented understanding. "Somatic medicine," he writes at one point, "only deals with the individual as a creature of nature. It examines and investigates his body as it would that of an animal. But psychopathology is constantly faced with the fact that the individual is a creature of *culture*" (GP, p. 709). Animals can indeed suffer from brain afflictions and nervous disorders, but mental illnesses are specifically human: "Medicine is only one of the roots of psychopathology (...) Whenever the object studied is Man and not man as a species of animal, we find that psychopathology comes to be not only a kind of biology but also one of the Humanities" (GP, pp. 35/36).

5.2.2   The Localization of the Mental

In his critique of somatic reductionism, Jaspers especially opposes every hasty attempt to localize mental processes to certain areas of the brain: "We should be particularly wary of regarding known cerebral processes as such direct bases for particular psychic events" (GP, p. 458). Every attempt at localization—the history of which Jaspers reports on thoroughly, from the 18th century on—was based on a presupposition that had not been well thought out, namely, that the arrangement and structure of psychic life had to correlate to the structure of the brain.[6] This presupposition, however, was just as unverifiable as it was pointless: "What is heterogeneous cannot coincide, but at best the one can only be used as a metaphorical expression of the other" (GP, p. 481 f.). The temporal, processual reality of the mental remained incommensurable with the spatiality of the brain's form (GP, p. 491).

Such somatic constructions have no real basis. Not one specific cerebral process is known which parallels a specific psychic phenomenon. Localization of various sensory areas in the cerebral cortex and of the aphasias in the left hemisphere only means that these organs must be intact for a specific psychic event to be possible. There is no difference in principle here from the equal necessity of having intact

---

[6] In this manner, Jaspers also characterized C. Wernicke's system (1906): "The elements and connections of psychic life are seen as identical with the elements and structures of the brain. The psyche becomes spatially represented. Holding such a view one will tend to turn not to the psychic life itself but to the brain and to neurology when one wishes for psychopathological comprehension. Psychic phenomena will only be used for the time being in the absence of direct access to the brain" (GP, p. 534).

function of the eye or of the motor mechanism, etc., which are also essential "tools" (GP, p. 18).

However, don't certain deficiencies occurring in correlation with localizable lesions in the brain also prove the localizability of the accompanying function? According to Jaspers, the answer is no; this is because the localizations established through attention to brain lesions can only account for "centres of disturbance, not centres of performance" (GP, p. 493). That which is localized proves to be only a tool of the mind, not the mind itself. "We only know conditioning factors for the psychic life; we never know *the* cause of the psychic even, only *a cause*" (GP, p. 459). The reality of the function itself may possibly depend "on an infinite number of relationships between the many parts and is nowhere essentially localized in a centre" (GP, p. 493). "Everything psychic is always a total event, it is not composed of partial functions but functions are the tools it uses and, when these are affected, the event in its totality becomes impossible (…). *Elementary psychic functions* that could be localized are unknown" (GP, p. 495).

The entirety of mental life cannot be assembled out of localizable partial functions. Wouldn't it then at least be appropriate to localize consciousness or the mind as a whole in the brain? Jaspers finds this notion just as pointless: There can be no fundamental "seat for the psyche" (GP, p. 226). Moreover, the notion is connected with the suggestion of absolutizing brain processes as the substance of what it is to be a person, or to take every human occurrence to be occurrences of the brain (GP, p. 496). From a phenomenological standpoint, brain illnesses are only "one of the causes of psychic disturbance among many. The idea that everything psychic is at least partially conditioned by the brain is correct but is too general to mean anything" (GP, p. 496). The only experienceable coincidence of mind and body, according to Jaspers, is to be found in events of expression (i.e., in the concrete, bodily encounters with others). In such moments, we can perceive directly in the corporeal appearance of the other, the psyche of the other (GP, p. 226). Once we have separated body and mind, however, then we shall never find a coincidence of the two again.[7]

5.2.3 *"Causal Knowledge Must Not Be Made into an Absolute"*

Jaspers' critique of the biological paradigm, as it was just detailed, is closely related with his well-known opposition to understanding and descriptive psychologies. Thus, he assigns, on the one hand, a significant role to causal explanations for psychopathology; on the other hand, he argues against making "causal knowledge (…) into an absolute," for which every mental disorder would only be a symptom of a researchable brain process (GP, p. 460)—one consequence of this would be that one holds every psychological interest (e.g., for schizophrenia), as obsolete as soon

---

[7] "To sum up, coincidence (and that restricted to what is an understandable manifestation) exists only at the point where in primary fashion we see and experience the psyche in the body and the body in the psyche. If we have separated body and psyche and are investigating their relationship, no such coincidence is to be found" (GP, p. 226).

as the disorder's somatic causes have been discovered (GP, p. 18). For the psycho-pathologist (if he does not want to be untrue to his primary duty), the primacy of understanding remains opposed to such a position. And yet, Jaspers does not remain opposed only to descriptive approaches, rather he continues his opposition in the sphere of therapeutic practice. The need for causality is namely based mostly on a longing for "the greatest therapeutic power" (GP, p. 461). Where material causes of mental disorders become accessible, medical interventions will also have an immediate effect; this underpins an important and justified motivation towards thinking in terms of causality. Nonetheless, Jaspers also addresses the problem of such an approach: "Causal knowledge, which grasps the non-understandable as it arises necessarily from its causes, can influence therapy decisively by measures *in which the psyche which is wanting help need take no active part*" (GP, p. 461, author's emphasis).

In complete contrast to such a causally effective, but absolutely impersonal therapy, Jaspers advocates therapy through personal influence on the afflicted person in regards to his internal reflections and resolutions. Causal, descriptive thinking attains possible effectiveness on the basis of general knowledge; however, it tends to distract one away from concrete encounters with the individual patient. Instead, he will only be treated as a case for application of the general principle. The understanding approach, on the contrary, is based on reenactment, on empathy, and (as a result) on the inner relatedness that the therapist experiences with the patient qua human being. "Causal thinking impinges on what is alien, not-understandable and on what can be manipulated; understanding of meaning impinges on myself in the other…" (GP, p. 462). "[T]he healthy person who keeps his psyche marginally exposed," encounters in sick persons, "what he potentially is" (GP, p. 786). In this encounter, one finds "the most intense presentation of what is entirely individual" (GP, p. 462).

5.3   The Relevance of Jaspers' Critique for Today

So much for an outline of the Jaspersian critique; now, to what do we owe its relevance today? It is not difficult to recognize in his dispute with the reductionism of his day positions that we can find in the dominant biological paradigms of neurosciences and psychiatry today. Even if the sophistication of their findings offers much more when compared with the relatively unrefined localization theory of 1900, the primary presupposition remains the same. Accordingly, the mental is assigned a solely symptomatic significance for the natural sciences; all psychological or phenomenological knowledge is simply a preliminary way of describing what is actually going on, namely material processes at the neuronal level. Thus, it is assumed that neuroscience has priority over phenomenology and psychology when it comes to describing experiences and behaviors, or to put it in Jaspers' own words: "Man is only comprehensible when he is understood in somatic terms" (GP, p. 18).

"But we do not know a single physical event in the brain which could be considered the identical counterpart of any morbid psychic event" (GP, p. 459). This warning still holds true today in the era of image-producing technologies. It is not in the brain that we discover conscious experiences, rather only the neuronal processes or correlates that we assign to them. Yet during this assigning, neuroscience can still make the mistake of overhasty localization, thereby arriving at a new form of "phrenology." Indeed, the activity of certain neuronal modules presents a function's *necessary* condition if it is shown that the modules are activated through this function or if, vice versa, a lesion leads to the function's *impairment*. Regardless, it remains impossible to conclude from this that these modules ever provide *sufficient* conditions for the *functions* as such, which, for example, can even involve completely different brain regions (Fuchs 2012, 72f.). The more complex the function, the more likely it will require the integration of differing and spatially disparate networks and centers. "We only know conditioning factors for the psychic life; we never know *the* cause of the psychic event, only *a* cause" (GP, p. 459).

These necessary differences in the relation between single brain processes and the whole structure of the psyche are, however, often neglected in anticipation of a universal biological explanation. Already in 1925, Karl Kleist rejected Jaspers' approach with the following:

> In my opinion, all "psychic processes" will merge with organic ones. This will happen when one has gained more of a perspective for the fact that the meaningful connections of psychic processes, which are prized so highly by Jaspers, are accompanied without exception by neuropathologically explainable symptoms. (Kleist 1925, p. 18, my translation)

That here, in the rapture of formulating his thoughts, Kleist asserts that every understandable mental process should be explainable *neuropathologically*, is a statement that is ironically shared by a current psychiatrist, as can be seen in this analogous statement:

> The foundational concepts of learning, thinking, imagining, and perceiving will become understandable—in the same way as the deviations of physiological processing patterns—as disorders of brain functions; they will become representable with the help of medical imaging (…) as states and processes of the brain. As a result, psychic disorders will increasingly become brain function disorders and will no longer differ fundamentally from other CNS illnesses. (Maier 2002)

Such points of view make it clear which consequences may result from a biological reductionist approach. If anxiety, compulsiveness, depression, or schizophrenia are *essentially* only neurobiochemical disorders, then psychiatry will become a specialized form of neurology and psychiatrists will become brain specialists. Psychopathology would then be exhausted by a listing of symptoms, which would be conceived of as simply reflections of disorders of the biological substrate. No longer would inherent meaning or significance be ascribed to mental phenomena and processes of the illness. They, like strokes and neurological syndromes of impairment, would no longer involve such categories.

5.4 Limits of the Jaspersian Position

Kleist's critique does simultaneously hit upon a problematic point in the Jaspersian position that we will now examine in conclusion. Said point is the retreat of the very first foundation of psychopathology into the refuge of conscious subjectivity. In the attempt to demarcate the phenomenal sphere of psychopathology and counter causal explanations of the mental, Jaspers surrenders the entire sphere of the unconscious and of the organic substrate to the natural scientific principle of causality:

> It is in the nature of all causal investigation that, as it advances, it penetrates deeper into the *extra-conscious foundations* of psychic life, whereas the psychology of meaning remains by definition within consciousness and *ends at the point where consciousness ends* (…). The extra-conscious element can only be found in the world as something somatic. (GP, p. 457, author's emphasis)

Jaspers' dualism of understanding and explaining[8] originates from an ultimately Cartesian dualism between psychic and corporeal, in that corporeality remains foreign to understanding's every attempt. As a result, the "meaningful connections" of psychic life run the danger of being criticized by researchers in the field of neurobiology as constituting nothing more than superficial epiphenomena (GP, p. 457f.). Jaspers was unsuccessful in searching for comprehensible motives in the unconscious processes and development of symptoms, as psychoanalysis had undertaken before him; simultaneously, his dualistic approach could not offer the possibility of seeing or (at least) postulating the impact of mental processes on the neurological processes themselves.[9] In so doing, subjectivity as such persisted as a, granted, impregnable citadel, whose study could be pursued by phenomenological psychopathologists at their leisure. This research, however, was in danger of losing its relevance for the development of psychiatry due to the increasing dominance of causal explanations in science. The loss of psychopathological experience, as is to be diagnosed everywhere today, has at least its roots in the dualistic presuppositions of the Jaspersian psychopathology.

The dichotomy of explaining and understanding appears to be unsustainable today in this form, and indeed for two reasons: First, at the latest since T. S. Kuhn's *The Structure of Scientific Revolutions* (1970), the view has asserted itself in scientific theory that the causal, explanation dimension of the sciences is itself subjugated to historically shifting paradigms. In other words, sociocultural structures of

---

[8] Cf. with this also the somewhat critical portrayal by Blankenburg (1991, p. 358).

[9] Indeed, Jaspers saw correctly that the principle of causality in the biological substrate needed to be reconsidered and expanded into a circular gestalt form: "Causal relations do not run only one way, but take reciprocal effect; they extend in this circular fashion so that they either build life up or as 'circulivitiosi' foster a process of destruction" (GP, p. 454). Yet, he continues with: "Now biological causality is not added to mechanistic causality as something fresh and new" (GP, p. 454). This statement should be understood as a verdict against vitalism; it surrenders, however, the field of the living processes in the end to a physicalistic understanding. Above all, the interplay between that which is subjective and that which is organic remains outside of Jaspers' horizon—e.g., in the form of an influence on the brain through interpersonal experiences or a "historical biology," of which Mitscherlich later spoke.

thought are built into the explanatory paradigms, which can then only be understood through hermeneutic comparison. Second, the discovery of neuroplasticity (i.e., the effects that subjective and intersubjective experiences, for example, in psychotherapeutic processes, have on the neural structure), has made it clear that "causes" and "meanings" (as that which is explainable and as that which is understandable) are only comprehensible when taken in constant interplay with each other. As a result, the Jaspersian dichotomy-based differentiation loses its selectivity when compared to a circular relation between influences of the psyche and influences of its substrate (i.e., the brain), which should be described biologically and hermeneutically (Fuchs 2011, 2012).

The advances of neuroscience and psychopharmacology have pushed psychiatry lately in the direction of causal explanations. Nevertheless, for a unified naturalistic model of mental disorders there is no end in sight. If anything, it is precisely the dependency of the brain on the psychosocial world (in a dialectic swinging back of the pendulum) that has opened up a new appreciation for the dependency of the brain on its psychological and social environment. It can increasingly be understood as a historically and socially constituted, meaning-carrying organ, which perpetually translates biological processes and intersubjective experiences back and forth. More than ever, neurobiology and psychiatry are becoming increasingly dependent on the integration of philosophical, biographical-hermeneutic, sociocultural, and systematic approaches. Precisely because the brain itself is the organ responsible for reciprocal translations or transformations of spheres of reality, which are only accessible to us through differing aspects, it cannot itself be adequately comprehended in one single paradigm. Thus, hermeneutic understanding receives a new, comprehensive task: namely, to make communication possible between the currently incommensurable perspectives and languages with which we attempt to grasp scientifically and clinically the state of being mentally ill. Psychopathology can only recover its importance, which was rightfully reclaimed by Jaspers, if it transcends the subjectivism of understanding and also understands the biological processes (within the brain) as socially and historically constituted.

References

Blankenburg, W. (1991). Karl Jaspers (1883–1969). In D. V. Engelhardt & F. Hartmann (Eds.), *Klassiker der Medizin (Vol. 2, pp. 350–365)*. Munich: Beck.
Fuchs, T. (2008). Jaspers' Reduktionismus-Kritik in der Gegenwart. In K. Eming & T. Fuchs (Eds.), *Karl Jaspers—Philosophie und Psychopathologie* (pp. 235–246). Heidelberg: Winter.
Fuchs, T. (2011). The brain—A mediating organ. *Journal of Consciousness Studies, 18,* 196–221.
Fuchs, T. (2012). *Das Gehirn—ein Beziehungsorgan. Eine phänomenologisch-ökologische Konzeption* (4th ed.). Stuttgart: Kohlhammer.
Griesinger, W. (1861). *Pathologie und Therapie der psychischen Krankheiten*. Stuttgart: Krabbe.
Janzarik, W. (1974). *Themen und Tendenzen der deutschsprachigen Psychiatrie*. Berlin: Springer.
Jaspers, K. (1984). *Philosophische Autobiographie*. Munich: Piper.
Jaspers, K. (1997). *General psychopathology* (trans: Hoenig, J., Hamilton, M. W.). Baltimore: Johns Hopkins University Press. German edition: Jaspers, K. (1973). *Allgemeine Psychopathologie* (9th ed.). Berlin: Springer.

Kleist, K. (1925). *Die gegenwärtigen Strömungen in der Psychiatrie*. Berlin: de Gruyter.

Kuhn, T. S. (1970). *The structure of scientific revolutions*. Chicago: University of Chicago Press.

Maier, W. (2002). Psychiatrie als Beruf—Wie sieht die Zukunft aus? *Der Nervenarzt, 73,* 96–97.

Meynert, T. (1884). *Psychiatrie. Klinik der Erkrankungen des Vorderhirns begründet auf dessen Bau, Leistungen und Ernährung*. Vienna: Braumüller.

Schneider, K. (1926). Die phänomenologische Richtung in der Psychiatrie. *Philos Anzeiger, 4,* 382–404.

Seidler, E. (1976). Die Medizin und ihre Auswirkungen auf Freud. In H. Balmer (Ed.), *Psychologie des 20. Jahrhunderts. Bd. I: Die europäische Tradition. Tendenzen, Schulen, Entwicklungslinien* (pp. 701–720). Zurich: Kindler.

Wernicke, C. (1906). *Grundriss der Psychiatrie in klinischen Vorlesungen* (2nd ed.). Leipzig: Thieme.

Chapter 6
Karl Jaspers Criticism of Anthropological and Phenomenological Psychiatry

Samuel Thoma

6.1 Introductory Remarks[1]

In the fourth edition of his *General Psychopathology (GP)* Karl Jaspers develops a critique of concepts advanced by Viktor E. von Gebsattels and Erwin Straus—thus criticizing two important representatives of the phenomenological movement in psychiatry. It may at first seem peculiar to engage a critique put forward by Karl Jaspers of the phenomenological movement in psychiatry, as it was Karl Jaspers who, with the essay "The phenomenological approach in psychopathology" (1968), and then with the first edition of his *General Psychopathology*, provided the first systematic introduction of phenomenology into psychopathology. In these works, Jaspers accords phenomenology with the task of empathizing with the psychic life [*Seelenleben*] of the patient and describing this in clear terms. From such a first-person perspective, singular psychopathological phenomena are intended to be clearly outlined and distinguished from one another—before the question can subsequently be posed as to under which nosological units they could be located (Jaspers 1997, pp. 564). Thus, for Jaspers, phenomenology has a basic function for each psycho-pathological task. Yet it would be wrong to identify Jaspers as a follower of the phenomenological-psychiatric school. This has to do with changes in phenomenology, which, starting in 1913 emerged as an eidetic science of transcendental consciousness (Husserl 2009). Jaspers' concept of phenomenology referred to the Husserl in the "Logical Investigations" of 1900, and Jaspers rejected phenomenology in its eidetic-transcendental form (Luft 2008). If we follow Arthur Tatossian, however, it

---

Translation: Kelly Mulvaney.

---

[1] Quotes from *General Psychopathology* are cited from the English translation (Jaspers 1997) and have been modified to include this author's (S.T.) corrections.

S. Thoma (✉)
Hermannstraße 154, 12051 Berlin, Germany
e-mail: samuel.thoma@gmx.net

T. Fuchs et al. (eds.), *Karl Jaspers' Philosophy and Psychopathology,*
DOI 10.1007/978-1-4614-8878-1_6, © Springer Science+Business Media New York 2014

is precisely this latter form of phenomenology, which—contrary to Spiegelberg's contention—delivered the decisive impulse for the emergence of phenomenological psychiatry (Tatossian 2002; Spiegelberg 1972, p. 96): after Tatossian, phenomeno-logical-psychiatric thought is no longer interested in the psychically actual, as it is found, but rather in the conditions of possibility of this actual—meaning the essence and the essential modifications of factual experience (Tatossian 2002, pp. 21–24). From this perspective, Jaspers' use of phenomenology solely corresponds to a de-scriptive psychology of inner life (Tatossian 2002, p. 18; see also Husserl 2009). The actual birth of phenomenological psychiatry is therefore, according to Tatos-sian, a conference held in 1922 by Eugène Minkowski and Ludwig Binswanger, at which both authors introduced the modified concept of phenomenology into psy-chiatry (Tatossian 2002, p. 18).

6.1.1   Psychiatric Historical Dimension of Jaspers' Critique

Precisely this distinguished use of phenomenology should from now on identify the fault line between the classical German psychiatric school and phenomenological psychiatry: in the classical psychiatric school, from Jaspers to Kurt Schneider and until Gerd Huber, phenomenology was only ever grasped as a descriptive method of subjective experience that served to classify various modes of experience as a basis for psychology and psychopathology. Phenomenological psychiatry, on the other hand, embraced a concept of phenomenology that described this subjective experience in more comprehensive and basic structures. There are many examples of authors of classical German psychiatry distancing themselves from this attempt (Jaspers 1997, p. 55; Schneider 1921, 1976, p. 132; Huber 2005, p. 4). This is the context in which Jaspers' critique of the first generation of phenomenological psy-chiatrists in the fourth edition of his *General Psychopathology* must be seen.

6.1.2   Is There Even a Singular Phenomenological Psychiatry?

The question already suggests that the answer is no. Just as there is no unified concept of phenomenology, there is no unified concept of phenomenological psy-chiatry. However, here we refer to Tatossian's hypothesis, which says that despite the differences between and the partial lack of a clear overview of phenomenolog-ical-psychiatric works, there are some basic features of this thought that justify the use of the term "phenomenological psychiatry." As indicated, this corresponds to Tatossian's concept of phenomenological psychiatry as a psychopathological eidet-ic science of modified subjective experience (Tatossian 2002, p. 22). In this sense, Tatossian decouples the term essence from its orthodox Husserlian properties: for Tatossian, essence solely implies that the subject's actual experiences are anchored in basic structures that should be examined by means of phenomenological analy-sis (Tatossian 2002). He identifies the structures as the condition of possibility for that which is concretely experienced (Tatossian 2002). Tatossian subsumes in this general concept of essence both the concepts of the first generation of phenomenological psychiatrists (including Straus, von Gebsattel, Minkowski, Binswanger, Kunz, and Storch) as well as newer authors (Blankenburg, Kuhlenkampff, Zutt, and Kraus). At the end of this article, Jasper's critique of Straus and von Gebsattel will give us reason to explicate Tatossian's concept of essence more closely.

6.1.3   Is Jaspers' Critique Directed Only at von Gebsattel and Straus or Does It Make a General Claim?

Our examination is complicated by the fact that Jaspers only explicitly develops his critique with reference to some of Viktor E. von Gebsattel's and Erwin Straus' essays (Jaspers 1997, pp. 540–546). Moreover, in his critique, Jaspers refers not to "phenomenological psychiatry," but rather to the term "constructive-genetic psychopathology" introduced by von Gebsattel (Jaspers 1997, p. 540). However, this should not belie his critique's claim to generality: first, Jaspers rubricates almost the entire first generation of phenomenological psychiatrists within "constructive-genetic psychopathology" (Jaspers 1997): Ludwig Binswanger, Erwin Straus, Viktor E. von Gebsattel, Alfred Storch, and Hans Kunz (Jaspers 1997), and speaks generally of this "trend of thought in psychopathology" (Jaspers 1997, p. 540). Second, in its applicability, Jaspers' critique does not intend to deal precisely with the works of Straus and von Gebsattel. Rather, Jaspers sets up general hypotheses and uses the terms of these two authors in their support.

For this reason, we will proceed in this investigation with two steps: first, we will explore Jaspers' direct confrontation with Straus and von Gebsattel (Sect. 6.3), and then in conclusion (Sect. 6.4) we will evaluate this critique within the broader framework of phenomenological-psychiatric thought in accordance with Jaspers' claim. Moreover, an assessment based on such a *general* concept of phenomenological psychiatry is justified by the fact that the structural terms of Jaspers' critique can be recognized in other authors of classical German psychiatry (Kurt Schneider, Gerd Huber). The basis for this further assessment is Tatossian's comprehensive determination of phenomenological psychiatry.

6.2   Locating the Critique in General Psychopathology

In order to understand Karl Jaspers' critique of phenomenological psychiatry, it must first be placed in the broader framework of his *General Psychopathology*. Thus, our initial task is to explore this critique in the modified context of the fourth edition of *General Psychopathology*. Subsequently, we will deal briefly with Jaspers' concept of phenomenology, genetic understanding (*Verstehen*), explanation (*Erklären*), his concept of theory, as well as the concept of the Illumination of Existence. From this perspective, his critique of von Gebsattel and Straus can be illustrated.

6.2.1   The Modified Context of the Fourth Version of General Psychopathology

Jaspers' *GP* undergoes significant change throughout the chronic of its editions. Of a total of nine versions, the largest relative differences are to be found between the first (1913) and fourth (1946) edition (for more on the relationship between these two versions, see Kirkbright 2008). This can be traced to multiple causes, which seem to be rooted in Jaspers' philosophical development. Whereas Jaspers writes the first edition, for the most part, as a psychiatrist with the quasi-philosophical aim of explicating a method specific to psychiatry, his purpose in 1946 (1942) is to place his philosophical standpoint of existential philosophy up against psychiatry as a whole: in simplified terms, Jaspers is primarily a psychiatric, and secondly a philosophical author. The development of his stance toward psychoanalysis and phenomenological psychiatry is grounded in this fact. Whereas this stance can be described as of 1913 as open and affirmative, as Jaspers developed his own philosophical standpoint, this gave way to a position of resignation and critique by 1946. This change is reflected in the structure of the book. While the significant methodical difference in psychopathological practice in 1913 lies between understanding (*Verstehen*) and explanation (*Erklären*), the difference stressed in 1946 is one between these two methods and the genuinely Jaspersian view of psychiatry from the focal point of *Existential Philosophy*. To this end, the book was extended to a sixth part (*The human being as a whole*) in 1946. This is the first year in which Jaspers added the critique of Straus and von Gebsattel considered in this article, which can be found in the third capital of the third part (*The explanatory theories—their meaning and value*).

6.2.2   Understanding (Static, Genetic) Explanation, Concept of Theory, and Illumination of Existence

Jaspers is considered the first author who introduced informed, methodical self-reflection to psychiatry (Binswanger 1994, p. 76). The strength of his psychopathology in the first edition lies less in having developed something methodically new than in setting up a *methodological* order for existing methods and relationships. This methodological conscience can be understood as the norm providing the grounds for Jaspers to call especially phenomenological psychiatry into critique, as it undermines the methodological lines of division he himself draws. These lines of division consist, as generally known, in Jaspers' distinction between understanding (*Verstehen*) and explaining (*Erklären*), as well as in the third dimension of the Illumination of Existence (*Existenzerhellung*) the latter which he added in the fourth edition. We would like to briefly consider this.

Static Understanding—Jaspers' Use of Phenomenology

As already mentioned, Jaspers uses phenomenology as a descriptive psychology of a patient's subjective and conscious ways of experiencing. On the whole this approach results in a static concept of experience: the description of the present condition, rather than how experiences arise from other experiences (see genetic understanding) and the extraconscious that underlies these experiences (Jaspers 1968, p. 1320 et seq.), matters. The latter in particular is significant for Jaspers' critique of phenomenological psychiatry. The essential methodical tool for a diagnostician is empathy (*Einfühlung*): through exploration, analysis of expression, or on the basis of self-assessments, the diagnostician should place oneself in the patient's way of experiencing, reflexively make this experience an outlook and arrange it in ordered terms (Jaspers 1968, p. 1320). As a histologist describes a preparation under a microscope, one should "account for every psychic phenomenon, every experience met with in our investigation" (Jaspers 1997, p. 56). It is critical for this description that "conventional theories, psychological constructions, interpretations and evaluations must be left aside." (Jaspers 1997)

A provisional result of this method is Jaspers' description of different (psychopathological) forms of awareness of objects, awareness of the self, experience of space and time, awareness of the body, and, finally, awareness of reality—just to mention a few (Jaspers 1997, pp. 60–104).[2]

Genetic Understanding—Emergence of the Psychic from the Psychic

Contrary to Jaspers' use of phenomenology as a static description of the conditions of psychic experience, genetic understanding aims to empathetically trace the *emergence* of one psychic state from another (Jaspers 1997, p. 302 et seq.). Thus, genetic understanding poses the question of the connection between individual psychic phenomena. According to Jaspers, these connections are evident as such and cannot be falsified through empirical research or theories of the unconscious. In this sense, for example, the effect of autumn in promoting suicide is, in understanding, an evident fact—even if this is generally and objectively statistically false (Jaspers 1997, pp. 714–715).

Commonalities of Genetic and Static Understanding

Empathy is typical of both static and genetic understanding, as even genetic understanding is based on a purely conscious level of experience (Jaspers 1997, p. 306).

---

[2] As already mentioned, Jaspers accords to phenomenology a fundamental task for psychopathology. The conviction that a truly specific and valid diagnostic is only possible through orientation around a first-person perspective is also reflected in Kurt Schneider's first-rank symptoms of schizophrenia, and from this it was also included in the ICD-10 Manual. Mainstream psychiatry today has distanced itself as far as possible from this supposedly unreliable first-person perspective, replacing it with an allegedly more objective third-person perspective.

In both cases, Jaspers claims it is possible that things which were heretofore unnoticed can become noticed through understanding. This distinguishes it from the actual unconscious, which he up to now characterizes as extraconscious (Jaspers 1997). Static as well as genetic understanding is compared to mechanisms outside of consciousness (Jaspers 1997).

Explanation

Jaspers uses term "explanatory psychology" to characterize all approaches dealing with mechanisms that determine conscious, psychic experience (Jaspers 1997, p. 451 et seq.). Explanatory psychology thus is interested in processes outside of consciousness and their causal relationship to conscious experience. Here, Jaspers understands causality not in a purely mechanistic and linear sense, and he distinguishes between various forms of causality (Jaspers 1997, pp. 451–452). "Extraconscious mechanisms," which determine conscious psychic experience in various ways, are, according to Jaspers, essentially of corporeal form (Jaspers 1997, pp. 457–460).[3]

Definition of Theory

With respect to Jasper's concept of explanation, it is necessary to explicate his definition of theory. For Jaspers, a theory embraces two moments: the adoption of a basic occurrence that forms the basis of (subjective or objective) phenomena, and thinking a *causal correlation* of this occurrence with the phenomena (Jaspers 1997, p. 530). Here, *forming the basis* is also meant in the case of *psychological theory* as *outside of consciousness*, and psychological theory according to Jaspers takes effect at the point where understanding based on consciousness ends (Jaspers 1997).

Causal correlation means two things for theory: first, the cause-and-effect relationship of that which is outside of consciousness on that which is outside of consciousness, as well as the effect relationship of that which is outside of consciousness on that which is known to consciousness (Jaspers 1997). For Jaspers, however, the causal relationship is only conceived and not, like subjective experience, directly given. Theories for Jaspers are always only imagined or conceived, not perceived (Jaspers 1997, pp. 530–531). According to Jaspers' definition of theory, hypotheses made with theory can always be verified or falsified through knowledge (*Erkenntnis*—Jaspers 1997, p. 545).

In the following, we will use the expression "theory" strictly in Jaspers' sense.

---

[3] It is interesting at this point that Jaspers considers the possibilities for understanding (verstehen) psychic phenomena to be limited (which can especially be seen in his understanding of primary experiences of delusion). However, he does not take up such a limit for explanation: "understanding is limited, explanation unlimited." (Jaspers 1997, p. 305)

Illumination of Existence

It is impossible here to discuss what Jaspers understands with respect to this concept. Illumination of Existence constitutes the core of his philosophy, and the explanations in the sixth part of the fourth edition of *GP* only allude to this. We will limit ourselves to a few comments.

According to Jaspers, the prospects of psychological understanding (*Verstehen*) are limited. In understanding, we come up against the unintelligible time and time again. At these points, Jaspers claims that we must revert to models of explanation based on that which is outside of consciousness. He moreover considers the prospects of explanatory psychology to be limited in a different sense: namely, in determining man as a whole. This whole is, for him, both incomprehensible (unverstehbar) and inexplicable. He identifies it as "the endlessness, individuality and *that which encompasses all things*" (Jaspers 1997, p. 754). However, this "other" of understanding and explanation demonstrates itself, according to Jaspers, in man himself—in that which Jaspers calls "existence" (*Dasein*), "consciousness" (*Bewusstsein*), and "spirit" (*Geist*) (Jaspers 1997, p. 759). According to Jaspers, these terms point to the openness and incompleteness of man and to the fundamental impossibility of knowing (*erkennen*) man completely. For this reason, Jaspers shies away from speaking at all of this "Encompassing" in an explicit manner: "If we put it into words we are likely to be tempted to make it into a theory of the components of human existence." (Jaspers 1997, p. 759) This ultimately clarifies how Jaspers understands the dictum Illumination of Existence: thinking in concepts that extend beyond the fixed meaning of scientific theoretical frameworks and point to a sphere that transcends these. Jaspers calls such thinking "transcendental thought" (Jaspers 1997, p. 756).

6.3   Jaspers' Critique of Straus and von Gebsattel

6.3.1   Explaining the Critique

In the explanations Jaspers added in 1946 it is clear that in pointing to "Existence" and "Encompassing," he intends to save the sciences from absolutizing thought with regard to man.

Jaspers' critique is aimed against all dogmatic, objectivizing and explanatory approaches used in the sciences with respect to man, to the extent that this approach is the result of a totalitarian claim. Such objectivization can, according to Jaspers, be avoided if the sciences themselves are *conscious* of their methodical approaches and limitations. This indicates figuring out what can be spoken of by means of a certain method (for example, that of understanding or explanation) as well as what eludes the method at hand (Jaspers 1997, p. 754 et seq.). Jaspers' critique of certain psychiatric schools thus applies to those in which such methodological self-awareness is lacking. For him, early phenomenological psychiatry arrived at the false conclusion of mixing the category of *explanation* with that of the *Illumination of Existence of man*. The fact that Jaspers' critique to this end can be found in the third part of the book, in the section "*The explanatory theories—their meaning and value*" (Jaspers 1997, pp. 530–555) makes it clear that Jaspers understands this method as part *of "explanatory psychology*." For Jaspers, this is a method that aims to identify the mechanisms—outside of consciousness and determining—of ostensively given subjective experience (see above).

With reference to Straus and von Gebsattel, Jaspers justifies this in the following manner: while praising the high level of descriptive capabilities made possible by the work of these authors, he criticizes that they take an error, as "basic events," "basic disturbance," "vital inhibition," or "disturbance in becoming a person," as the basis for such descriptions (Jaspers 1997, p. 540). Modified experience (for example, compulsively ill) is derived from the adoption of this basic disturbance, without itself being directly experienced by the affected (Jaspers 1997, pp. 541–542). Out of the impossibility of realizing the determining basic events from the experience of the affected—as Jaspers' own concept of phenomenology would require—Jaspers concludes that this basic event can only be only be made accessible and imagined as something outside of consciousness. Thus, the elements of an explanatory theory, for Jaspers, are fulfilled. This analysis of Jaspers leads to an interesting contradiction in his critique, which we will now analyze more closely.

Jaspers takes up the theoretical-explanatory claim that he attributes to von Gebsattels and Straus and puts forward five critiques. *First*, Jaspers points out that the basic disturbance documented by Straus and von Gebsattel is ill defined and of shifting significance. Being outside of consciousness and biological, it is determined, yet it is not determinable by means of biological observation. Thus, basic disturbance "in the end (…) only becomes the mysterious whole of life, inaccessible to science" (Jaspers 1997, p. 544). *Second*, the authors, however, would maintain that this shifting basic disturbance becomes visible *in* direct experiences. Yet were it the case, this basic disturbance would have to be able to be proven or refuted through an observation of these experiences—which, however, is not the case. Due to this difficult empirical verifiability, *third*, its relationship to concrete experience appears to be arbitrary and disputable: "*It is not known why the same basic disturbance can bring about sometimes one sometimes the other manifestation.*" (Jaspers 1997, p. 542) However, the concept of basic disturbance according to Jaspers refers to scientific and explanatory knowledge—a kind of knowledge that refers to the whole of man. Both Straus and von Gebsattel aim at creating a "phenomenological-anthropological structural theory" of man (von Gebsattel 1954, p. 533; Jaspers 1997, p. 543). However, for Jaspers, as already mentioned, *fourth*, "*the totality of human life and its ultimate origin cannot be the object of any scientific research*" (Jaspers 1997, p. 543). In this sense, *fifth*, the corresponding knowledge solely *appears* to be knowledge (*Scheinerkenntnis*), as it makes a claim to something—the whole of human existence—that is fundamentally beyond its scope (Jaspers 1997, p. 545). In this area, Jaspers claims, it is not possible to know—and where this is feigned, true philosophy becomes lost (Jaspers 1997, p. 546).

We will now attempt to put these points of critique in order. It is clear that the first three refer critically to Straus' and von Gebsattel's results derived from description *as theory*: the terms *basic disturbance* or *disturbance of becoming*, used by the authors in reference to the experience of the affected persons, cannot be united with the notion of a coherent theory that could explain the given by pointing to (not given) fundamental, clearly defined processes. The insufficient scientific precision of theory thus becomes the bone of contention for Jaspers. This theory does not meet the norm of clearly formulated scientific knowledge, because scientific knowledge "must always look for definite connections that can either be verified or refuted" (Jaspers 1997, p. 545), which, for Jaspers, is impossible given the concept of basic disturbance.

Jaspers' latter two arguments criticize Straus' and von Gebsattel's claim to refer to human existence as a whole. Here, it seems that to Jaspers that the connection is made between the basic disturbance—to which he had already ascribed the function of theoretical explanation—and the concept of human existence that already extends beyond explicability. This human existence as a whole is presumed in Jaspersian thought of *philosophical Illumination of Existence*, and it eludes determination of causal-scientific knowing, whether this meets the Jaspersian criteria for scientificity or not. In basic terms, Straus' and von Gebsattel's concept of basic disturbance is, in Jaspers' view, poor science making the wrong claim.

Developing a "comprehensive theory of human life," as Jaspers criticizes Straus' and von Gebsattel for doing, would clearly be objectionable at the point when such a theory fixes and determines man as a whole to clear functions and thus precludes "thought of transcendence." Jaspers' critique first makes clear that these functions—basic disturbance or disturbance of becoming—*are* not at all clear and their relationship to that which is directly experienced is highly *imprecise*. He turns this imprecision, however, into an allegation, and this critique results from having initially defined phenomenological-psychiatric thought as *theory*, and thus *measuring it on the norms associated therewith*. At this point, Jaspers' view of von Gebsattel and Straus leads to a philosophical *double-bind*: after Jaspers interprets their results as causal theory about human existence, these appear to be untenable *both* as an explanatory causal-scientific claim *as well as* in a philosophical sense, pointing to the wholeness of human existence. Thus, for Jaspers, this approach can only fail.

6.3.2   Assessment of the Critique

The resulting question is whether Jaspers was even right in understanding "constructive-genetic psychopathology" (Jaspers 1997, p. 540) as theory. Might there not be a possibility that its terms about human existence lie in a realm very similar to that of Jaspers' Illumination of Existence? We can best approach this idea in a passage in which Jaspers analyzes Straus' idea of the future-oriented nature of human becoming (Jaspers 1997, p. 545).

According to Straus, the development of our life narrative and in particular our relationship to the past is dependent on our future-oriented nature (Jaspers 1997;

Straus 1960a). According to Jaspers, the prospects resulting from this observation apply, "with proper understanding to phenomena which in the last resort have their roots in the very Existence of Man in its historical, absolute and irreversible aspect. They have to be seen in light of this" (Jaspers 1997, p. 545).[4] The reader may ask at this juncture wherein Jaspers' "proper understanding" is distinguished from that which is supposedly improper. Jaspers further adds: "If however such experiences are grounded instead in the vital processes of becoming and their disturbances in a concrete objectivization of what can never be understood, then the vital substrate, a factor both impenetrable to understanding and obscure, replaces Existence itself, that which is understood but capable of an infinite illumination." (Jaspers 1997, p. 545).[5] Proper understanding would therefore be understanding of Existence and its infinite illumination; improper understanding, on the contrary, would be one that apprehends the affected person according to vital processes of becoming. Yet of what does the difference between Existence and vital processes of becoming consist? Evidently it consists in the first being an "unlimited incomprehensible that becomes illuminated," and the latter, contrarily, an "unilluminable incomprehensible" (Jaspers 1997). The latter is a "concrete objectivization," the former is not. However, this distinction is not further justified by Jaspers, and it thus remains almost arbitrary. It shows that Jaspers delineates something that shows commonalities: why should the Strausian concept of "becoming life" not similarly point to the moment of man that eludes scientific knowledge (*Erkenntnis*)? Were this so, Jaspers' entire critique would be inaccurate: these terms would then have to be understood in terms of "transcendental thought" (Jaspers 1997, p. 756), and they would *not* have to be measured according to the norms of scientific knowledge and they would *not* need to be criticized for attempting to scientifically determine man as a whole. Yet Jaspers overlooks this possibility in his critique. Thus, in the best case, his critique is incomplete.

Furthermore, if we consider the texts of Straus and von Gebsattel that Jaspers analyzed, it becomes clear that the contradictions of the Jaspersian critique point to an underlying ambivalence in these texts: the extent to which the terms developed here (basic disturbance, disturbance of becoming) are thought by these authors as "scientific theory" and "explanation" of mechanisms outside of consciousness, is, in our opinion, not clearly distinguishable (even if Jaspers claims this is so). For example, von Gebsattel calls the "endogenous barrier" on the one hand the "biological grounding" of clinical compulsive symptoms, yet he is oriented almost exclusively toward clinical observations and the "basic experience of the sick person" of the "passage of time" (von Gebsattel 1954, pp. 7, 18). Straus similarly claims on the one hand that there is a "vital barrier" in the basic disturbance, from which the affective symptoms of a human with a compulsive disorder can be "derived," yet he distinguishes his psychological and anthropological approach from the classical

---

[4] Incorrect translation: "im richtigen Verstehen" translates more accurately to "with proper understanding" rather than "rightly understood. " The quotation reflects this revision.

[5] "Gegenständliche Verdinglichung" translates more accurately to "concrete objectivization" rather than "concretization." The quotation reflects this revision.

approach of the natural sciences, as his thought is based solely on the norm of the "questioning and erroring human" (Straus 1960a, p. 136; Straus 1960b, p. 223). In the articles mentioned, it ultimately becomes evident that the work of both authors is closely oriented around clinical observations and subjective experiences of patients, and that they give relatively little attention to the associated hypotheses mentioned above. As it were, the postulates of the "disturbance of becoming" is distinguished from the patient's own experience, yet this does not *necessarily* mean that according to Jaspers, the "vital basic event which *cannot be experienced* but can only be *grasped*"[6] must be a causal theory (Jaspers 1997, p. 542). Thus, we arrive at the problem that in the totality of von Gebsattel's work and in the early work of Straus, only little attention is given to questions of method (Spiegelberg 1972, pp. 249–279). Therefore, it can be justified to count them as part of a branch of phenomenological psychiatrists who deal more with the comprehensive and realistic description of clinical conditions than with the philosophical and methodical categorization of such studies' results (Tatossian 2002, pp. 18–19). This makes it even more remarkable that Jaspers develops a critique intended as a general critique of concepts and methods of this "trend of thought in psychopathology" of authors who themselves give little thought to reflection on methods. Reference to other authors mentioned by Jaspers, such as Kunz, Storch, and not least Binswanger, would have been more fruitful, as this is not the case for them.

6.4 General Views of Phenomenological Psychiatry on Jaspers' Critique

The contradictory nature of Jaspers' critique is grounded in the determination of the concept of basic disturbance as a causal mechanism outside of consciousness. This is an approach that can also be found later in Kurt Schneider's reference to Hubertus Tellenbach's concept of phenomenon as well as in Gerd Huber: similar to basic disturbance in Straus and von Gebsattel, Tellenbach's concept of phenomenon, as well as the concept of Eidos in general, is rejected (Schneider 1976, p. 132; Huber 2005, p. 4). This is justified by the claim that these concepts might not be related to conscious clinical experience and are only delivered as theory to back up such experience. We would like to consider in closing whether this corresponds to a general self-understanding of phenomenological psychiatry. Because further individual observations cannot be made here, we would like to limit ourselves to Tatossian's general identification of phenomenological psychiatry.

---

[6] In this sentence, Jaspers' use of the German term "erschliessen"was originally translated into English as "deduced." This English translation does not contain a second meaning of the term "erschliessen," which refers to attaining knowledge through experience or practice, as opposed to by means of scientific method. This second meaning of "erschliessen" has been demonstrated by Heidegger in *Being and Time* (Heidegger 2008).

6.4.1   Closer Determination of the Concept of Essence and Phenomenological Psychiatry in Tatossian

With his study "la phénoménologie des psychoses"—which has been little observed outside of France—Tatossian attempted to write less an history of phenomenological psychiatry like Spiegelberg as to critically develop the actual purposes of phenomenological psychiatry as a whole based on basic psychopathological phenomena. For Tatossian, the concept of essence or eidos is definitive for the meaning of phenomenological-psychiatric research. Such research deals with fundamental structures of our experience which must be made observable by analysis. Tatossian refers to Straus' and von Gebsattel's concepts of basic disturbance, disturbance of becoming, etc. in terms of such structures (Tatossian 2002, pp. 90–103). However, he argues against the use of these concepts as mechanisms outside of consciousness or causal models of experience. For him, these are precisely *not* to be understood in terms of the "concrete objectivization" of experience, as Jaspers claimed with respect to Straus' disturbance of becoming (Jaspers 1997, p. 545). Straus' attempt to create a "phenomenological-anthropological theory," which Jaspers criticizes, does not occur in the sphere of the natural sciences according to Tatossian (von Gebsattel 1954, p. 533; Jaspers 1997, p. 543). Thus, it cannot be contrasted as a whole with Jaspers' philosophy of Existence.

This becomes clear in the following: for Tatossian, the basic disturbance is not a substructure of conscious experience, it is immanent to this experience. He illustrates this with a mathematical example: when the mathematician derives the function of a speed curve from the function of its acceleration, he adds "nothing new" to the speed curve. "Just as the acceleration curve is not the *origin*, but the *principle*, so is the eidetic structure which demands a phenomenological approach not the origin of that which is psychologically given. Rather, this approach plainly shows what it makes possible [...]" (Tatossian 2002, p. 22). The use of the concept of essence thus remains in the realm of experience—it has the status of a not causal but structural condition of the possibility of this experience. For Tatossian, revealing this condition is the actual task of description of direct subjective experience (Jaspers 1997, p. 14). Phenomenological psychiatry is thus interested in *clarification (Klärung)*, not *explanation (Er-klärung)* of experience (Jaspers 1997, p. 22).

Tatossian's reference to phenomenology as a "science of essence" (*Wesenswissenschaft*) therefore does not intend to explain reality by looking to that which is outside of consciousness. Rather, *within* experienced reality and its "how," a structure must be sought out. Thus, with the notion of an eidetic method, Tatossian aims not to consider something *different than* conscious reality, but rather to consider conscious reality *differently*. As in Goethe's claim "that experience is but the half of experience," it is the *structure* of experience, which can be viewed in each experience beyond this experience, whereas a natural-sciences approach would tend to reduce experience to its "whereby" or "why" (Goethe 2006, p. 166; Tatossian 2002, p. 22).

Tatossian names Rümke's well-known praecox-feeling as an example of this—in the case of praecox-feeling the impression of a schizophrenia does not arise on the basis of a psychopathological description of individual symptoms, but through the properties connecting all symptoms and the structure of these symptoms (Tatossian 2002, p. 26). This is moreover the structure which, for Tatossian, leads to the fact that the psychiatric symptom cannot be separated from or added to other symptoms (as is done in contemporary diagnostic manuals that proceed in terms of algorithms). Rather, its value can be found only in the *total image* with the other given facts: "the incoherence [as a single symptom, S.T.] of the delirious is not that of the schizophrenic, whose blunted affect, in turn, is not that of the melancholic" (Tatossian 2002, p. 25). In this sense of clarifying but not explaining, Tatossian contrasts phenomenological psychiatry with the instrumental interests of a natural-sciences approach in psychiatry: in the last instance, the natural-sciences approach aims at the domination of nature by reducing experience to models which are underlaid (Tatossian 2009). Phenomenological psychiatry, however, does not want to dominate the experienced, but simply bring this to bear. For this reason, Tatossian speaks of the "glorious non-utility" of phenomenological psychiatry for the instrumental thought of the natural sciences (Tatossian 2002, p. 237). Phenomenological experience itself is "not a theory" but a "critique of psychiatric reason" (Tatossian 2009, p. 131). Here, Tatossian ultimately points to the interactional and ethical meaning of the phenomenological-psychiatric approach: "phenomenological psychiatry is not a kind of Sunday psychiatry that limits itself to purely cognitive work; just because it becomes whole in and through daily experience (…), it makes "true positivism" possible, which can make the encounter with the psychically ill more appropriate" (Tatossian 2002, p. 83).

In Tatossian's critique of a natural-sciences approach to man, as well as in his reference to a heterogenous and ultimately interactional mode of experience that always exceeds simply factual experience, surprisingly, significant parallels are to be found to Jaspers' critique of science as well as his philosophy of existence (see above). Thus, it becomes evident in conclusion that Jaspers' philosophical aims and those of phenomenological psychiatry, as formulated by Tatossian, display, from a contemporary perspective, many more commonalities than contradictions—as Jaspers yet made it appear in his critique of Straus and von Gebsattel.

Acknowledgement   Special thanks to Johanna Thoma for insightful remarks.

References

Binswanger, L. (1994). Lebensgeschichte und Lebensfunktion. In L. Binswanger (Ed.), *Ausgewählte Werke in Vier Bänden* (Vol. 3, pp. 71–94). Heildelberg: Asanger.

Goethe, J. W. v. (2006). *Maximen und Reflexionen*. Munich: Deutscher Taschenbuch Verlag.

Heidegger, M. (2008). *Being and time* (Reprint). New York: Harper Perennial Modern Classics.

Huber, G. (2005). *Psychiatrie: Lehrbuch für Studium und Weiterbildung* (7., vollst. überarb. u. aktualis. A.). Stuttgart: Schattauer.

Husserl, E. (2009). *Ideen zu einer reinen Phänomenologie und phänomenologischen Philosophie* (1st ed.). Hamburg: Meiner.

Jaspers, K. (1968). The phenomenological approach in psychopathology. *The British Journal of Psychiatry*, 114(516), 1313–1323. doi:10.1192/bjp.114.516.1313.

Jaspers, K. (1997). *General psychopathology* (trans: Hoenig, J., Hamilton, M. W.). Baltimore: Johns Hopkins University Press. German edition: Jaspers, K. (1959). *Allgemeine Psychopathologie*, 7. unveränderte Aufl. Berlin: Springer.

Kirkbright, S. (2008). Ein kritischer Vergleich zwischen den verschiedenen Auflagen von Karl Jaspers Allgemeiner Psychopathologie. In S. Rinofner-Kreidl & H. Wiltsche (Eds.), *Jaspers' Allgemeine Psychopathologie Zwischen Wissenschaft, Philosophie Und Praxis*. Würzburg: Königshausen und Neumann.

Luft, S. (2008). Zur phänomenologischen Methode in Karl Jaspers' Allgemeiner Psychopathologie. In S. Rinofner-Kreidl & H. Wiltsche (Eds.), *Karl Jaspers' Allgemeine Psychopathologie Zwischen Wissenschaft, Philosophie Und Praxis*. Würzburg: Königshausen und Neumann.

Schneider, K. (1921). Pathopsychologische Beiträge zur phänomenologischen Psychologie von Liebe und Mitfühlen. *Zeitschrift für die gesamte Neurologie und Psychiatrie*, 65, 109–140.

Schneider, K. (1976). *Klinische Psychopathologie*. Stuttgart: Thieme.

Spiegelberg, H. (1972). *Phenomenology in psychology and psychiatry: A historical introduction* (1st ed.). Evanston: Northwestern University Press.

Straus, E. (1960a). Das Zeiterlebnis in der endogenen Depression und in der psychopathischen Verstimmung. In *Psychologie Der Menschlichen Welt: Gesammelte Schriften* (1st ed.). Heidelberg: Springer.

Straus, E. (1960b). Ein Beitrag zur Pathologie des Zwangserscheinungen. In *Psychologie Der Menschlichen Welt: Gesammelte Schriften* (1st ed.). Heidelberg: Springer.

Tatossian, A. (2002). *La phénoménologie des psychoses*. Paris: Le Cercle Hérméneutique.

Tatossian, A. (2009). Pratique psychiatrique et phénoménologie. In P. Fédida & M. Wolf-Fédida, Mareike (Eds.), *Phénoménologie, Psychiatrie, Psychanalyse* (pp. 131–140). Paris: Le Cercle Hérméneutique.

von Gebsattel, V. E. (1954). *Prolegomena einer medizinischen Anthropologie: Ausgewählte Aufsätze* (1st ed.). Heidelberg: Springer.

Wiggins, O. P., & Schwartz, M. A. (1997). Edmund Husserl's influence on Karl Jaspers's phenomenology. *Philosophy, Psychiatry, and Psychology*, 4(1), 15–36.

Chapter 7
Perspectival Knowing Karl Jaspers and Ronald N. Giere

Osborne P. Wiggins and Michael A. Schwartz

7.1 Jaspers' Multiperspectivalism

A passage in the Introduction to the Eighth edition of the book clearly expresses Jaspers' intention of his book (*die Absicht meines Buches*) (Jaspers 1965, p. 36). In this passage Jaspers refers to and quotes a paragraph in the edition of 1913, the edition we celebrate in this volume. He writes:

> I wrote in 1913 the meaning of my system of methodology: "Instead of forcing the whole domain into a system on the ground of a theory, we ought to seek to separate neatly the individual paths of research, points of view, and methods. Only in this manner can we bring to presentation the many-sidedness of psychopathology and allow this many-sidedness to stand forth clearly. Therefore, we can exclude neither theories nor in general any kind of point of view. Each image of the whole should be grasped, its meaning and its limits understood, and recognized in its legitimacy (Geltung). However, what prevails throughout (Umfassende) remains always investigative thinking. Only out of this thinking is each image of the whole legitimate, and legitimate only from one standpoint. Finally the methods and categories of investigation rule over and restrain (beherrschen) the images of the whole. Thus psychopathological investigations can be organized only according to the different methods and categories out of which the images of the whole arise." (Jaspers 1965, p. 36 (translation ours), 1997, pp. 41–42)

The above passage—the statement of *the basic intention* of the first edition—shows Jaspers to be firmly dedicated to his perspectivalism, and we shall argue later that this perspectivalism, expanded and reconceived, will remain central to his later philosophizing.

The passage describes perspectives as limited methods and sets of concepts. No one perspective can possibly reveal the whole of psychopathological reality; each perspective discloses only a restricted set of aspects of reality. Thus each perspective

O. P. Wiggins (✉)
University of Louisville, Louisville, KY 40292, USA
e-mail: opwigg01@gmail.com

M. A. Schwartz
Texas A&M Health Science Center College of Medicine, Round Rock, TX 78665, USA
e-mail: michael.schwartz@mas1.cnc.net

T. Fuchs et al. (eds.), *Karl Jaspers' Philosophy and Psychopathology,*
DOI 10.1007/978-1-4614-8878-1_7, © Springer Science+Business Media New York 2014

provides only a one-sided and partial depiction of reality. Other "sides" and "parts" of reality can be revealed only through research guided by other perspectives. Some psychopathologists may think it embarrassing that the field is furnished with multiple perspectives rather than just one systematic and comprehensive theory on which all researchers and practitioners can agree. But not Jaspers. He almost celebrates the "many-sidedness" of the field. It should simply be kept vigilantly in mind that this many-sidedness of theories and methods comes pared with the one-sidedness of each separate theory and its method.

Not only psychopathology but also the entire field of psychology is confined to research projects occurring from a particular point of view. Each approach in psychology highlights its own characteristic concepts and disregards others. The three main schools of psychology to which Jaspers refers are association psychology, intentionalist psychology, and gestalt psychology. About them Jaspers writes:

> The schools of thought which have developed one after the other (as the psychology of association, of intentional thought, or as gestalt-psychology) and which have all attacked each other, can in fact be brought together. We can make use of all of them, each one within its own limitations, as a means of describing phenomena and posing new questions for analysis. None of these psychologies can claim to explain everything or provide an all-embracing theory of psychic life as it really is. They fall down entirely as an explanation of the psyche, but show their value nonetheless if one employs them for a clear presentation of the relevant psychic facts. They cohere, they can be combined and do not have to contradict one another. (Jaspers 1965, p. 135, 1997, p. 161)

In this last sentence Jaspers has in mind that the methodological and conceptual differences of the various schools of psychology often clash with one another. He sees these clashes not as inevitable outcomes of the differences. Rather they occur only when one of these schools claims to explain the entire field of psychological phenomena. When several different schools populate a discipline like psychology, i.e., when a *plurality* of approaches prevails in a discipline, for one of them to claim *total* validity is for it to claim *exclusive* validity. As a consequence, polemical attacks and counterattacks by the different schools plague the discipline, and it, embarrassed and weakened by the irresolvable polemics, fails to advance. Hence Jaspers seeks to secure the path toward advancement in psychopathology by showing why claims to exclusivity and universality must give way to more modest claims to validity within the limits of a particular perspective.

As Jaspers asserts, the different perspectives, as long as they do not claim more for themselves than their particular point of view warrants, i.e., as long as they allow the others their own spheres of legitimacy, need not contradict one another: "They cohere." Hence Jaspers' perspectivalism, by insisting that different perspectives are only one approach to the psyche, creates a field of consistency in multiplicity. We wish to emphasize this feature of Jaspers' perspectivalism because some present-day writers would argue that different perspectives often contradict others and thus cannot possibly be true. Indeed, some authors would assert that different perspectives are "incommensurable" with one another, that they depict "different worlds" (Giere 2006, pp. 82–84). Jaspers contends that, while different perspectives may initially present incompatible elements, what is valid in each can be made compatible with the others, thus preserving the formal-logical conditions of truth.

Given the perspectivalism of all inquiry, scientists must resist the temptation to extend their favored perspectives beyond their domains of legitimacy. Jaspers could be said to see it as a natural, difficult-to-restrain human tendency to for investigators to work in the confidence that their point of view can, with sufficient endeavor, be extended to the whole of the field. Psychiatric perspectives may certainly contain manifold truths about human beings and their mental disorders. But each has its limits, the points at which its concepts cease to accurately capture real facets of mental difficulties. If psychiatrists insist on applying these perspectives beyond their inherent limits, their concepts become mere analogies and, at the extreme, mythic images. Hence we need to remain mindful of this temptation of the mind and to be vigilant in recognizing when the limits of the applicability of a perspective have been reached. The recognition of a perspectivism in psychiatric theories should prompt psychiatrists to remain reluctant to commit themselves to any particular perspective. They should, on the contrary, maintain a willingness to consider other views. No doubt is needed, but rather a hesitation to commit oneself uncritically to any particular perspective. Self-critique and a readiness to examine other approaches are useful tools of the scientific mind.

It might be easier to assent to the thesis that psychopathological theories are perspectival than to accept the same position regarding the natural sciences. For after all, the psychopathological theories can more easily qualify as "soft sciences" while the natural sciences are generally thought to count as "hard sciences." Expressed differently, the natural sciences are believed to possess a firm epistemological cogency that psychopathology does not. The evidence that allows for the choosing between competing scientific hypotheses is more decisive in the natural sciences than it is in the psychopathological sciences.

7.2   A Comparison of Jaspers and Ronald Giere on Scientific Perspectivism

This general assumption is what makes it so interesting to come upon a highly regarded philosopher of science, Ronald N. Giere, arguing for perspectivism, indeed a perspectivism *at all levels of natural scientific investigation* (Giere 2006). He finds such perspectivism present in scientific *instrumentation* by which evidence is gathered, the scientific *theories* in which propositions are logically systematized, and in the *"Laws of Nature"* which define the foundational bedrock of a scientific worldview. Giere is professor of philosophy emeritus at the University of Minnesota, a former Director of the Minnesota Center for Philosophy of Science, and a past president of the Philosophy of Science Association as well as the author of many books. In other words, he is recognized as one of the leaders in the field of the philosophy of science. His contentions thus carry real weight regarding issues of scientific methodology.

Giere treads his own distinctive middle path between what he calls "objectivist realism" and "social constructivism." Objectivist Realism asserts that scientific claims do faithfully represent features of the real world. Social Constructivists advocate a skepticism regarding scientific claims, arguing that contingent social factors such as ambitious drives for reputation and prestige, rhetorical manipulation, etc., motivate the community of scientists to accept claims to proven knowledge. Giere takes both of these opposing positions seriously and fairly appraises the arguments of each (Giere 2006, pp. 1–16). As a consequence, however, he thinks that a more adequate position consists in, as we mentioned, a middle path between them that he calls "perspectival realism" (Giere 2006, p. 88). We shall attempt to explicate such a perspectival realism, one that both Jaspers and Giere could accept.

Giere, like Jaspers, does not attempt to straightforwardly define his concept of "perspectivism." He probably refrains from trying to provide one because he discloses a perspectivism at every level of natural scientific thinking, and it is difficult to imagine a single characterization of that would adequately cover all of these levels. Instead of a general definition Giere demonstrates a perspectivism in color vision that he explains in detail (Giere 2006, pp. 17–36). Color vision is a basic level of encounter with the world—a level that Giere calls "commonsense" (p. 40). He seems to believe that if he can show perspectivism at this level, the reader will be more readily persuaded of its prevalence at "higher" experiential levels, such as observation through technologically advanced instruments and mathematically designed laws and theories.

In view of the fact that we live in an age soaked in "social constructionism," we should probably emphasize that perspectives, for Jaspers as well as for Giere, are the "conditions for the possibility of knowledge of *real* objects." Without them, human knowledge of reality would be impossible, unattainable. They are "enabling conditions" of our knowing the real. This is so because of the finitude of human reason and the infinity of the realities to be comprehended. All comprehension for Jaspers occurs from a point of view. Just as Giere has shown for color vision, the human intellect as such can make sense of something only from a point of view. We may be able to conceive of God, as an infinite intelligence, being able to grasp the whole of reality in an all-encompassing mental act: "From God nothing is hidden." However, humans, as finite intelligences, can grasp the whole only partially and one-sidedly. From humans much is hidden. As Giere expresses it, "We simply cannot transcend our human perspective, however much some may aspire to a God's eye view of the universe" (Giere 2006, p. 15).

This one-sidedness of every form of access to the world need not lead to Post-Modern skepticism. Granted, we know only those aspects of reality to which the chosen perspective furnishes access. Nevertheless, these are *aspects of reality*. And therefore, when we grasp them through the concepts or methods of the perspective, *we grasp truth.* For this reason Giere can propose his "perspectival realism" (Giere 2006, p. 88): it is *reality* that can be known through a perspective, even if it is *only from a particular perspective* that reality can be known.

Comparing the positions of Jaspers and Giere, we could get the impression that arguing for the thesis that access to reality is available to humans only through multiple perspectives is inherently unsatisfying to the human mind. For in both Jaspers and Giere we find a strong tendency to claim that *the world as a unique whole* is the center which brings together and unites the multiplicity of perspectives. They both maintain, however, that the idea of the world as the whole of reality plays solely *a methodological role.* The idea of the world provides only a *method for further investigation.* The world as a real being, the world as the unique whole of all that is, the world as the whole that unites all the perspectives because they all are "about it, that they all refer to and explain it" is tempting. For both Jaspers and Giere, however, the world is an idea of method, an idea that regulates our various inquiries, but is not the ultimately object of reference. For Jaspers, the world-whole is only a Kantian idea *(Idee),* a guiding conception of how to proceed further, but this idea does not refer to reality (Jaspers 1971, pp. 463–486, 1997, p. 560). The whole is not given *(gegeben);* it is rather posited as a task *(aufgegeben)* for further investigations. Giere, for instance, writes, "Now, the uniqueness of the world is a clear example of what would typically be taken as a metaphysical doctrine. But it need not be so regarded. It can be understood as merely a methodological presumption" (Giere 2006, p. 34). For Giere, the world as the unique whole that ultimately unites all our many points of view on it is simply "a presumption of our actions" (Giere 2006, p. 34).

7.3   The Multiplicity of the Cultural Symbolisms

In his later thought, Jaspers emphasized the need for philosophers to take up the pressing problems of the day and to reflect on politics (Jaspers 1958, 1964, 1986, pp. 124–131). To do so was to confront inevitably the threat of large-scale destruction through nuclear attack. Jaspers sees the enormity of this threat as so great that he believes it requires markedly new ways of conceiving the relationships among nations and individuals across the globe. He expresses this unprecedented human threat as follows:

> In the past, folly and wickedness had limited consequences; today they draw all mankind to perdition. Now, unless all of us live with and for one another, we shall all be destroyed together. This new situation demands an answer appropriate to it […]. It is not enough to find new institutions; we must change ourselves, our characters, or moral-political wills. I do not believe that I am exaggerating. Whoever continues to live in the manner in which he has lived up to now has not grasped the menace. Merely thinking this intellectually does not yet mean absorbing it into the actuality of one's life. Men must turn their lives around; if they do not want to lose them. If they want to continue living, they must change. (Jaspers 1958, p. 24, 1986, p. 409)

This danger only grows as we watch different cultures throughout the world acquire nuclear weapons and harden their particular cultural outlooks in such a way as to oppose nations to one another in uncompromising conflicts. In brief, the danger lies in part in the various cultures absolutizing their religious and political differences to such an extent that only deadly antagonisms would ensue. Jaspers, of course, had in mind Russian Communism and German Nazism (Jaspers 1986, pp. 429–440). However, the same processes of ideological hardening can be found all too ominously today in various parts of the world.

Jaspers had explicitly criticized the absolutization of perspectives that created dogmatisms warring against one another. The following passage from the *General Psychopathology* could also be applied to Jaspers' stance regarding the different world cultures:

> Looking over this series of basic wholes we are first struck by their multiplicity; no one whole is the whole; each complex unity is but one among others and relative. Secondly we see the universal tendency to turn each complex unity into an absolute, to find in it the psyche as such or at any rate the focal point, the dominating factor. Every conversion into an absolute contains some truth which is in this way only destroyed. (Jaspers 1997, p. 750)

Philosophy could contribute to avoiding such a disastrous outcome by studying the variety of the major religious, political, and philosophical orientations around the world and uncovering in each what was of lasting value and thus should be appreciated by all societies. Philosophy could also contribute to world peace by showing why no culture had a monopoly on the truth because each culture had grasped only a part of the whole of ultimate Being. In other words, each culture had a perspective on reality which, like all perspectives, expressed a *one-sided* and *limited* understanding of the whole. Arguing that the worldviews of the major cultures across the globe embody only partial perspectives seems to carry the danger of advocating a *relativism of beliefs* in which no culture can claim to have grasped the truth. Confronting and accepting the relativity of cultural perspectives seems to many people to entail a *skepticism* regarding all claims to truth. Jaspers refuses to accept this chain of logical implication: *pluralism* of worldviews implies *relativity* of worldviews implies *skepticism* toward all worldviews. Jaspers seeks a history of the great philosophers to uncover and emphasize the lasting truths which each has unearthed, however misunderstood this truth may be in its indigenous literal form. In this manner truth is definitely attainable by the human mind. However, it remains only the truth of a specific perspective; it is not the truth of the whole. Jaspers insists that the search for truth always sustains its energy and intensity only as long as it is driven by a desire to know the whole. Human understanding is teleological: it aims at its eventual completion in systematically knowing the entirety of being, being both temporal and eternal. However, this completion is unattainable. As a consequence, no culture or institution possesses the entire and final truth even though it may think it has. Hence the philosophical task is to demonstrate the partiality of any worldview while also arguing that, contrary to skepticism, truth is attainable, albeit a partial and limited truth (Jaspers 1986, pp. 437–440).

Jaspers aims to appreciate the plurality of religious and cultural worldviews without the pernicious absolutisms that tend to produce conflicts and even war. The dangers of absolutisms are addressed by Jaspers' conception of cyphers. Each presents an idea or image which refers to a reality, but the idea or image is not a literal or exact representation of the reality to which it points us. Only in vague respects is the representation "similar to" the reality it makes us aware of. Through this "deliteralization" ideas and images are conceived by Jaspers as "cyphers" which refer beyond themselves to realities which cannot be described literally and univocally (Jaspers 1986, pp. 438–440).

Jaspers obviously was already moving toward this pluralism of perspectives in his psychiatry, in the first edition and in the repeated revisions of it. This concern with the multiple ways by which we have access to reality, whether it be to the empirical realities of science and everyday life or to the metaphysical reality of Being itself, Jaspers deems the human mind confined to particular and differing points of view. In the latter stages of his philosophy he focused his attention on an analogous plurality in political, religious, and philosophies. This was Jaspers' faith in human freedom and reason to rise to the challenges that confront it, even the ultimate challenge that faces us today, nuclear war.

References

Giere, R. N. (2006). *Scientific perspectivism*. Chicago: The University of Chicago Press.

Jaspers, K. (1958). *The future of mankind*. Chicago: The University of Chicago Press.

Jaspers, K. (1964). *Die Atombombe und die Zukunft des Menschen*. Munich: Deutscher Taschenbuch Verlag.

Jaspers, K. (1965). *Allgemeine psychopathologie* (8th ed.). Berlin: Springer-Verlag.

Jaspers, K. (1971). *Kants Ideenlehre, Psychologie der Weltanschauungen* (6th ed., pp. 463–486). Berlin: Springer-Verlag.

Jaspers, K. (1986). *Karl Jaspers: Basic philosophical writings*, edited by Ehrlich, E., Ehrlich, L., and Pepper, G., Athens, OH: Ohio University Press.

Part II
Psychopathology and Psychotherapy

Chapter 8
Karl Jaspers on Primary Delusional Experiences of Schizophrenics: His Concept of Delusion Compared to That of the DSM

Alfred Kraus

8.1 Introduction

By and large, definitions of "delusion" in the *Diagnostic and Statistical Manual of Mental Disorders* (DSM)—along with various other theoretical, explicative attempts thereof—adopt Karl Jaspers' definition of schizophrenic delusions, which he defined as "false judgements" in his *General Psychopathology* (Jaspers 1959/1997)[1]. Thus, DSM-IV-TM defines schizophrenic delusions generally as "erroneous beliefs" (1994, p. 275). Concurrent with his work on GP, however, Jaspers came into conflict with his own definition of schizophrenic delusion as false judgements, which he had adopted from his contemporaries. This accepted and general definition had its foundation in the so-called three criteria of delusion with explanations of the real "psychological nature" ("Wesen," HH p. 80) of delusion. Going further, he differentiated between incomprehensible "primary delusional experiences" (HH p. 82)[2,3] and comprehensible delusional assumptions often originating from these. Following from this differentiation, he showed that primary delusional experiences are quite different than those delusional meanings arising from false judgements. For Jaspers, these are much

Herrn Prof. Dr. Werner Janzarik mit den besten Wünschen zum 92. Geburtstag.

[1]All page numbers marked with "own translation" relate to our own translation of *Allgemeine Psychopathologie* (1965) with the original page numbers. English translations of Jaspers' *General Psychopathology* of Hoenig & Hamilton (1959/1997) are marked with "HH" and the page number.

[2]This is the original title of Chapter B of Paragraph 4, translated and shortened by Hoenig and Hamilton (1997). Primary delusions leave out the most important "experiences" (HH p. 82).

[3]Whether there are possibly different meanings of primary delusional experiences is a topic that was recently discussed extensively by Gorsky (2012a, 2012b) and by Stanghellini (2012). For us it is decisive that the "contents of delusional ideas" (HH p. 80) resulting from false judgements of primary experiences are "a secondary product" (HH p. 80).

A. Kraus (✉)
Klinik für Allgemeine Psychiatrie, Zentrum für Psychosoziale Medizin,
Universitätsklinikum Heidelberg, Voß-Str. 4,
D-69115 Heidelberg, Germany

T. Fuchs et al. (eds.), *Karl Jaspers' Philosophy and Psychopathology*,
DOI 10.1007/978-1-4614-8878-1_8, © Springer Science+Business Media New York 2014

more characteristic of a later stage of delusion. In the case of delusional perception, for example, the delusional meaning occurs as an "immediate intrusive knowledge of meanings" (own translation p. 83) and does not, as the DSM states, "involve misinterpretation of perceptions and experiences" (DSM p. 275). In other words, primary delusion has a different formal structure when compared to secondary stages of delusion. The definition of schizophrenic delusion as "erroneous beliefs" (DSM p. 275) and as consisting in "disease-induced misjudgement" (AGP system 58) relates almost exclusively to the delusion described by Jaspers as secondary. Due to a lack of appreciation about this distinction between judgement-based delusions and primary delusional experiences, the DSM neglects completely to discuss *primary* delusional experiences. Moreover, DSM adopts the three criteria of delusion posited by Jaspers but conceives of these with a total lack of phenomenological specificity. In other words, the definition is almost exclusively quantitative without Jaspers' attempt to conceptualize this also in a *qualitatively* specified way.

Besides this explicative purpose of distinguishing Jaspers' definition of primary delusional experience from the general, judgement-based definitions of the DSM, a secondary topic to be discussed is the possibility that the disturbance of the ego (or of the basic or bodily self), which one takes as characteristic of schizophrenic delusions[4], takes place as a result of alterations of existential a prioris (i.e., basic categories of human existence). That would indicate a shift from being in the sense of Heidegger's "Dasein" in the direction of a "reification" ("Verdinglichung") of being. If this shift were indeed the case, then it would underline the importance of Jaspers' phenomenological specificity regarding the criteria of delusion. Also, it would shed light on the specific formal structure of the schizophrenic primary delusion while partly reducing its incomprehensibility. To conclude this section concerning the secondary topic, some consequences for psychotherapy of delusion will be discussed.

Jaspers' concept of delusional experiences of schizophrenics is highly significant for present psychiatry because he differentiates primary delusional experiences from the results of these, which occur when a patient tries to understand his (even for him) strange new experiences at the beginning of his delusion. In his own language, the primary delusional experience, that is, the "vivid givenness of the delusional contents," occurs before changing into "solidified delusional judgements, only reproduced, discussed, dissimulated on any opportunity" (own translation p. 80); these later developments are often referred to as the so-called secondary delusion(s). This differentiation is important for two reasons:

1. The emphasis on primary delusional experiences enables Jaspers to distinguish a definition of delusion based on criteria from what he called the "psychological nature of the delusional ideas behind these more superficial characteristics" (own translation p. 80). In contrast to Jaspers, the diagnostic glossaries emphasize without doubt the operational definition of delusion, thereby neglecting the real nature of delusion.

---

[4]This is particularly the case for so-called "experiences of being made" ("Erlebnisse des Gemachten").

Table 8.1 Comparison of Jaspers definition of schizophrenic delusions and modern diagnostic manuals such as DSM-IV-TM and the AGP-System

Jaspers' definition of schizophrenic delusion	DSM-IV-TM: definition of Schizophrenic delusion (p. 275)
"Delusion manifests itself in judgements; delusion can only arise in the process of thinking and judging. To this extent pathologically falsified judgements are termed delusion." (HH p. 80) ("Wissen")	Schizophrenic delusions (Criterion A1) are "erroneous beliefs that usually involve *misinterpretation of perceptions or experiences*"...
"The term delusion is vaguely applied to all false judgements that share the following *external characteristics* to a marked, though undefined, *degree*: they are held with *an extraordinary conviction*, with an *incomparable, subjective certainty*. there is *an imperviousness* to other experiences *and to compelling counter-argument.*	Ad (1) "the distinction between a delusion and a strongly held idea depends... *on the degree of conviction* with which the belief is held". Ad (2) "*despite clear contradictory evidence* (275)" (p. 275). Ad (3) "*Delusions are deemed bizarre*, if they are clearly *implausible* and *not understandable* and do not derive from ordinary life experiences" (p. 275).
their content is *impossible*. If we want to get behind these mere external characteristics into the psychological nature of delusion, we must distinguish the *original experience* from the judgement based on it, i.e., the delusional contents as presented data from the fixed judgement which is then merely reproduced, disputed, dissimulated as occasion demands." (HH p. 96)	*AGP-system*
"For any true grasp of delusion, it is most important to free ourselves from this prejudice that there has to be some poverty of intelligence at the root of it" (HH p. 97)	In the AGP-system delusion (in general) is defined as a "disease-induced misjudgement of reality" and delusional ideas as "isolated, irrational or delusional thoughts" (p. 58).

2. Separating the primary delusional experiences from secondary delusional ideas (as a product of the patient's working through these experiences) made it possible to distinguish the former as incomprehensible. Therefore, the primary delusional experiences could be considered as beyond our understanding, despite the comprehensibility of the contents of the delusional ideas, which the patient may disclose in an interview. These disclosed ideas are "always a secondary product [...] coming from the primary experiences in an understandable way" (own translation p. 81).

8.2 Definition and Nature of Schizophrenic Delusion

The relevance of Jaspers' concept of delusion is shown by the continual importance of his three criteria for the definition of schizophrenic delusion in the diagnostic manual of DSM-IV-TM. In the Table 8.1, we compare Jaspers' definition of schizophrenic delusion to the definition in the DSM. However, if we take into consideration his own commentaries to his criteria, we recognize the far extent to which Jaspers' concept of the real nature of schizophrenic delusion deviates from its definition in the DSM manual.

The general definition of schizophrenic delusions in the DSM as consisting in "erroneous beliefs" that usually involve misinterpretations of perceptions or experiences seems confirmed by Jaspers, for he states that delusion is communicated by judgements ("pathologically falsified judgements," HH p. 80). In the same chapter on "delusion and awareness of reality," however, he comments and criticizes his own statement, and thereby also implicitly the definition in the DSM, when he posits: "To say simply that delusion is a mistaken idea which is firmly held by the patient and which cannot be corrected gives only a superficial and incorrect answer to the problem. The definition will not dispose of the matter" (HH p. 93). The psychological nature of delusion, according to Jaspers, is not sufficiently explained by the mere external characteristics of the pathologically falsified judgements. We have to take into consideration also the original experiences on which the judgements are based as a "secondary product." This becomes particularly clear, when he speaks about the primary experiences of delusional perception: "We have here not to do with interpretations of the character of judgements....[5] The meaning is experienced immediately..." (own translation p. 83). Thus, primary delusional experiences do not "involve a misinterpretation of perception or experiences" (275) as formulated in DSM-IV-TM. Misinterpretations are characteristic for a secondary stage of delusion. In its formal structure, primary delusional experience is different from secondary stages of delusion, at which delusion may involve erroneous judgements. Evidently, the general definition of delusion of the DSM neglects the primary delusional experience completely, if accept Jaspers' point that erroneous judgements are different from delusions when considered according to their nature ("Wesen"). For Jaspers, proper delusions are "elementary," "immediate and final experiences" (own translation p. 110), as opposed to erroneous judgements arising only secondarily via thinking: "The elementary experiences psychologically cannot be influenced opposite to that which is mediated by thoughts. They are primarily without content" (own translation p. 110). Erroneous delusional interpretations of the secondary delusional stage are often called "extra explanatory delusion."[6] This secondary stage remains, however, intrinsically connected with a delusion proper insofar as its content relates to primary delusional experiences. The erroneous interpretations present the patient with a means to adapt his primary delusional experiences to common reality. This understanding of schizophrenic secondary stages of delusion maintains validity (as we will show below) regarding the inability to correct these delusions, which in its specificity also relates to the primary delusional experience. If we adhere to Jaspers' general definition, then the definition of delusions as "erroneous beliefs" in the DSM and its foundation can be questioned.

---

[5] "Character of judgements" is left out in the translation of Hoenig and Hamilton.
[6] Because the delusional ideas as falsified judgement are based in the pathological primary experiences, Jaspers speaks also of "pathologically falsified judgements" (p. 80). This does not mean, as cognitivists sometimes suppose, that falsified judgements are as such pathological."

The question whether delusion is merely an erroneous belief characterized by erroneous interpretations is not only important for conceptual and diagnostic reasons but also for psychotherapy. If convinced that his delusional assumptions are solely erroneous beliefs, then the patient finds himself in self-contradiction due to his attempts to "normalize" his primary delusional experiences. By trying to adapt his primary delusions to be normal, the situation can even worsen; for the self-created erroneous reality may return him back to his primary delusional experiences, which, in turn, become more dreadful because they seem impossible to alter. Without this differentiation, we, as psychiatrists, would fail to recognize that the primary delusional experience is the main "generator" of delusion, rather than the errors revealed in one's judgements.

Now let us return to our table. Jaspers' three characteristics of false judgement are summarized under criterion A1 in the DSM-IV-TM. Criterion A1 is given if delusions are bizarre. Further, hallucinations are considered bizarre if these involve "commenting" or "conversing" voices. This single criterion of bizarreness is judged as being so important for the diagnosis of schizophrenia that "only this symptom is needed to satisfy criterion A1 for schizophrenia" (p. 275). "Bizarre" is defined as being "clearly impossible and not understandable, not deriving from ordinary life experiences" (p. 275). It comprises delusions that express a loss of control over mind or body, or the patient's beliefs that "his or her thoughts have been taken away by some outside force ('thought withdrawal'), that alien thoughts have been put into his or her mind ('thought insertion'), or that his or her body or actions are being acted on or manipulated by some outside force ('delusions of control')" (p. 275). We will return to this topic of bizarreness below.

8.3   Primary Delusional Experiences

Let us cover what Jaspers says about "primary delusional experiences" (own translation p. 82) ("primäre Wahnerlebnisse"). "Primary" here is used in the sense that the delusion occurs *before* its development into false judgements. In the description of these experiences, Jaspers places the emphasis on formal aspects, that is, on the "how" of experiences and not so much on the "what" (or the content) of those experiences—the latter of which takes up the foreground of the diagnostic manuals today. The "how" of experiences, in the wider sense of our understanding, relates not only to symptoms (e.g., first rank symptoms and Jaspers' criteria of delusion), but also to the relationship of the patient to himself, to the world and to others.

8.3.1   Delusional Atmosphere

Jaspers starts the pertinent section in Chapter § 4 of his GP with a restriction: "We cannot really appreciate these quite alien modes of experience, they remain largely incomprehensible, unreal and beyond our understanding" (HH p. 98). "Patients feel uncanny and that there is something suspicious afoot." Everything "gets a new meaning. The environment is somehow different—not to gross degrees—perception is unaltered in itself, but there is some change, which envelops everything with a subtle pervasive and a strangely uncertain light. A living room which formerly was felt as neutral or friendly now becomes dominated by some indefinable atmosphere" (HH p. 98). "This general delusional atmosphere ('Wahnstimmung') with all its vagueness of content must be unbearable" (HH p. 98) (see also Fuchs 2005). With this delusional "indefinable atmosphere," "the awareness of meaning undergoes a radical transformation" (HH p. 99) and "there is an immediate, intrusive knowledge of the meaning and it is this which is itself the delusional experience" (HH p. 99). Jaspers continues that already in the delusional atmosphere "we always find an 'objective something' there, even though quite weak, a something which lays the seeds of objective validity and meaning" (HH p. 98).

8.3.2   Delusional Perception

It is important to mention that Jaspers does not consider delusional perceptions ranging from experiences of vague meanings to experiences of clear, but delusional observation and reference "as interpretations of the patient in the way of judgements"[7] "completely[8] separated from the perceived object. The delusional meaning is rather immediately experienced within the completely normal and unchanged perception" (own translation p. 83).

"Particularly at the beginning of processes in very many cases, no clear definite meaning accompanies the perceptions. Objects, persons and events are simply eerie, horrifying, peculiar, or they seem remarkable, mystifying, transcendental. Objects and events signify something, but nothing definite" (HH p. 100).

These undefined meanings already in the delusional atmosphere ("Wahnstimmung") do not signify doubts in the sense of uncertainty about the fact that something has happened, but only uncertainty about the definite meaning of the fact. In other words, one is certain that the event must have a definite meaning. Müller-Suur (1950) spoke of an absolute "certain uncertainty" about the definite meaning of the events, respectively of everything that the patient experiences in primary delusion. This absolute certain consciousness of uncertain certainty for Müller-Suur is very important from a diagnostic point of view because it differentiates schizophrenic delusion from paranoid delusion ("paranoia" in the traditional sense, where this basic experience of delusion is not present). The patient, therefore, does not believe with a certainty of 100% in his delusional system, rather only with a more or less relative certainty (even if his certainty increases in the course of the illness).

---

[7] Hoenig and Hamilton omitted in their translation (HH p. 100) the decisive suffixes "urteilsmäßig".
[8] "völlig" (Jaspers 1959).

Jaspers says about "delusional perceptions" that the delusional meanings are "not interpretations in the sense of judgements, but are immediately experienced in a completely normal and unchanged perception what concerns the senses" (HH p. 99). Also, he explains that normal perception is "never a mechanical image of sensory impression, but at the same time a perception of meaning" (HH p. 99). The primary delusional experiences "are analogous to this seeing of meaning, but the awareness of meaning undergoes a radical transformation. This is an immediate, *intrusive* knowledge of the meaning and it is this which is itself the delusional experience" (HH p. 99). He says further: "Is the meaning immediately given in the sensorial perception, in the imagined, in the memorized, then this meaning has the character of reality" (own translation p. 83). If in delusional perceptions we have to do with completely normal perceptions, then this offers grounds for criticism of a theory of a primary dysfunction of perception as a cause of the disease.

In contrast to the mere "delusion of meanings ("Bedeutungswahn") [by which] objects and events signify something but signify nothing definite," the "delusion of reference" is when the "patient recognizes more distinct meanings with an obvious relation to himself" (own translation p. 84). We think Jaspers' concept of delusional perception is different from K. Schneider's, even if the latter also considers perception as such to be normal in delusional. Nevertheless, Schneider insists on a double-tracked structure when speaking on delusional perception (Schneider 1967). The decisive difference is that, according to Jaspers' view, the abnormal meaning is "perceived directly with the senses," thus "having the character of reality." What Jaspers understands as "reality" is factual normal reality; it is not to be confused with reality of abnormal experience (cf. Müller-Suur 1950 and Schmidt-Degenhard 2009), nor should it be confused with the definite delusional content, which "impresses nearly like a symbol for something else" (own translation p. 88). This is very important in for the following reasons:

Firstly, if with sensuous perception the abnormal meaning is analogous to normal meaning and so becomes the character of reality for the patient, this must increase his certainty about the abnormal meaning: the patient has "seen" the meaning. Secondly, this explains the high diagnostic significance of delusional perception when compared to mere delusional ideas. Thirdly, the patient cannot easily forget these delusional meanings in delusional perceptions which are much more present in secondary states than mere delusional ideas. This is particularly true for delusional experiences of "being-made" (Erlebnisse des "Gemachten") if these are felt in a bodily way. When Schmidt-Degenhard (2009) speaks of a particular evidence of the fictional imaginary world in delusion being taken as real by the patient; this results partly from this sensuous foundation of delusional meanings in delusional perceptions, which the patient is secondarily working on by giving them explanations. Fourthly, the character of reality, analogous to normal reality, makes these experiences in primary delusion, apart from the "vagueness of content" mentioned by Jaspers, so extraordinarily dreadful and "unbearable" that it results in extreme anxiety. From this follows that anxiety here is not primary, as some authors of the affective theory approach to delusion would maintain. Instead, it is secondary to the threatening "sinking" of his former normal world ("Weltuntergang") and also to the "sinking" of his personality ("Untergang seiner Persönlichkeit") (own translation p. 248).

As an aside, Jaspers' refusal of a primary affective influence in schizophrenic delusion is clearly demonstrated when he contrasts schizophrenic delusion to melancholic and manic delusional ideas, the former not counting as delusions proper because they would originate from affects, desires, and fears in an understandable way.

8.4   Is Schizophrenic Delusion a Disturbance of Cognition?

The other widespread theory of schizophrenic delusion is that of the cognitive approach. When Jaspers speaks about delusion from the perspective of a psychology of achievement, he formulates without a note of ambiguity that with delusion we are not dealing with "a disturbance of intelligence" currently defined often "as the reason for false judgements. […] The apparatus of thinking and power of judgement of the patient is in order, but in his thinking there is something that gives her/him an unshakeable evidence, where others and also other patients would have an insight of error. […] Even if the psychological aspect of achievement comes first, that shows exactly negatively that delusion is not a disturbance of achievement but originates from a depth which appears in delusional judgements, but itself has not the character of a judgement" (own translation p. 164). This sentence can easily be misunderstood. What Jaspers wants to say, in our understanding is: delusion for the moment seems to be the result of a disturbance of an achievement, but in itself is not.

"Phenomenologically," Jaspers says "we observe in delusion an experience that is radically alien to the healthy person, something basic and primary, which comes before thought, although it becomes clear to itself only in thought" (HH p. 196). These very differentiated statements of Jaspers show that there is more to be considered in delusion than primary cognitive disturbances in the sense of biologically founded functional disturbances, which stand now in the foreground of modern research. All these statements of Jaspers we hold to be particularly important in the context of cognitive psychotherapy of schizophrenic delusion.

A main criticism of the concept of delusion in the DSM as well as in Jaspers' GP is the assumed unspecificity of the three items of schizophrenic delusion in the DSM and of the "characteristics" for the diagnosis of schizophrenic delusion in the GP. This may be the reason why these are not to be found in ICD-10.

We saw that Jaspers differentiated between "characteristics of false judgement" in delusion, which he called "external," and the "psychological essence" ("Wesen") (own translation p. 80) of delusional ideas. It would seem that Jaspers might have two kinds of phenomenology in mind: one in which the term phenomenon is synonymous with symptom, and the other in which phenomenon relates to the essence, the "Wesen," of something. Despite Jaspers wanting to avoid eidetic phenomenology in a Husserlian vein as a method of eidetic variation when speaking of "Wesen," his phenomenology here comes closer to an eidetic one.

8.5   The Nature of Schizophrenic Delusion from the Perspective of Its Three Characteristics

8.5.1   Incomparable Certainty

Jaspers differentiates in schizophrenic delusion an immediate experience of reality from a judgement of reality. He also distinguishes certainty of immediate experience from one that is the result of an intellectual processing of experience. Whereas the first kind of certainty is characteristic for the primary state of delusion and is completely incomprehensible and thus a qualitatively different "incomparable subjective certainty" ("unvergleichliche subjektive Gewissheit," Jaspers 1959/1997, p. 80), the second one is that of a later stage of delusion and is partly understandable, characterized by a quantitatively high certainty.

When first speaking of the definition of delusion, he characterized the subjective certainty of the deluded patient as being incomparable in a quantitative sense to normal convictions. Also, the other two characteristics of schizophrenic delusion (incorrigibility and impossible content) are given in a "marked, though undefined degree of a quantitative characteristic." We find a similar assertion of quantitative characteristics in the DSM, according to which the difference between a strongly held idea and a schizophrenic delusion depends only on the degree of conviction. However, when later describing primary delusional experiences,[9] Jaspers says: "If we try to come nearer to these primary delusional experiences, we very soon notice that we cannot intuitively represent[10] these completely alien modes of experience" (HH p. 82).

"There always remains a big leftover of something incomprehensible, intuitively not being representable, not understandable" (own translation p. 82). When translating "anschaulich vergegenwärtigen" with "intuitively represented," we see the influence of Husserl's phenomenology on Jaspers, even if, as Wiggins et al. (1992) show, Jaspers' understanding of these terms is in some way different from Husserl's. Jaspers underlines how difficult it is for the diagnostician to understand experiences of the patients and also to determine the kind of certainty of the patient (i.e., the quality of his conviction). Relating to delusional perception, Jaspers refers to an "immediate, intrusive knowledge of the meaning" (HH p. 99) (i.e., the uncertainty here must also have an intrusive character). When Müller-Suur (1950) says, regarding the absolute certainty in schizophrenic delusion, that we are faced with a kind of certainty relating merely to the reality of experience ("Erlebniswirklichkeit"), which is isolated from its object and thus not related to a reality of common sense understanding, this is only valid for delusional ideas. By contrast, in delusional per-

---

[9]The translation Hoenig and Hamilton omitted "experiences" in the title of this chapter speaking only of "primary delusions" and, not as Jaspers does, of "primary delusional experiences."

[10]translated: "cannot really appreciate these quite alien modes of experience. They remain largely incomprehensible, unreal and beyond our understanding" (HH p. 98).

ception the abnormal meaning is founded in the sensuously unchanged object (i.e., in common sense reality).

8.5.2 Incorrigibility of Schizophrenic Delusion: Is It Specific?

In our view there is a strong relationship between the qualitatively incomparable subjective certainty of the patient and his condition's "imperviousness to other experiences," which is called by Jaspers a "specific schizophrenic [incorrigibility]" ("spezifisch schizophrene Unkorrigierbarkeit" p. 88). Both characteristics help explain each other. Jaspers in this context demonstrates how the "whole world"[11] of the deluded patient has been transformed. A changed knowledge of reality ("Realitätswissen") has transformed the world to such a pervasive extent that any "correction would mean a collapse of being itself, insofar as for him it is his actual awareness of existence" (own translation p. 88).

"Man cannot believe something that would negate nihilate his existence" ("Dasein"[12]). Jaspers also maintains that the "delusion proper," that is, the schizophrenic one, is incorrigible because of an "alteration of personality" (p. 88). He points out that we are "unable to describe the former, let alone to formulate it conceptually conceptually; instead, we [can] only assume it" (own translation p. 88). If the incorrigibility is specific, we think that the certainty of the patient must also be incomparable in a qualitatively abnormal sense (i.e., not merely in a normal sense). In the DSM, however, this characteristic is adopted only in its quantitative sense. We mentioned already Jaspers' differentiation between delusion and error. Error can also be incorrigible, but in delusion there is always something beyond normal incorrigibility. [...] Until now it was not possible to describe it" (own translation p. 342).

8.5.3 Impossibility of the Content of Delusion: Is It Specific?

In his definition of delusion as false judgements, Jaspers first speaks of the impossibility of the delusional content in a merely unspecified way. This impossibility could also be the result of an error or a lack of knowledge. However, he then denotes this definition as more of an "external characteristic" (own translation p. 80) and

---

[11] When Jaspers speaks of the world of schizophrenics, this is never meant in the sense of a uniform schizophrenic world; there are always many worlds.

[12] When Jaspers speaks of Dasein, this is meant in a more concrete, not categorial sense, particularly not in the sense of Heidegger (1963). Thus, also when he speaks of "Daseinsverwandlung," this is not in the sense of a "transformation of one's existence" (Jaspers 1959/1997, p. 592). Only in the context of border situations ("Grenzsituationen") unchangeable situations of "Dasein," he comes near to an understanding of Dasein like that of daseinsanalytic authors when he maintains that in psychopathy, neuroses, psychoses we have to do not only with "deviances from a norm of health, but also with the origins of human possibilities in general" (own translation p. 275).

specifies the impossibility of the delusion's content by referring to it as a different kind of "knowledge of reality" ("Realitätswissen," p. 88). He states: "The sense of reality" (der Sinn der "Wirklichkeit," p. 88) for the patient "does not always carry the same meaning as that of normal reality. With these patients persecution does not always appear quite like the experience of people who are in fact being persecuted" (HH p. 105). Another example offered by Jaspers is delusional jealousy: "The jealousy of these patients does not seem like that of some justifiable jealous person, also there is often some similarity of behaviour" (HH p. 105). The DSM adopts also this characterization of the impossibility of content as only in an unspecified way. Further, the characterization of delusion as "bizarre" in the sense of "clearly impossible, not understandable and not deriving from ordinary life experience" (HH p. 275) could also be applied to non-delusional contents.

Moreover, the behavior of deluded schizophrenics goes against what one would expect if one understood the delusional contents as concretely as the patient expresses them. Sullivan, reported my Mundt (1996), shares the story of a schizophrenic patient who maintained to be Jesus Christ. The director of the clinic on a visit said to him: "If you are Jesus Christ please take the keys of the clinic." The patient answered: "One of us must be crazy."

According to Jaspers, the definite content of the delusion strikes one like a "symbol for something quite different" (HH p. 105). Kepinski spoke of a metaphysical taint of the theme of delusion in schizophrenia, which can be divided into three interrelated trends: an ontological trend, an eschatological trend and a charismatic trend (referred to extensively by Bovet and Parnas (1993)). Several authors, as well as Jaspers himself (GP p. 288), point to the character of schizophrenic delusional experiences being similar to that of a kind of revelation. According to Jaspers, the primary experience of delusion has a peculiar ontological status. Because of secondary thoughts about these primary experiences and by additional false judgements, the primary experiences become transformed but are in some way also preserved. The patient tries to adapt them to common sense reality. Speaking of delusion proper, Jaspers says: "Different from to that which what is mediated by thoughts, the elementary (i.e., experiences) cannot be influenced psychologically. [...] Opposite to the genetically incomprehensible not understandable stands what became understandable and developed itself" (own translation p. 110). Thus, in secondary delusion, that is, the further development of delusional ideas, the deluded patient tries more and more to adapt his primary experiences and delusional ideas to the facts of our common sense reality. In this way, not only the memory of the primary experiences decreases, but also the quantitative and qualitative incomparable certainty about them. More and more doubts about the primary delusional ideas may arise, and they can in turn lead to a double orientation toward reality, which is described well by Schwartz and Wiggins (1992): the patient "believes and disbelieves in the reality of the consensually validated world" (p. 309). This "co-experience of doubt and beliefs" (p. 309) produces a heightened anxiety; thus, according to these authors, the afflicted strive for certainty.

What we worked out as a phenomenological specificity of the three characteristics of schizophrenic delusion is summarized by Jaspers in the so-called theory of partial incomprehensibility of schizophrenic delusion. This theory of incomprehensibility has been criticized, first because the problem of communication with the patient ("Verständigung") is not sufficiently considered, and second because the subjective incompetence, that is, the not being able to understand, is made a criterion of an objectivity claiming diagnostics (Blankenburg 1984). Above all it has been criticized that the theory excludes completely the whole context of the life-world of the patient, his personality, his lifestyle and his social relations. Thus, the incomprehensibility is simply the effect of a depersonalized understanding of the patient's condition (Stanghellini 2004). Yet every critic in this case must consider that what Jaspers means with incomprehensibility is not any non-understanding or not-yet-understanding, but is a non-understanding of a particular kind ("auf eigene Weise unverständlich"). Müller-Suur (1950) rightly spoke of a definite incomprehensibility, which is empathetically inaccessible. Jaspers says that a particularly static understanding of certain psychic qualities and of states in primary delusion is impossible, or empathetically inaccessible ("nicht einfühlbar"); it can in principle never be made visible vivid ("prinzipiell nie anschaulich werden"). He warns that to understand the pathological psychic life ("pathologisches Seelenleben") of schizophrenics merely as a quantitative increase or decrease of phenomena known to us would be insufficient (own translation pp. 483 and 384). Just this, however, is as a dimensional against a categorical approach the agenda of modern psychiatry with all its advantages and disadvantages. Currently, pathology often seems to be only a question of degree. Examples for this are the items for schizophrenic delusion and also for affective disorder. The main question is: with which method is it possible to gain access to that which is incomprehensible in schizophrenic delusion, so as not to miss something that could be important for therapy and also for empirical research (e.g., biological research)?

8.6   Is Delusion a False Judgement of Reality?

One of the most momentous differentiations in Jaspers' understanding of schizophrenic delusion is a sort of twofold givenness of reality: on one hand, an original prereflexive experience of reality in the sense of a "consciousness of reality" ("Realitätsbewusstsein") or a "knowledge of reality" ("Realitätswissen," p. 88), and on the other hand, reality as an object of judgement ("Realitätsurteil"), that is, as the result of an "intellectual working on immediate experiences" (own translation p. 79). As already shown, the definition of schizophrenic delusion in the diagnostic manuals is based completely on "false judgement of reality" (AMDP), and on "erroneous belief" in the DSM-IV-TM. The characterization of schizophrenic delusion as "bizarre" is very weakly operationalized as "being completely implausible," "incomprehensible" and not derivable from experience of ordinary life and expresses a disturbance of judgement. In none of these statements, however, is the patient's primary delusional experience as such taken into account. These definitions relate to Jaspers' definition of delusions as "falsified judgements." Nevertheless, they leave out the same questioning that Jaspers pursued in his own definition, which led him to refer to it as being "vague" and only a first impression. Later, he clearly spoke of primary delusion as a "change ("Verwandlung") of the comprehensively altered consciousness of reality, which shows itself secondarily in judgements of reality" (own translation p. 80).

This seeming discrepancy between both statements can be easily explained. If we consider Jaspers' three characteristics of schizophrenic delusions in their true nature, these do not relate to common reality, but according to him show a specificity that is not taken into account in the diagnostic manuals. As we showed, according to Jaspers' understanding the incomparable certainty, the incorrigibility and even the contents of delusion are of a qualitatively specific sort. They point to a strange, incomprehensible experience, deviant from a normal one. How should the schizophrenic be able to form normal judgements of reality on the basis of a consciousness of reality that is altered in such an abnormal way? Inevitably such a consciousness must lead to false judgements, assuming of course a lack of any functional disturbance in performing judgements. Even in delusion of perception, the abnormal meaning is not an issue of interpreting judgements because it is already given within the perception. But what's about the secondary contents of delusion? If these were "unreal," Jaspers would certainly point to the fact that, on one hand, these were always a secondary product of primary delusional experiences, and, on the other hand, could be the product of erroneous, but not necessarily delusional, judgements involved in adapting these to common reality. Erroneous judgements, according to Jaspers, are not identical with delusional ones and are as such ubiquitous.

8.7   Epilogue

In 1931, Hans Kunz stated that Jaspers understood more of delusion than he expressed (Kunz 1931). We already pointed to that which stayed undeveloped in his very restricted kind of phenomenology (see also Blankenburg 1984). This has become apparent in the last 30 years due to the enormous phenomenological development initiated by his General Psychopathology. We cannot deal with this topic here; instead, we only wish to return to his statements about functional disturbances of perception and cognition as well as ego-disturbances, which are discussed often in modern psychiatry.

We first compare the concepts of Straus and of Jaspers about the question of disturbances of perception, of cognition or of judgement in schizophrenic delusion. Our goal is to clarify Jaspers' position through a comparison of the similar issues that the two authors consider. The central idea in Straus' "Vom Sinn der Sinne" (1978) is "impression" ("Empfindung"). Unlike Jaspers, Straus does not distinguish between a pathic and an active part of perception, but between impression and perception as two separate acts. Impression according to Straus is a pre-logical act, which gives particular meanings to some object or person (e.g., in the sense of luring and scaring, of separating and unifying, of being able to and failing, and so on). In Straus' understanding, these experiences are particularly prominent in psychotic states (e.g., expressed in several schizophrenic symptoms). Impression is a "sympathetic experience" in which ego and world unfold themselves at the same time. Whereas in impression the individual stays in a certain union with the world, in perception, as a "recognizing act," there is more distance between the individual and the perceived world. Impression, in which reality is experienced in a pre-logical kind of communication with the world, immediately precedes perception. Thus impression leads to a subjective, sensuous certainty, which has only a private validity; by contrast, in perception the world is given as an objective, general reality. Normally, a transition is possible from impression to perception. However in schizophrenics this transition can be reduced to such an extent that the patient, isolated in the idios kosmos of his impression, lacks access to a world perceived jointly with others. Janzarik (1959, 1974, 1999) was one of the first to point to the loss of control over the impressive mode of perception in the productive psychosis.

Straus' and Jaspers' concepts overlap in the fact that, according to Straus, the person is, on one hand, part of the world in impression, while he is, on the other hand, also before the world in perception. Thus, similar to Jaspers' concept, in the case of the delusional person the abnormal meaning possesses a unique kind of evidence that is implanted in the act of impression. Straus says: "Impression is connected with certainty" in the sense of "it happened to me in the world" (377). However, it is a private certainty different from that of perception, which provides the individual with a certainty of a seemingly objective, general reality (a reality of judgement in Jaspers understanding). Because impression is pre-logical, it comes up "immediately, not hypothetically, before doubt" (327) (i.e., before judgement is possible).

Now, coming to the question of ego-disturbance, it was certainly an important step to conceive of the special "being-made" experiences—that is, experiences of being influenced or controlled in one's will, thinking, feeling and movements, mostly by technical means—not only under the aspect of delusion, but also as an ego-disturbance in the way of a permeability of the borders of the ego. A further step occurred in conceiving of schizophrenia as such from a phenomenological point of view as a disorder of self (i.e., a basic and bodily self). But some questions have to be clarified. Does this mean that we are still left with the concept of a disturbance of the ego? Are ego and self here taken as identical? What is the relationship between them? The notion of self is nearer to that of the person than to that of the ego. But what is the difference between disorders of depersonalization in schizophrenia (e.g., disorders of depersonalization in depressive phases) and the latter characterized by Schneider as a change of personality and not as a disturbance of the ego, as is the case in schizophrenics?

These and other questions lead us in our studies of delusional experiences regarding "being-made" (Kraus 2008a, 2008b, 2010) first to investigate the alteration of the existential a priori conditions for the possibility of experience, which in our view are much more fundamental in schizophrenics than disturbances of the ego or self, which may secondarily result from the alteration of these conditions. "Being-made" experiences are described verbally and categorically as a relation to things, not to human beings. In fact, the patient, in such experiences, feels himself being treated like a thing. Thoughts, feelings, acts of the will of others, for example, are transformed to rays and felt to be implanted into the brains of the patients, as if they were their own. Because the patients are the objects of the effects of these technical influences, they can feel forced to stay in contact with others, who influence them and expose them to the public in intimate respects, regardless of the time or the place. But these intrusive, controlling others stay anonymously absent in presence. Heidegger (1963) differentiated two kinds of being: the being in the way of "Dasein" as a human being, as a being-in-the-world open to other beings, and being in the way of "occurrentness" ("Vorhandenheit") as merely that being which is available in the world. He described Dasein by categories different from those of other things in terms of existential a priori conditions for experience (being-in-the-world, being with others, temporalization and spatialization of being, and so on). Thus, in delusional experiences of "being-made" we observe a certain shift in schizophrenics from being in the way of Dasein to that of non-Daseinesque things via a certain kind of hypostatization ("Verdinglichung") of one's being. The alteration of the existential a priori conditions in schizophrenic delusion makes it understandable why we are dealing with a definite incomprehensibility here, and how the phenomena of delusion and hallucination, as well as the experiences of "being-made," are constituted. As a phenomenological method, the Dasein-analytical method (à la Heidegger) is, in principle, independent of the empathic faculties of the diagnostician, even if these ameliorate the understanding of the deluded patient in general. The alteration of existential apriori conditions (e.g., a general lacking of openness for being-in-the-world and being with others) and, thus, a generally diminished involvement therein, leads consequentially to a decreased resistance against the influences of an exclusively impressive mode of experiencing in cases of delusion. This lack of resistance is probably one of the singular most important conditions for the possibility of delusion and hallucination occurring at all. The absence of resistance might also be the reason for the lacking desactualization of delusion in the sense of the structural-dynamic theory of Janzarik (1959, 1999).

The existential a priori conditions are the structural preconditions that make certain concrete experiences possible. Elsewhere, we will show in detail the structural affinity between the alteration of the existential a priori conditions as structural aspects for the openness of being-in-the-world and structural aspects of the contents of delusion. Here, it is enough to point out as consequence that delusional contents in persons with schizophrenia arise from the self-explication of these fundamentally altered categories of being-in-the-world. As such, they are also important for psychotherapy. For this purpose, we must distinguish two kinds of pre-predicative delusional expressions (Wahnaussagen):

1. Such relating to concrete life problems, blocked topics of life, etc., which have been described by Mundt (1996)
2. Such relating to the altered being-in-the-world, i.e., the alteration of the existential a priori conditions, these also partly constituting those of (1).

References

Blankenburg, W. (1984). Unausgeschöpftes in der Psychopathologie von Karl Jaspers. *Nervenarzt*, 55, 447–460.

Bovet, P., Parnas, J. (1993). Schizophrenic delusions: a phenomenological approach. *Schizophrenic Bulletin*, 19, 579–597.

DSM-IV-TM (1994). American Psychiatric Association. Washington, DC.

Fuchs, T. (2005). Delusional mood and delusional perception—A phenomenological analysis. *Psychopathology*, 38, 133–139.

Gorski, M. (2012a). Karl Jaspers on delusions: Definitions by genus and specific difference. *Philosophy, Psychiatry, & Psychology*, 19(2), 79–86.

Gorski, M. (2012a). The real definition of delusion. *Philosophy, Psychiatry, & Psychology*, 19(2), 97–101.

Heidegger, M. (1963). *Sein und Zeit*. Tübingen: Niemeyer.

Janzarik, W. (1959). *Dynamische Grundkonstellationen in endogenen Psychosen*. Berlin: Springer.

Janzarik, W. (1974). Probleme der strukturell-dynamischen Kohärenz in der Zyklothymieforschung. *Nervenarzt*, 45, 628–638.

Janzarik, W. (1999). Wie ist Wahn und psychopathologisches Verständnis möglich?. *Nervenarzt*, 70, 981–986.

Jaspers, K. (1959). *Allgemeine Psychopathologie*, 7.unveränderte Auflage. Berlin: Springer. English edition: Jaspers, K. (1997). *General psychopathology* (trans. J. Hoenig & M. W. Hamilton). Baltimore: Johns Hopkins University Press.

Kepinski, A. (1974). *Schizophrenia*. Warsaw: Panstwowy Zaklad Wydawnictw Lekarskich.

Kraus, A. (2008a). Der Wahn Schizophrener bei Karl Jaspers im Vergleich mit der operationalen Diagnostik (ICD 10 Kapitel V (F) und DSM-IV-TR) sowie neueren psychopathologischen Ansätzen. In S. Rinofer-Kreidl, H. A. Wiltsche (Eds.), *Karl Jaspers' allgemeine Psychopathologie zwischen Wissenschaft, Philosophie und Praxis* (pp. 127–145). Würzburg: Königshausen & Neumann.

Kraus, A. (2008b). Die moderne Diagnostik und Klassifikation (ICD und DSM) im Licht der Allgemeinen Psychopathologie von Karl Jaspers. In J. Eming, T. Fuchs (Eds.), *Karl Jaspers—Philosophie und Psychopathologie* (pp. 209–233). Heidelberg: Winter-Verlag.

Kraus, A. (2010). Existential a prioris and the phenomenology of schizophrenia. *Dialogues in Philosophy, Mental and Neuro Sciences*, 3(1), 1–7.

Kunz, H. (1931). Die Grenze der psychopathologischen Wahninterpretation. *Zeitschrift für die gesamte Neurologie und Psychiatrie*, 135, 671–715.

Müller-Suur, H. (1950). Das Gewißheitserlebnis beim schizophrenen und beim paranoischen Wahn. *Fortschritte Der Neurologie Psychiatrie*, 18, 44–51.

Mundt, C. (1996). Zur Psychotherapie des Wahns. *Nervenarzt*, 67, 515–523.

Schmidt-Degenhard, M. (2009). Wandlungen des Unverständlichen in der schizophrenen Wahndynamik. In R. Schulz, G. Bonanni, M. Bormuth (Eds.), *Wahrheit ist, was uns verbindet. Karl Jaspers' Kunst zu philosophieren*. Göttingen: Wallstein.

Schneider, K. (1967). *Klinische Psychopathologie* (8th ed.). Stuttgart: Georg Thieme.

Schwartz, M. A., & Wiggins, O. P. (1992). The phenomenology of schizophrenic delusions. In M. Spitzer, F. Uehlein, M. A. Schwartz, & C. Mundt (Eds.), *Phenomenology, language & schizophrenia* (pp. 305–318). New York: Springer.

Stanghellini, G. (2004). *Disembodied spirits and deanimated bodies: The psychopathology of common sense*. Oxford: Oxford University Press.

Stanghellini, G. (2012). Jaspers on "Primary" Delusions. *Philosophy, Psychiatry, & Psychology*, 19(2), 87–89.

Straus, E. (1978). *Vom Sinn der Sinne. Ein Beitrag zur Grundlegung der Psychologie*. Berlin: Springer.

Wiggins, O. P., Schwartz, M. A., Spitzer, M. (1992). Phenomenological/descriptive psychiatry. The methods of E. Husserl and K. Jaspers. In M. Spitzer, F. Uehlein, M. A. Schwartz, C. Mundt (Eds.), *Phenomenology, language and schizophrenia*. New York: Springer.

Chapter 9
Delusion and Double Book-Keeping

Louis A. Sass

> *"For any true grasp of delusion, it is important to free ourselves from this prejudice that there has to be some poverty of intelligence at the root of it."*
>
> (Jaspers 1963, p. 97)

> *"Les non-dupes errent."*
>
> (Jacques Lacan 1973/1974, seminar XXI)

9.1   Introduction

One of the most curious features of the history of psychopathology is the attitude Karl Jaspers adopted toward schizophrenia and, in particular, toward *delusion*—a key symptom that he considered to occur, in its "true" or "primary" form, only in this particular illness. Schizophrenia, aptly termed the "sacred symbol" and "sublime object of psychiatry" (Szasz 1976; Woods 2011), has been the major preoccupation of psychopathologists over the course of the last century; phenomenologists have been particularly fascinated, devoting great effort to exploring the subjective lives of people with this diagnosis. Jaspers' *magnum opus*, the *General Psychopathology* (a work of genius whose first version was published in 1913), is typically seen as the inaugural monument of this crucial movement of modern psychiatry and clinical psychology.[1] It is curious, then, that in this very book, Jaspers

---

[1] Jaspers (p. 48) demurred: "It is wrong to call this book 'the principal text of phenomenology.' The phenomenological attitude is one point of view and one chapter has been devoted to it .... But the whole book is directed to showing that it is only one point of view among many and holds

---

L. A. Sass (✉)
Rutgers University, Graduate School of Applied and Professional Psychology,
152 Frelinghuysen Road, Piscataway, NJ 08854-8020, USA
e-mail: lsass@rci.rutgers.edu

T. Fuchs et al. (eds.), *Karl Jaspers' Philosophy and Psychopathology*,   125
DOI 10.1007/978-1-4614-8878-1_9, © Springer Science+Business Media New York 2014

declares schizophrenia to be essentially *closed* to the very possibility of empathy, thus setting it *outside* the domain of possible or legitimate phenomenological inquiry, on the other side of "a gulf which defies description" (Jaspers 1963, p. 447). Though well aware of the many attempts to offer psychological explanations of the strange symptoms and demeanor of such individuals, Jaspers was skeptical that one could do more than register an essential mysteriousness: "We call the behavior crazy or silly," he wrote, "but all these words simply imply in the end that there is a common element of 'the ununderstandable'" (p. 581).

Jaspers believed that schizophrenia was, essentially, a brain-based illness, and that the neural abnormality in question (which was and remains unknown) altered the coordinates of schizophrenic experience in so fundamental a way as to place it beyond the empathic or imaginative capacity of normal persons. This meant that schizophrenia could not on principle be "understood" but only "explained" through causal analysis of a neurobiological sort.

We need not assume that Jaspers believed persons with schizophrenia to be *entirely* opaque to us: he surely knew that they are "simply human" as well as "otherwise" (in the famous phrasing of Harry Stack Sullivan 1953, p. 32), sharing many of the perceptions and concerns of normal individuals. But there is, he thought, a central kernel that lies beyond all empathy or psychological comprehension; this kernel is the core of the illness, the very thing that makes them schizophrenic. Although Jaspers was not the first to describe the strangeness of schizophrenia, his formulation crystallized the notion of an essential bizarreness that has been prominent in psychiatry ever since—whether conceived as an inability to *make sense* out of the schizophrenia patient's action or speech, to *imagine* what she might be going through, or simply to feel a minimal sense of *emotional attunement* (Rümke 1990).

The issue of empathy and related questions about psychological comprehension or explanation constitute an obscure and highly contested domain in the psychopathological literature, both classic and contemporary. A few contemporary philosophers, relying on a particular interpretation of the philosopher Ludwig Wittgenstein (e.g., Read 2001; Thornton 2004), would indeed place schizophrenia beyond the pale of the comprehensible. There are many psychiatrists whose adoption (often unthinking) of a pure-deficit model and neurobiological reductionism places them in a similar camp. But many subsequent psychopathologists who have thought about these issues (Henriksen in press; Sass 2003, 2004a) are disinclined to accept the *radical* nature of Jaspers' distinction, or his view about schizophrenia in particular.

The issue of the understandability or comprehensibility of delusions is not unitary, as has been noted (Conrad 1958). One might speak, for example, of the comprehensibility of the *content* of the delusion, the course of its *development*, its putative *triggering experience*, or even of overall *ontological status*. And as already indicated, one might distinguish between *modes* of comprehension: some more empathic and involving imaginative reliving or "simulation" of the experience at issue, others involving more distanced and intellectualized analysis.

---

a subordinate position at that." The chapter to which Jaspers refers is, however, 100 pages long, and many passages elsewhere in the book bear upon the phenomenological perspective.

But whatever one's view on these questions, several things seem fairly clear and un-contentious: there are certain experiences that, if not unique, are at least highly *distinctive* of schizophrenia; these experiences tend to have a quality of the bizarre; and this bizarreness is often apparent in their delusions (Cermolacce et al. 2010). In this spirit, we need not take Jaspers' account of schizophrenic incomprehensibility literally, but may look to it as a guide to what may be, at the same time, most *difficult* (yet not impossible) to understand yet most *crucial* for grasping the distinctive nature of this key disorder.

9.2   Derealization

The features of schizophrenia that Jaspers considers so difficult and distinctive fall into two broad domains. The first involves loss or diminishment of what seems the most basic sense of existing as a self or first-person perspective: "though he exists," wrote Jaspers, the schizophrenic individual "is no longer able to feel he exists. Descartes' '*cogito ergo sum*' (I think therefore I am) may still be superficially cogitated but it is no longer a valid experience' (Jaspers 1963, p. 122). This has been operationalized at both the psychotic and sub-psychotic levels—in Schneider's "First Rank Symptoms" (Mellor 1970) and the Examination of Anomalous Self-Experience or EASE (Parnas et al. 2005). The second domain is perhaps even more difficult to operationalize. It pertains to what might be termed the "phenomenality" or "worldhood" of the experiential world and its objects, and is particularly bound up with the classic issue of the nature of schizophrenic delusion.

In *General Psychopathology*, Jaspers describes two modes of *worldly* experience that are, in his view, associated with the "true" or "primary" delusions found in schizophrenia. One involves experiential mutations of the perceived world that typically proceed, and lay the foundations for, the subsequent development of delusions. Objects and events become abnormally salient or "just so," taking on intensified significance. This has been termed the predelusional state, delusional mood, or *Wahnstimmung* (Berrios 1996, pp. 115–125; Fuchs 2005; Sass & Pienkos in press). The second pertains especially to the patient's attitude or belief in the reality of her delusional objects or world. This is the topic of the present chapter.

Standard approaches to delusion generally define it as a form of "mistaken belief," as in the current DSM IV-R definition of delusion as "a false personal belief based on incorrect inference about external reality and firmly sustained in spite of what almost everyone else believes and in spite of what constitutes incontrovertible proof or evidence to the contrary" (American Psychiatric Association 2000, p. 821). Most definitions of "belief" (what analytic philosophers call the "doxastic" attitude) imply commitment to the actuality of a particular state of affairs in the external or inter-subjective world and imply, in concert with this, a promise of action (where appropriate) with regard to this state of affairs and an implicit acceptance of at least the *potential* relevance of evidence either in favor or against the truth value of the belief in question.

But as Jaspers pointed out, the "true delusions" of schizophrenic patients do not seem to fulfill these criteria (see also Berrios 1996, p. 112–115). Such patients will frequently demonstrate a degree or kind of certitude, and their delusions a sort of "incorrigibility" (p. 105), that goes beyond any possibility of doubt. "Well, that is how it is; I have no doubts about it," says the patient. "I know it is so" (Jaspers 1963, p. 97). Yet at the same time the patient does not, at least in the typical case, act on what he (seemingly) so confidently asserts, as if the belief, or pseudo-belief, pertained to some other realm. Eugen Bleuler (1911/1950, pp. 378, 127–130), coiner of the term "schizophrenia," described a kind of "double orientation," "double registration," or "double bookkeeping"—the phenomenon whereby the patient who seems to be convinced of her delusion nevertheless acts or reacts as if the delusion were either untrue or irrelevant. Thus the savior of humanity worries about not getting his grounds pass; the creator of the universe does not balk at lining up at the cafeteria. A schizophrenia patient may experience others or even himself as dying, but then as coming back to life again and again (Tatossian 1997). Bleuler remarks as well on a quality of emotional experience or expression, the "striking ... indifference of patients toward their own delusional ideas and strivings," giving the example of a patient who complains "in peculiar tones" that his children are being killed but does not manifest an appropriate emotional reaction (p. 369).

From these facts—the combination of absolute incorrigibility with inconsequentiality, together with a seeming lack of normal emotional response[2]—one might well conclude, with Jaspers, that the patient's overall experience of the world must be not simply mistaken but somehow altered or transformed in some overall way. "Reality for [the patient] does not always carry the same meaning as that of normal reality," wrote Jaspers (1963, p. 105). The patient's "world has changed ... a changed knowledge of reality so rules and pervades it that any correction would mean a collapse of Being itself, in so far as it is for him his actual awareness of existence." Speaking of "the incorrigibility of delusion," Jaspers writes:

> So far, however, we have not succeeded in defining what this is. ... we simply give a name to something which we can neither see nor comprehend. And yet it is precisely this problem that gives us no peace. ... This constitutes what is called 'being unhinged or mad ... '. (Jaspers 1963, p. 411)

Here, it seems, we are concerned not just with alterations in the quality of objects, events, or bodily sensations, such as the "uncanny particularity" and "phantom concreteness" characteristic of the delusional mood (Sass 1994), but with challenges to (what Husserl called) the "natural attitude" itself—namely, to the very sense of encountering an objective or shared world and thus to its ontological status in the full sense of that term. We are dealing here with the ontological dimension that, as Heidegger teaches us, is so easily forgotten or ignored in what he termed the "forgetting of the ontological difference" (Sass 1992). Although this may be the most *crucial* aspect of delusion in schizophrenia, it is perhaps the most difficult to characterize or to comprehend.

The ontological dimension, it seems, is not only a *fact* of the delusional world; it can also come to be its theme—expressed in the content of the delusion itself. Thus Jaspers (p. 107) mentions the prominence and the problem of "metaphysi-

---

[2]Reimer (2011) mentions three forms of detachment in delusion: from action, emotion, and web of belief.

cal delusions," noting that "patients may display their delusions in some supra-natural mode and such experiences cannot be adjudged true or untrue, correct or false." Schizophrenic delusions in particular tend to involve encompassing issues of a philosophical or religious nature. These include metaphysical, epistemological, or eschatological themes that are typically suppressed by common-sense assumptions and the exigencies of practical life. Typically, the metaphysical delusions do not make reference merely to some empirical or "ontic" fact occurring *within* the normal framework of the "natural attitude," but concern some more encompassing (ontological) sense or grasp of the entire universe, self, or self-world relationship. Jaspers mentions delusions expressing both "the shattering of the self" and "the end of the world" (p. 10). To treat such delusions as mere errors or falsehoods hardly does them justice. It is in fact uncomfortably reminiscent of attempts to reduce religious or mythic intuition to a crass conception of magical belief, and may involve similar forms of condescension and over-simplification (see Wittgenstein 1979).[3]

The challenge of understanding "true delusion" is exacerbated by the fact that there is no *single* delusional alternative to the lived-world of the natural attitude, but a gamut of ways in which things or the world may be "derealized"—that is, may lack or otherwise deviate from the normal experience of objective and inter-subjective reality. Each of these ways is itself both strange and ambiguous; and these latter, disconcerting qualities are compounded by the fact that the experiential modalities may, at times, slip and slide one into the other. The overall feel of the world of the delusional patient has been aptly described as "peculiarly insubstantial, evanescent, and hovering" (Schmidt 1987, p. 115), and as having the "conceptual halo of the fantastic" (Ey 1996, p. 214).

One statement from a person with schizophrenia, "Sophie" (whom I will quote extensively below), will serve as a first example: "I often feel that certain people physically enter my brain through my ear canals and then proceed to rearrange various parts of my brain—albeit not in a truly literal way" (email to author, 2010–11).[4] Sophie's reference to experiencing a *physical* event that was nevertheless not *literal* suggests the potential complexity of delusional or so-called delusional experiences, as well as the difficulty of knowing how to capture such experiences in standard words and categories. Patients themselves often complain of the ineffability of their delusional or pre-delusional experiences (Møller and Husby 2000), and may sometimes despair of the very possibility of communication (Aviv 2010, p. 41). "There are no words,"

---

[3] One important *difference* between the delusional and religious contexts is the idiosyncratic and isolated nature of the former as against the conventional and shared nature of the latter. The religious person may have a special role or relationship with the divine, but not *so very* special that it would amount to denying the very existence of other consciousnesses or other persons—as may sometimes (but only sometimes) occur in schizophrenia.

[4] All subsequent quotations from Sophie are from emails sent to the author in 2010 or 2011. Some are in response to earlier drafts of this article. Sophie is well read in philosophy and psychology. As her reports will make clear, she not only *describes* her experience with considerable eloquence but is, in a sense, *doing* phenomenology herself. I am extremely grateful and indebted to Sophie for her crucial contribution to this article.

says a patient named Chloe, referring to the delusional state, "It's like trying to explain what a bark sounds like to someone who's never heard of a dog."

Sophie herself used the term "derealization," and states that, based on her own past experience and careful reflection, this is the universal and defining feature of psychotic or delusional experience: "the single most pervasive, enduring, and desta-bilizing 'world-disturbance' in schizophrenia." But what, precisely, *is* derealization, and how does it manifest in schizophrenic delusion?

In a recent report, one patient with schizophrenia is described as trying to explain to herself why people seemed to her to be "so phony and lifeless and small, as if they could be manipulated in her fingers" (Aviv 2010, p. 46). In order to explain this experience, she considered various possibilities: Were the people only drawings? Were they marionettes, robots, or automatons? Were they "agents of an omniscient godhead"? Eventually she settled on the idea of paper figurines, though this never really satisfied her: it only seemed "to border on reasonable."

Sophie explains, however, that derealization—at least for her—can take many forms and is not restricted to experiences involving obvious forms of diminished in-tensity or vitality; it may also involve "*increases* in metaphysical dynamism, univer-sal animism, emotional resonance, human and/or divine purposiveness"—these too "have clearly and unambiguously led me to feel that the world is profoundly unreal."

> To make my point a little clearer (perhaps), let me emphasize that the feeling of unreality I get when I perceive others as transformed into paper maché chess pieces …, is absolutely no different from (the same feeling of derealization I get) when I perceive them as gods, manifes-tations (faces) of a single god, mental projections, one dimensional stage trappings, physical instantiations of my thoughts, phony or fake, superhumanly powerful, changed in size and/or shape, etc. The common factor is not a loss of dynamism or vitality, but simply radical change. Faced with people who no longer feel anything like 'normal' people—the people one has lived with one's whole life—for any reason, the logical conclusion is that they are simply not real.

It seems clear enough that the "radical change" to which Sophie refers—whereby things seem "simply not real"—involves a loss of the *standard* reality with which one is most familiar and feels most at ease. Sophie speaks in fact of not feeling "at home." The hovering strangeness and ambiguity that tends to transfix and unhinge the patient is clearly ontological in nature. But does it necessarily involve a loss of the sense of things possessing the objectivity implied by Husserl's notion of the "natural attitude"—that is, the quality of existing "out there" in the world, inde-pendent of the mind that experiences them? Might it even be described, in fact, as a subjectivized or even solipsistic reality—as a realm felt to exist only for, or even perhaps to be created by, the patient or person who witnesses it?

The answer to this question must, as we shall see, be both yes and no. Though indispensable, such words as "subjective" and "objective," "unreal" and "real," or "internal" and "external," are hardly adequate and can even be misleading in dis-cussing delusional experience; they presuppose something like normal experience or the common-sense world-view; and as we shall see, this is precisely what is obliterated or at least suspended in delusion.[5]

---

[5] One recent philosopher coins the term "bimagination" (Egan 2009). Some would argue as to whether we should classify delusions as "beliefs" or not (Bortolotti 2009). From a Wittgensteinian

Let us first look at some of the more extreme and clear-cut forms of derealization. Later we shall consider forms that are more ambiguous, and more likely to confuse both patient and theorist.

The present chapter is qualitative and exploratory. It relies heavily on analogical comparisons and on reports from a schizophrenia patient of unusual articulateness (Sophie) with whom the author is in dialogue. The reader is hereby warned that, as we proceed, some early claims will seem to be revised or even reversed. As we uncover the diversity and complexity in the phenomena at hand, some threads of the argument may even seem to come unraveled, then to intertwine in unexpected ways. But this is as it should and must be: Jaspers was right to stress the difficulty of understanding schizophrenic delusion, and, perhaps, not *entirely* wrong to insist on some irreducible element of the incomprehensible.

9.3 Double Book-Keeping

A particularly clear description of a delusional world is offered by Daniel Paul Schreber, perhaps the most famous psychotic or schizophrenic patient in the history of psychiatry (analyzed in Sass 1994). In his *Memoirs of My Nervous Illness*, more accurately translated as *Great Thoughts of a Mental Patient* (*Denkwürdigkeiten eines Nervenkranken*), Schreber (1988) describes an elaborate delusional world consisting of "souls" and "gods" and of "nerves" and "rays" that span the cosmos, connect him with God, and, often, monitor or control his thoughts and actions. He speaks of losing his stomach and having it reappear repeatedly, and of foreign beings who inhabit his consciousness and control his thoughts. A key delusion is of being transformed into a woman. He sometimes experienced the actual people around him as being mere "fleeting-improvised men" who had been set down by God to fool him (M 43n). These delusions have often been taken as clear instances of poor reality-testing—as, for example, when in a legal brief, the superintendent of the asylum wrote of Schreber, "What objectively seen appears as delusions and hallucinations is to him (a) unassailable truth and (b) adequate motive for action" (M 301).

Schreber clearly took these delusional realities very seriously indeed (he describes his revelations as bringing him "infinitely closer to the truth than human beings who have not received divine revelation"; M 41); and is confident of their truth value. But he does not seem to have ascribed to them the kind of reality-status or ontological weight of something objectively real, or in which he could be said fully to believe—at least in the standard sense of that term. In a legal document Schreber himself rejects the superintendent's characterization:

> I have to confirm the first part (a) of [the superintendent's] statement, namely that my so-called delusional system is unshakeable certainty, with the same decisive 'yes' as I have to counter the second part (b), namely that my delusions are adequate motive for action,

---

as well as phenomenological standpoint, this emphasis on semantics and conceptual analysis can seem somewhat beside the point. The important question is: "What is it like?"

with the strongest possible 'no.' I could even say with Jesus Christ: 'My Kingdom is not of this world,' my so-called delusions are concerned solely with God and the beyond, they can therefore never in any way influence my behavior in any worldly matter…. (M 301)

The non-literal nature of Schreber's delusion is apparent in his account of being transformed into a woman. As he explains in the memoir, this event occurred when he stood before a mirror looking at himself while stripped to the waist and wearing feminine jewelry. As Schreber stared at his own torso, he would feel the approach of "the rays," which constitute an important center of consciousness in his delusional world, and then "my breast gives the impression [*Eindruck*] of a pretty well-developed female bosom" (M 207) Attentive reading of Schreber's description makes it clear the he is *not* describing an actual anatomical change, but something more like a way of seeing or construing an unchanged physical reality. ("Naturally hairs remain… on my chest…; my nipples also remain small as in the male sex.") Indeed, he even describes it as an illusion [*Illusion* in German]. Thus he speaks of getting "the undoubted *impression* of a female trunk—especially when the illusion [*Illusion*] is strengthened by some feminine adornments" (M, 207). Elsewhere in his *Memoir*, Schreber describes what he calls "picturing" (*Zeichnung*) or "representing," which may occur in a more passive or a more active manner and which involves "use of the human imagination for the purpose of producing pictures [*Bilder*]" (M 180–181). Typically Schreber does *not* make claims about the external or interpersonally shared world, claims that could be supported or refuted by evidence independent of the experience itself. His delusional beliefs are often described in a way that gives them a coefficient of subjectivity—as when he says not "I am a scoffer at God" or "I am given to voluptuous excesses," but I am "represented" [*dargestellt*] as one of these things (M, 120).

Schreber was also acutely aware of the difficulty of conveying the precise nature of his experiences and the likelihood of being misunderstood by his readers: "Again it is extremely difficult to describe such changes in words because matters are dealt with which lack all analogies in human experience and which I appreciated directly only in part with my mind's eye [*mit meinem geistigen Auge*]" (M 109, 117, 124, 137, 181f, 227). "To make myself at least somewhat comprehensible I shall have to speak much in images and similes, which may at times perhaps be only *approximately* correct" (M 41). In accord with this recognition, Schreber peppered his original text with such phrases as "in part," "on the other hand," "so to speak," "up to a point," and "in a way"—all of which imply a certain non-literal and self-aware quality that is apparent in the original German.[6]

We see, then, that the delusions of at least this classic case lack the kind of straightforward objective or inter-subjective referentiality that would seem to be implied by the standard "poor reality testing" formula, with its use of such terms as "false," "incorrect," and "absurd." What is suggested, rather, is something akin to Bleuler's double book-keeping, where the patient experiences the delusional reality as existing in a different ontological domain from that of everyday reality. In an email to the

---

[6] Since the translators found these phrases distracting and felt they did "not add to the sense," they omitted them from the English translation (M p. 26).

present author, Sophie states this explicitly: "I often feel that many of my aberrant pseudo-perceptions feel the way they do because I am actually perceiving them taking place in a parallel reality that only partially overlaps with this one." She continues:

> For instance I can feel absolutely certain that space and time (and hence physical reality) no longer or never did exist, and yet understand that in order to get to a psychiatry appointment I have to walk down the street, get on the train, and so on (in other words, physically navigate or move through the "objective" world). Or I can feel certain, even as I am talking to my psychiatrist, that I killed him five minutes earlier (fully aware that he is sitting a few feet from me talking). The strangeness is that both "beliefs" exists simultaneously and seem in no way to impinge on one another (nor have I ever figured out any way of consciously reconciling them)—which is not to say that the very simultaneity isn't rather deeply disturbing (it is, and it often drives me to self-consciously engage with and elaborate on the delusional in order to escape this painful contradiction).

Speaking also of a friend with schizophrenia, Sophie says:

> "John" described to me in detail a time when he walked to the store to buy some groceries (in spite of, in his own words, feeling "absolutely convinced" that aliens were gunning the streets) and yet was conscious of the strange absence of expectable negative affect (fear or anxiety). (Likewise he confirmed that he was quite aware that others would not be affected by the alien bullets and was thus utterly unsurprised to see them walking around unfazed.) [He proceeds to tell a number of related stories from the half-decade he spent homeless ...]

9.4 Two Analogies: Epoche, Imagination

The standard "natural attitude," in normal life, involves the sense that the objects one perceives are *intersubjectively* present—that is, present to the gaze of awareness of *other* persons who are separate from and similar to oneself. But as we have seen with both Schreber and Sophie, the derealization of the delusional realm *can* imply a certain subjectivization, a sense that the realities in question are true *for me* (in "my mind's eye"), as immediate experiential realities rather than as entities existing somehow "out there" and directly accessible to other consciousnesses—or, at least, to other consciousnesses in the *actual* world (more on this point below). Two analogies are worth exploring in order to clarify the distinct nature of the universe or experiential stance in question. (Some disanalogies—and another analogy—will come later.)

Various phenomenologists (Blankenburg 1971, Tatossian) have pointed out the affinity between this kind of delusional stance and the fundamental nature of phenomenological "bracketing" or the phenomenological "reduction" itself, which are the key methodological moves of Husserlian phenomenology. In phenomenological bracketing, one sets aside the objectivist claims of the "natural attitude" in order to isolate an immanent realm of pure experiencing, a realm from which doubt can presumably be expunged and within which "apodictic" or absolute certitude can be achieved. Another close affinity (but not, as we shall discuss later, an identity) is with the experiential stance or modality of imagination.

As the philosopher Edward Casey (2000) points out in his book, *Imagining: A Phenomenological Study*, the imaginary is characterized by the qualities of self-containedness and self-evidence. Imagination's self-containedness involves a felt discontinuity or delimitation from other psychological acts or orientations, such as perception and memory. It implies as well a certain "unexplorability": Insofar as it exists at all, the imagined object is given all at once, without a backside or hidden depth. It is also self-evident in the sense of being non-corrigible (non-falsifiable, non-verifiable) and apodictic: containing a kind of indubitable presence and certainty. Hence "I cannot doubt that what I imagine is appearing to me precisely as it presents itself to me" (p. 98). Casey compares this to Husserl's description of self-evidence in his *Cartesian Meditations* as "the quite pre-eminent mode of consciousness that consists in the *self-appearance*, the *self-exhibiting*, the *self-giving*" of a phenomenon. Imagining, writes Casey, is "all appearance and nothing but appearance," for "there is no extra-imaginal state of affairs with which to compare the imaginative presentation" (p. 95). As Casey further notes, this gives imagining a somewhat problematic relationship to the standard, correspondence mode of truth, but does not separate it entirely from issues of truth or veridicality: "In making a true report of one's imaginative experience, one is *not* reporting what was not experienced and *is* describing what was experienced" (p. 97).

Another interesting feature of imagining mentioned by Casey is its combination of spontaneity and controlledness—of a certain effortless, surprising, and self-generating quality that coexists or changes place with a sense of being able somehow to initiate, guide, and terminate a given process or flow. This is consistent with one patient's report of a quasi-delusional or quasi–hallucinatory experience that a bust of Plato was talking to her: "It wasn't as if this bust suddenly started talking to me out of thin air.... I wanted him to, and then I sort of convinced myself that he did. I didn't feel like I was passively being subjected to another reality. It felt like I somehow actively engaged in creating it" (Aviv 2010, p. 36). Like imagination, delusion can involve what Sophie nicely described (in a response to a draft of this chapter) as "the give and take of passive subjection and control."

Drawing these parallels may help to explain a feature of many schizophrenic delusions that might otherwise seem strange: the characteristic combination of what Jaspers called "certitude" with "inconsequentiality"—and especially the seemingly odd fact that it is often the delusion about which the patient is *most certain* with regard to which he is *least likely* to act. If the delusion occurred within a natural attitude, this would make no sense: surely one ought to act in relation to that whose existence one must assumes. But if the delusion is felt, on some level, to be true only for me, in my mind's eye and for me alone, then the contradiction is resolved: One need hardly seek evidence for an experience (akin in this sense to the imaginary) that makes no claim with regard to objective or intersubjective reality. And one will hardly take action *in actuality* with regard to what one knows to exist in a purely virtual realm.

This provides a phenomenological way of accounting for at least *some* instances of the famous "double bookkeeping" of which Bleuler spoke. The patient who insists he is god or Napoleon, yet willingly sweeps the floor, would presumably recognize, in some manner or level of awareness, that this god-status is purely subjective—only a kind of imaginary truth or a truth holding within his own mind's eye world, and therefore irrelevant to the daily routine of his life on the hospital ward.

Such a patient may also sense that delusional events, like imagined ones, may come and go without the usual consequences. Hence, people may die yet come to life, or one may travel to the sun without being burned. An additional feature of many schizophrenic delusions is that, in the main, such patients do not proselytize or attempt to convert others to their beliefs, as if they sensed or somehow knew that the delusional reality was not only inaccessible but irrelevant to others.

In his cogent critique of standard definitions of "delusion," the psychiatrist Manfred Spitzer (1990) offers an alternative definition of the Jaspersian "true delusion" as involving "statements about external reality which are uttered like statements about a mental state, i.e., with subjective certainty and incorrigible by others" (p. 147). Here we make the further, phenomenological suggestion that this certainty and incorrigibility, together with the typical inconsequentiality, are not just *reminiscent* of a mental state (Spitzer goes no further than this), but are actually consequences of the delusion being experienced *as* a kind of mental state, namely, in a somewhat or somehow subjectivized fashion. The certitude, incorrigibility, and inconsequentiality of such delusions are more reminiscent of the realm of the imaginary than of that of perception or belief: like imaginary reality or the immanent reality of phenomenology, delusional reality can have an apodictic quality that can place it beyond justification or doubt.[7]

But the status of the imaginary is also *different* from that of delusion. For the normal individual, and even for the artist or writer (except perhaps in the throes of creative trance), the imaginary realm remains somehow *subordinated* to the primacy of the natural attitude. No matter how fascinating it may be, the imaginary continues to be experienced as lacking the ontological weight we associate with the word "reality." As a result, the "suspension of disbelief" characteristic of imaginary or esthetic experience is never complete enough to allow the imaginary to become the dominant realm—to eclipse "reality" and replace it with something else.

The metaphor of double book-keeping implies the existence of two distinct realms that, like an accountant's two ledgers, are kept strictly apart:

1. the real world (perhaps boring, perhaps threatening) of *actual* intersubjective reality;
2. the imaginary or virtual world (often more serene, perhaps more satisfying) which is *felt* or *implicitly recognized, by the patient,* to be imaginary.

This does appear to approximate the condition of certain chronic patients for whom delusional reality affords reliable escape from both the content and the form of the real. At times, it appears, the patient may have a sense of relative confidence about this

---

[7] The psychiatrist Müller-Suur (1950, p. 45) asked his paranoid and schizophrenic patients how certain they were about their delusions. Paranoiacs believed in their basic experience (*Grunderlebnis*) with a relative certainty, and this certainty increased only gradually with the passage of time. By contrast, his schizophrenia patients claimed to be absolutely certain (100 % certainty; as certain as that $2 \times 2 = 4$) about their delusions, even when these delusions seemed absurd to the listener. Müller-Suur describes the delusional certainty of schizophrenics as something that is "suffered"— that is, registered passively, akin to feeling a sensation—whereas the paranoid's was "achieved" or "hard-earned." (For this reference, I thank Claudia Welz, whose account is paraphrased here.)

subjective aspect of the delusional world, and this may permit her to exist either simultaneously or successively in two rather distinct spheres/realms, without much confusion or uncertainty. Sophie describes herself and her friend John as feeling, at times, considerable confidence about the distinction between delusional and social reality:

> Finally, both John and I agree that it is generally quite easy (except during periods of what John calls "extreme self-indulgence") to act "normal" precisely because the non-coincidence of the delusional and the consensual/intersubjective is so obvious. I have never once, for example, when talking to my therapist, ever expected her to actually agree with me, or express some kind of shared sense of my alter-realities…

At times, they would even adjust their avowed commitment to these different worlds or orientations with some aplomb:

> Both of us, at any rate, have, on any number of occasions both pretended to believe in things we don't actually believe in (or to believe in and insist on them to clinicians without acknowledging how self-consciously subjectivistic we felt them to be) AND pretended not to believe things we actually did. … Until I had discussed this with John I really felt pretty horribly guilty about it (and tended to think that I was maybe the only one and/or that there was something horribly manipulative about me), but with his reassurance I'm beginning to suspect it's much more common…. In both our cases, as we discussed, we've tended to feel that clinicians are quite predictable—if you want them to take you seriously, to express empathy or concern (etc.), you have to express "full" conviction (without insight); if, on the other hand, you want to avoid hospitalization or further coercion re medications (or simply to get out of the hospital) you play the other side and pretend that you are experiencing no delusional thoughts whatsoever.

Sophie emphasizes what she calls "this strange form of doubled belief or quasi-belief."

> Last week I spent an entire hour trying to convince my therapist, for example, that one could be simultaneously convinced of two competing "realities" (and thus that insight should *not* be understood as something that simply increases only as delusional conviction decreases) and yet I clearly failed to get this point through to her. (I will undoubtedly have to resort to my usual strategies in the future.) John (who, I should emphasize, clearly was and is quite "crazy") describes the whole thing repeatedly as "performance" and "theatre."

But in the same email exchange, Sophie indicates that she, at least, was not immune to being unhinged by the uncomprehending psychiatric environment—which sometimes contributed to her sense of being truly insane and utterly beyond the pale. "The resounding consensus (among clinicians and researchers, especially CBTists, in my experience)," she writes, "seems to be that insight and delusional conviction are inversely correlated"; and as a result, she notes, they assume that "the (my) combination of high insight and high conviction is either categorically impossible or reflective of some kind of profound self-conscious moral failing." (CBT refers to cognitive-behavioral therapy.) She is grateful for phenomenological work that explains this possibility: "If I hadn't had [the] work on double bookkeeping and subjectivism to turn to, I almost certainly would have been forced to conclude that I was somehow even 'madder' (or simply more psychologically messed up) than 'real' schizophrenics."

9.5 Double Exposure and Dream

We see, then, that the analysis in terms of double book-keeping may sometimes fit the case. But more often—it must be admitted—things are not so clear-cut, nor so potentially reassuring for the deluded patient. Often the parallel realities can be more difficult to distinguish one from another: the patient may feel uncertain as to which track he is on, or may even feel that the different tracks are intersecting or even fusing with each other in unanticipated ways. Often persons with schizophrenia do seem to be making truth claims—albeit somewhat ambiguous ones—about the objects of their delusional realm. As Sophie herself states: "often I feel like a big part of the problem is precisely that I lose my conceptual (metaphysical and experiential) grasp of what reality is, was, or should be." "Isn't the general (unconscious) confusion of perception, fantasy, memory, and imagination simply an ubiquitous part of each and every delusion?" she asks.

There is the possibility, in fact, that rather than double book-keeping, the patient will experience something closer to a kind of photographic *double exposure*, a merging or crossing of two perspectives on reality such as is found in the famous "contamination" response on the Rorschach test. Does this in effect bring us back, after all, to the original poor reality-testing formula that we thought we had rejected—according to which the patient is mistaken or unable to distinguish because he takes the imaginary for the real?

The notion of poor reality-testing generally implies that the patient takes the imaginary for real—that is, that he *believes* in his imaginary objects with essentially the same form of belief as we address to our surrounding world (as when the DSM speaks of "a false personal belief based on incorrect inference about external reality"). Double book-keeping implies that the patient is well aware of the distinction between the imaginary and the real. But what often occurs may fit neither of these formulae. It may involve less a sense of everything being real than of everything being unreal. Not only one's own thoughts and body, but also the actual external world that surrounds one may contain more than a tinge or accent of unreality. Thus Schreber experienced actual people in his asylum as what he called the "fleeting-improvised men," namely, beings who only existed when he laid eyes on them, and in the "wasp miracle," he experienced "miracled-up" insects as appearing only before his gaze (M 233).

Taking action toward something is too readily taken as an index of belief in the reality of that thing, but this need not be the case. A patient may feel that just as his actual objects are but dream-objects so his real actions are but dream-actions, lacking the consequentiality or finality of *real* actions in the real world. Indeed this may help to explain how some patients can perform unthinkable acts of self-mutilation without seeming to register the finality of what they have done. Here it is not that fantasy seems real, but that even reality is somehow incorporated into the *unreality* of a delusional realm—a realm in which serious injuries can be fleeting events, in which even death loses its finality and one can perish and yet be resurrected an infinity of times (Tatossian 1997, pp. 127, 120). An apt analogy is, in fact, the state of dreaming, in which one turns away from the world—world of shared and practical reality in favor of a private realm that lacks the normal constraints of time, space, causality, and identity—a realm that is felt to be, in some sense, both real and unreal at the same time.

As just noted, the confusion of worlds may reflect the derealization/subjectivization of both delusional and *actual* reality, which undermines the distinction between the two. But it may also reflect the objectification of "inner" mental threads, for this renders them similar, on the ontological level, to objects in the world. In addition to a (potential) subjectivization of the external world, then, there is an objectivization of the internal world of thought and sensations; and this also contributes to an effacement of distinctions and boundaries.

Given this potential for nearly universal yet ambiguous forms of derealization, it is understandable that the very distinction between realms might seem to come into question. There is likely to be an alternation between periods of distinction and of confusion, in what Sophie (in reflecting on this article) called different "periods of time or even stages in the 'life' of a delusion." She states: "the quality of one's experience of (even the same) delusion can change and shift (over the long and short-term) ... from an almost haughty sense of control, to total confusion re boundaries." The generalized derealization and associated ontological insecurity—of uncertainty about the reality-status of all one's experiential objects—is perhaps the most profound source of anxiety in schizophrenia, and a common feature of the delusional world.

This potential for confusion becomes easier to understand if one recognizes that the two (or more) worlds may differ not in the objects they contain, but only in the attitude that it taken *toward* these objects.

The double book-keeping notion might be taken to imply that the patient shifts attention from a set of *real* persons and objects to a quite different set of *delusional* persons and objects. This is, in fact, what sometimes does occur—as in the case of a famous asylum patient named Adolf Wölfli, who moved back and forth between the real world of doctors, nurses, and asylum walls to that of his delusional memories, where he traveled through imaginary cities and vast cosmoses of his own making (Sass 2004b). This is analogous, in a way, to the normal person's shifting between a waking attitude and that of the sleeper who dreams. But Sophie makes it quite clear that what she typically experienced was not a matter of two different realities, whether side by side or successive. She speaks rather of the "coexistence" of her "aberrant perceptions"—psychotic or deluded—and her true perceptions, and goes on to explain:

> The term co-existence is not meant to imply a literal or qualitatively symmetrical 'doubling' of phenomena—i.e. it's not like literally seeing both a distorted chair and normal chair at the same time (or as somehow superimposed on each other). Instead a single chair may seem perceptually distorted and yet if one checks oneself one realizes that it really isn't (somehow it appears radically changed and perfectly normal at the same time but the former apperception is considerably more vague, amorphous and/or 'unbookable').

Here is an important disanalogy with dreams. The normal person alternates between the two distinct realms of waking life and dream life, in one of which external reality is shut out. But in the *waking* dream (or nightmare) of schizophrenic delusion, there is something more like an awareness of two distinct ways of seeing things, of ways things can appear and going along with this, a sense that, as Sophie puts it, "even the most fundamental conditions of possibility of the world [can seem to be both] (profoundly) changed *and* unchanged."

There is a variety of experiential possibilities. Here, at least, the "aberrant perceptions" were experienced *neither* as straightforward facts within the natural attitude *nor* as merely imaginary projections set clearly apart from the realm of the real. Sophie describes what might be called perceptual abnormalities in schizophrenia as, in reality, "*pseudo*-perceptual":

> Aberrant perceptions, that is, very rarely seem to truly "replace" or even approximate (the feeling or quality of) normal perceptions, but rather they co-exist beside them and/or occupy that grey zone between a very vivid and seemingly automatically generated *imagined* scenario and a true perception.

There certainly is potential for confusion between the realms she calls "aberrant" and "normal" (more on this below). But it is crucial to recognize that there was also the sense of a meaningful distinction—albeit equivocal and wavering, more disconcerting than reassuring—between two or more realms; one involving something closer to the standard reality of the natural attitude, and the other (or others) involving various forms of derealization often including subjectivization. Often (though not always) the patient does retain a residual, often disconcerting sense of the finality of physical or intersubjective reality, of the existence of a realm, always difficult to discern, in which *irreversible* injury might *actually* result if one fails to pay the right kind of attention.[8] One man with schizophrenia said, "During the decades I've felt the unreality of the outside world, I still never walked in front of buses."[9] But the awareness that prevents such accidents can also infuse delusional experience with a kind of background anxiety—the anxiety of what *might* occur if one were fully to lose one's bearings.

A related issue concerns the potentially *intersubjective* nature of the delusional world. Some delusions do have a solitary and de-substantialized quality. One patient I treated, for instance, would feel that he was traveling down his own trachea and exploring his inner organs—which now constituted the entire world and which he described as having the two-dimensional appearance of architect's drawings. But this is not always the case. Sophie states that her delusional world is typically a peopled world in which others do have a quite tangible presence; and this she maintains even while acknowledging that the delusional world is indeed derealized and even in some sense subjective. For as she acknowledged (responding in an email), her delusions are peopled by others whom she describes as "radically derealized and/or ontologically changed from 'real' people—for example, individuals who can transform into leaves, or enter my mind from the other side of the country."

---

[8] A passage from the photographer Diane Arbus captures, on a non-psychotic, schizoid level, the sense of actual vulnerability that accompanies all but the most total experiences of derealization: "I have this funny thing which is that I'm never afraid when I'm looking in the round glass [of the camera lens]. This person could be approaching with a gun or something like that and I'd have my eyes glued to the finder and it wasn't like I was really vulnerable. It just seemed terrific what was happening. I mean I'm sure there are limits. God knows, when the troops start advancing on me, you do approach that stricken feeling where you perfectly well can get killed" (pp. 12–13).

[9] From article in *The Advocate*, statewide newsletter of N.A.M.I.—Oregon, July/August 1998, p. 7.

Here again the dream analogy is of interest. As the phenomenologist Alfred Schutz (1945, p. 563) has noted, dreams can indeed contain other persons—but he insists that the others are not *true* others. Schutz speaks of "an empty fictitious quasi-We relationship," and writes that the other person in dreams "is an alter ego only by my grace. Thus, the monad, with all its mirroring of the universe, is indeed without windows while it dreams." Although the others may well exist in the round, they are not, it seems, in the real. Yet this analogy, too, must be qualified—as Sophie would surely insist.

One problem with applying Schutz's account of dreams to schizophrenic delusions is that his phrasing ("by my grace," for example) exaggerates the sense of control the person has both in dreams and in delusion. Another is that dreams and delusion can *differ* in a crucial way. For sometimes, we must recall, the delusional other of what Sophie calls an "aberrant perception" is superimposed on a *real* object or a *real* other person; and that quasi-real other may therefore be actually touched, or may even act on its own. As Sophie pointed out in her response to a draft of this chapter, there is "less of a distinction [than one might think] between delusional perception and delusions proper [since] experientially the two are more or less inextricably interwoven." "In delusions," she writes, "there is this external perceptual reality (albeit in a very strange sense) that needs to be included. Closer, I still feel to a dream [than to imagination or the phenomenological epoche]—a dream in which one moves, and feels, and explores"—that is (as she later clarified), in which "one does have some sense that one is discovering (and not merely projecting or imagining) the texture and quality of things."

To the extent that delusion bleeds into delusional percept, or double book-keeping into double-exposure, distinctions and boundaries will dissolve. And with them disappears the sense of utter aloneness, but also the security, of feeling oneself to be a solitary or even god-like center.

9.6   Incomprehensibility

I have tried to make some sense out of the overall ontological feel of the delusional world, in a way that might help to explain certain features: the combination of incorrigibility/certainty with inconsequentiality, the fleeting/fantastical quality, the combination of insight with certitude, and so forth. But, I freely confess, one is not left with the clearest of pictures. This question of ontological status, and of how it can or should be described, is complicated by various factors, including the diversity and complexity of the possible states and also the fact that schizophrenic subjectivity and worldhood can be altered at the most basic levels. When alterations as fundamental as this can occur, the meaning of distinctions we normally take for granted—such as subjective vs objective or active vs passive—are called into question. A term such as "subjective," for example, does not have its usual meaning if we consider the possibility of experiencing one's own experience as somehow belonging to another being—that is to say, as being subjective yet alien at the same time. Consider Schreber's experience of a "seeing" or representing of the femininity of his own torso: a "seeing" that is somehow not his own even though it is he himself who stand before the mirror doing the staring. The very meaning of such terms as "real" or "subjective" are altered when one applies them in a context whose ontological dimensions have shifted so dramatically. The technique, used by Heidegger and Derrida, of writing certain metaphysical terms while simultaneously crossing them out (in our case, subjective, objectivity, and real) would seem appropriate in discussing this realm of "true" delusions.

Schizophrenia in general, and "true delusions" in particular, certainly pose a special challenge to the project of hermeneutic comprehension, for the latter project, by its very nature, seems committed to finding forms of coherence in its object; this is known as the principle of charity: it describes both the goal and the enabling method (the criterion of truth or validity) of interpretive comprehension. Schizophrenia, however, seems to involve forms of experience and expression that, by the very nature, are at the limit of emphatic or interpretive comprehension, since they involve forms of experience and expression that involve contradiction of a very fundamental kind (see Ey 1996, p. 167). As Sophie writes: "There's a sense in which the law of contradiction—that something can't be X and not X at the same time—has ceased to matter. ... What I know and what I believe no longer coincide and I can't make them."

As noted in the introduction, some philosophers writing on psychosis have argued that language loses all meaning under such circumstances as these. They go on to defend an updated version of Jaspers' "doctrine of the abyss"—the notion that schizophrenia must lie beyond our comprehension or empathic grasp, and that claims to understand it are purely illusory.

An alternative view, which I prefer, would reject this polarized approach, with its equation of convention with comprehension, in favor of a more relaxed view of communication and understanding. Like many other notions, "real" and "subjective" would seem to involve family-resemblance concepts devoid of any single, essential feature yet not, for all that, totally lacking in meaning or use. The challenge is to develop forms of interpretive understanding that help us comprehend the overall structure, the inner logic or coherence, such as it is, of schizophrenic experience without slighting or denying the forms of paradox or contradiction that are nonetheless present. The principle of charity, we must remember, demands only as much coherence as is compatible with the phenomenon being understood.

It can help to compare the delusional condition with other, more familiar conditions—so long as one recognizes that these offer only partial analogies that should not be taken too far. The normal person may not be able fully to grasp precisely what it is like to have the experience of one's body mutating or being destroyed, then snapping back to normalcy, or of the world ceasing to exist yet continuing all the same. Still, one can have inklings, and one can pursue certain analogies, and in doing so one approaches far closer to an understanding of the other than if one had never made the effort in the first place.[10]

---

[10] One issue I cannot discuss in detail is the question of motivation or defense: Is delusion something that simply *happens* to a patient, as a kind of affliction, or something that has a purposive or even purposeful quality? Should it, in any important sense, be understood as an act, albeit an unconscious act whose defensive or compensatory purpose may or may not be consciously recognized by the patient herself? This question is complicated by the diversity of types of delusional

9.7 Multiple Realities

In "On multiple realities," an article from 1945, the phenomenologist Alfred Schutz makes the point that, for the normal individual, the natural attitude of the working world provides a primary grounding, "the specific reality of everyday life" (p. 546), which is also the "paramount reality" (p. 533), since other modes—dream, imagination, religious belief, even scientific theorizing—are experienced as its "modifications" (p. 554). The very meaning of imagining, for example, would lose or transform its meaning or lived quality if it lacked this form of contrast (p. 658). "Only he who lived in experiences [of the natural attitude] and reaches from there into the world of phantasm can, provided that the phantasms contrast with the experienced, have the concepts fiction and reality." Schutz is enough of an *existential* phenomenologist to emphasize our human predicament, and specifically, our mortality as a central organizing vector: "I know that I shall die and I fear to die." This he calls the "fundamental anxiety"—the "primordial anticipation from which all the others originate," thereby providing "the many interrelated systems of hopes and fears, of wants and satisfactions, of chances and risks which incite man with the natural attitude to attempts the master of the world, to overcome obstacles, to draft projects, and to realize them." (p. 550)

Obviously this is an eminently pragmatic orientation, and one that instills a basic lack of interest in anything that would go beyond practical reality or call it into question. "It is characteristic of the natural attitude that it takes the world and its objects for granted…." In this attitude, "We are not interested in finding out whether this world really does exist or whether it is merely a coherent system of consistent experiences" (p. 550). All this is simply assumed.

But interestingly enough, Schutz himself does not always present this grounding condition as an inevitable framework or residual state into which one inevitably and naturally sinks, as if with the force of gravity itself. Rather he suggests that the person living in the practical attitude must engage in a "specific epoche" that is quite differ-

---

experience. The sheer immediacy of classic "delusional percept" might, for example, preclude the prominent compensatory motivations present in the more elaborated, late-stage delusions of a patient who (like Wölfli) finds a kind of psychic equilibrium through withdrawal from the common world. The notion that wish-fulfillment can motivate the occurrence of delusions is an ancient idea. The emphasis has typically been placed more on content than on form. In recent years preservation of self-esteem is often mentioned—as may fit the case of a patient who bolsters his self-esteem by, say, imagining himself a great scientist. Phenomenology would certainly not deny such motivations, which can indeed be important. Its particular contribution, however, is to emphasize formal or structural features of experience. In *Psychology of Imagination*, for example, Sartre (1950) describes the "morbid dreamer" who is drawn to the delusional world precisely *because* of its unreality, since this allows escape from the very "form of the real." The delusional memories of Adolf Wölfli afford excellent examples (Sass 2004b). It is noteworthy as well that in at least *some* schizophrenic delusions, the unreal or subjective nature of reality (whether delusional or actual) may emerge as the overt *theme* of the delusion itself, which may express a certain solipsism. This was the case of Wölfli's "omnipotence horn," a device whereby he himself created worlds (Sass 2004b). Here, however, we must bear in mind a distinction suggested to me by a man who suffers from schizophrenia: this is between the "triumphant solipsism" expressed by Wölfli, and the mostly "miserable lonely solipsism" that was more typical of himself (email to author, May 2007).

ent from the phenomenological reduction: "He does not suspend *belief* in the outer world and its objects but on the contrary: he suspends *doubt* in its existence" (p. 551, emphasis added). Schutz calls this "the epoche of the natural attitude" (p. 551).

Schutz's analysis is of considerable interest in relationship to schizophrenic delusion in which the natural attitude seem to lose its unequivocal or grounding status. In delusion everything can seem quasi-imaginary, yet there is no "imaginary world" as such. There may be no mortality; no finality of any kind, and above all no suspension of doubt in the everyday.

The standard explanations for *why* such an eclipse of common sense and the natural attitude sometimes does occur in schizophrenia, points to a supposed cognitive deficiency, some inability to monitor external reality or the boundary between the internal and the external world. Seldom, however, do schizophrenic delusions seem to involve quite the state of confusion this would seem to imply.

Both Sophie and John agree that "general reasoning deficits," such as the inferential biases postulated by cognitive-behaviorists, almost certainly have nothing to do with delusional thinking or elaboration.[11] They both experience themselves, according to Sophie, as "actively engaged in trying to create meaning and make sense of things, in John's words, to 'maximize rational outcomes'." Far more important, or perhaps more basic and primary, says Sophie, is "rather the dissolution of the (commonsense) assumption of certain metaphysical premises that, as John says, any philosopher knows (knows but ironically cannot, unlike the schizophrenic, *believe*) are fundamentally unsubstantiable."

Here it may be more apt to emphasize a matter of attitude or orientation, namely, an idiosyncratic, perhaps autistic stance that fails or refuses to accept the organizing horizon of intersubjectivity and the natural attitude. The capacity to adopt two or more distinct attitudes toward reality—a kind of double book-keeping—is common enough in normal human existence as well (Manonni 2003). The mark of delusion in schizophrenia may be the fact that such persons put more or at least equal faith in their own private experiences rather than in the shared, objective world. Although this can sometimes involve a willful element, at its core it seems to be something the patient can neither alter nor escape. Unlike the normal person, who only sojourns in the imaginary, the individual with schizophrenia does not have the same anchoring and unshakeable faith in the public, the objective, and the ordinary. But this means that delusional experience may not fit the model of either the real or the imaginary, since the standard and defining distinction between the two has been radically displaced.

In *La découverte du quotidien* (Bégout 2005), the philosopher Bruce Bégout develops these points in some detail, and in a way that undermines any inclination to confuse schizophrenic detachment-from-the-everyday with dementia-like intellectual decline or simple error. For Bégout, the suspension of doubt or specific epoche of the ordinary is, in an important sense, a defensive and a self-deceiving act, albeit one that is required for successful functioning within the practical and social reality of common sense. A certain abridgment of possible perspectives is a prerequisite for smooth and graceful action—for the flow, spontaneous yet habitual, that is the basis

---

[11] For a similar critique, from an eminent psychiatrist, of the emphasis on supposed "inferential failures," see Berrios (1996, p. 114).

of so much of our activity. Further, shared rapport with the everyday allows human beings to recognize their shared humanity and feel they live not in a private universe but in one common to all (pp. 94, 202).

Bégout describes the quotidian as consisting in everything in our environment that we experience as immediately comprehensible and familiar. It is defined less by its particular contents than by a specific attitude or orientation, the latter involving a familiar balance between the familiar or habitual, on the one hand, and openness toward the novel or unknown, on the other. Practical life must obviously be concerned with the unexpected, which must be noticed and coped with if the organism is to survive. But what is new will typically conform to a set of more general expectations about the *sort* of things that can occur, and within a set of dimensions that constrain possibilities. Further it will be quickly assimilated to a general set of prototypes, through the process of "typification," and in this sense the familiar always "emerges victorious from its confrontation with the strangeness of the world." Indeed, the everyday life-world tries, in some sense, to suppress or domesticate the unknown, giving it a standard form, agreed and acceptable, in the order of things (p. 45). In this sense, we might say that everyday life requires one to live the lie— the essential lie being that things are as they generally appear to be, that the working world of everyday reality just *is* reality, and all else but whimsy or delusion.

Trauma would seem to be one exception to this rule, schizophrenia is another. In the latter case, it is less an eruptive event than a persistent orientation that undoes the victory of the quotidian. And this orientation, in turn, is both affliction and act, involving both disruption of "passive genesis" (Husserl 2001) and various forms of more active involvement—sometimes, and at some levels, the consequence of neurocognitive abnormalities in integrating expectation with attentional focus (Hemsley 2005), but at other levels involving a quasi-choice, a principled or preferential refusal to restrict oneself to the banality of the everyday (Sass 2011).

Sophie illuminates a schizophrenic modality when she describes what she terms the "conditions of possibility of certain events or structures (e.g., causal relations, conditional inferences)" as changing, so that common-sense knowledge and assumptions no longer constrain expectations and therefore one feels that almost anything could happen. The issue, she says, is not an inability to predict but a detachment from the normal horizons of experience in favor of a hovering stance.

> If I no longer believe in gravity, it's not that I fail to anticipate something when I don't expect an apple to drop from the tree, but that I simply think that the apple could just as easily float or fly and therefore have no reason to anticipate it falling.

Sophie rejects ignorance or intellectual incapacity as the source of her perspective:

> I cannot count the number of times I've been told 'but Sophie, X is impossible' and all I ever want to say in response is 'yes, I am perfectly capable of appreciating why you think X is impossible, but your conceptual or metaphysical constraints are simply not mine'.

Earlier we mentioned Sophie's sense of things "taking place in a parallel reality that only partially overlaps with this one." There is, she says, "… the sense that the world/universe/reality is doubled/multiplied (that there are parallel worlds and/or multiple alter-realities and/or that reality as such is actually fractured." After reading a draft of this chapter, Sophie asked what one should make of the fact that derealization itself seems to instigate a process of alternative (delusional) explanation, and create or strengthen the sense that there is a 'more real' reality somewhere else? Conversely, does the direct personal relevance of other (delusional) worlds, itself lead or contribute to a sense that this world lacks something—a pointedness, directedness, a certain kind of depth...? Indeed [she asks], which world is really the 'flat' or uni-dimensional one?

Those who are unable to endorse, or who refuse, standard constraints will be opened up to a plethora of alternative possibilities, akin, in a way, to the "multiverse" postulated in contemporary physics (Greene 2011). But this openness and insight, such as it is, will hardly aid in navigating the realities of actual life. And this, essentially, is the meaning of Lacan's paradoxical dictum about the psychotic condition: *les non-dupes errent*—namely, that those who are *not* duped are doomed to wander, lost and in error.

Bégout, following the early Heidegger, interprets the normal suspension of doubt as a kind of universal (or near-universal, as we have seen) and utterly foundational defense mechanism that human beings adopt not only in the face of mortality and fear of meaninglessness, but in connection with practical needs to cope with life's demands. It is in the very nature of this defense mechanism of domestication that it hides its own working through a process of auto-dissimulation (Bégout 2005, p. 337). The reasons for this are structural (the limited capacity of conscious awareness) but also motivational: if one is to lie to oneself effectively, the process of lying must also be obscured. Yet for most of us, most of the time, the victory of the everyday and the ordinary is usually so complete that we even "doubt that there is any doubt to overcome" (p. 308).

Still, the banality that this every day brings does not "abolish the agitation of the original disquietude (*l'inquiétude originelle*), but serves only to mask it" (Bégout 2005, p. 45). This assumption of a primary uncertainty and a fundamental angst (pp. 272, 275)—of a primordial condition of doubt rather than belief, of being a stranger to oneself and to one's world (p. 277)[12]—is a somewhat controversial claim. (Even the later Heidegger seems to have rejected it.) But if accepted, it suggests that at least some modes and some moments of schizophrenic experience might be seen as involving not only superior insight (albeit a largely "dysfunctional" one), but also a sort of heightened authenticity, a keeping faith with what we all know to be the truth of our existence.[13]

Acknowledgments For helpful comments on drafts of this article, the author thanks Greg Byrom and Nev Jones.

---

[12] Bégout (2005, p. 428) quotes a line from Hölderlin to which Heidegger devoted much attention: "... for the spirit is at home/Not in the beginning, not at the source. He is consumed by the homeland./Colonies loves..." (*"nehmlich zu Hauss ist der Geist/Nicht im anfang, nicht an der Quell, Ihn zehret die Heimath./ Kolonien liebt ..."* (in Melberg 1999 p. 343; Heidegger 1996 p. 126). Hölderlin, the poet Heidegger most admired, suffered from schizophrenia in the final decades of his life; his mental troubles had begun at the time he wrote these lines (1803 or 1805) (Hölderlin 1984, p. 267).

[13] Here is another comment Sophie made on reading a draft of this chapter: "Yes, and this is such a struggle in therapy—it would always be so much easier to simply capitulate and agree that such and such is not reasonable, even though one continues to experience it... I often feel like the stereotypical political prisoner in the Gulag undergoing psychological torture who is told again and again to repeat (and evince true belief) that the sky is pink or that $2+2=5$...."

References

American Psychiatric Association. (2000). *Diagnostic and statistical manual of mental disorders (DSM IV-R)*. Washington, DC: American Psychiatric Association.

Aviv, R. (Dec. (2010). Which way madness lies: Can psychosis be prevented? *Harper's Magazine*, 35–46.

Bégout, B. (2005). *La découverte du quotidien*. Paris: Editions Allia.

Berrios, G. (1996). *The history of mental symptoms: Descriptive psychopathology since the 19th Century*. Cambridge: Cambridge University Press.

Blankenburg, W. (1971). *Der Verlust der Natürlichen Selbstverständlichkeit: Ein Beitrag zur Psychopathologie symptomarmer Schizophrenien*. Stuttgart: Ferdinand Enke.

Bleuler, E. (1911/1950). *Dementia praecox or the group of schizophrenias* (trans: J. Zinkin). New York: International Universities Press.

Bortolotti, L. (2009). *Delusions and other irrational beliefs*. Oxford: Oxford University Press.

Casey, E. (2000). *Imagining: A phenomenological study*. Bloomington: Indiana University Press.

Cermolacce, M., Sass, L., & Parnas, J. (2010). What is bizarre in bizarre delusions: A critical review. *Schizophrenia Bulletin, 34*, 667–679.

Conrad, K. (1958). *Die beginnende Schizophrenie: Versuch einer Gestatlanalyse des Wahns*. Stuttgart: Thieme.

Egan, A. (2009). Imagination, delusion, and self-deception. In T. Bayne & J. Fernandez (Eds.), *Delusions and self-deception* (pp. 263–280). London: Psychology.

Ey, H. (1996). *Schizophrénie: Études cliniques et psychopathologiques*. France: Synthelabo.

Fuchs, T. (2005). Delusional mood and delusional perception—A phenomenological analysis. *Psychopathology, 38*, 133–139.

Greene, B. (2011). *The hidden reality: Parallel universes and the deep laws of the cosmos*. New York: Knopf.

Heidegger, M. (1996). *Hölderlin's Hymn "The Ister,"* (trans: W. McNeill & J. Davis). Bloomington & Indianapolis: Indiana University Press.

Hemsley, D. R. (2005). The schizophrenic experience: Taken out of context? *Schizophrenia Bulletin, 31*, 43–53.

Henriksen, M. (in press). On incomprehensibility in schizophrenia. *Phenomenology and the Cognitive Sciences*.

Hölderlin, F. (1984). *Hymns and fragments* (trans: R. Sieburth). Princeton: Princeton University Press.

Husserl, E. (2001). *Analyses concerning passive and active syntheses* (trans: A. Steinbock). Boston: Kluwer.

Jaspers, K. (1963). *General psychopathology* (trans: J. Hoenig & M. Hamilton). Chicago: University of Chicago Press.

Lacan, J. (1973/1974). *Les non-dupes errent*. (Lacan's Seminar XXI, 1973–1974, unpublished but available in various forms on the internet.).

Manonni, O. (2003). "I know well but all the same…" In M. A. Rothenberg, D. A. Foster, & S. Zizek (Eds.), *Perversion and the social relationship* (pp. 69–92). Durham: Duke University Press.

Melberg, A. (1999). Turns and echoes: Two examples of Hölderlin's poetics. In A. Fioretos (Ed.), *The solid letter: readings of friedrich hölderlin* (pp. 340–355). Stanford: Stanford University Press.

Mellor, C.S. (1970). First rank symptoms of schizophrenia. *British Journal of Psychiatry, 117*, 15–23.

Møller, P., & Husby, R. (2000). The initial prodrome in schizophrenia: Searching for naturalistic core dimensions of experience and behavior. *Schizophrenia Bulletin, 26*, 217–32.

Müller-Suur, H. (1950). Das Gewissheitsproblem beim schizophrenen und beim paranoischen Wahnerleben. *Fortschritte der Neurologie, Psychiatrie under ihrer Grenzgebiete, 18*, 44–51.

Parnas, J., et al. (2005). EASE: Examination of anomalous self-experience. *Psychopathology, 38*, 236–258.

Read, R. (2001). On approaching schizophrenia through Wittgenstein. *Philosophical Psychology*, *14*, 449–475.

Reimer, M. (2011). Only a philosopher or a madman: Impractical delusions in philosophy and psychiatry. *Philosophy, Psychiatry & Psychology*, *17*, 315–328.

Rümke, H. (1990). The nuclear symptoms of schizophrenia and the praecox feeling. *History of Psychiatry*, *1*, 331–341.

Sartre, J. P. (1950). *Psychology of imagination*. London: Rider.

Sass, L. (1992). Heidegger, schizophrenia, and the ontological difference. *Philosophical Psychology*, *5*, 109–132.

Sass, L. (1994). *The paradoxes of delusion: Wittgenstein, Schreber, and the schizophrenic mind*. Ithaca: Cornell University Press.

Sass, L. (2003). Incomprehensibility and understanding: On the interpretation of severe mental illness. *Philosophy, Psychiatry, & Psychology*, *10*, 125–132.

Sass, L. (2004a). Some reflections on the (analytical) philosophical approach to delusion. *Philosophy, Psychiatry, & Psychology*, *11*, 71–80.

Sass, L. (2004b). Affectivity in schizophrenia: A phenomenological perspective. *Journal of Consciousness Studies*, *11*, 127–147.

Sass, L. (2011). Autonomy and schizophrenia: Reflections on an ideal. In C. Piers (Ed.), *Personality and psychopathology: critical dialogues with David Shapiro* (pp. 99–131). New York: Springer.

Sass, L., & Pienkos, E. (in press). Delusion: The phenomenological approach. In W. Fulford, et al. (Eds.), *Oxford handbook of philosophy and psychiatry*. Oxford: Oxford University Press.

Schmidt, G. (1987). A review of the German literature on delusion between 1914 and 1939. In J. Cutting & M. Shepherd (Eds.) *The clinical roots of the schizophrenia concept* (pp. 104–134). Cambridge: Cambridge University Press.

Schreber, D. P. (1988). *Memoirs of my nervous illness* (trans: I. Macalpine & R. Hunter). Cambridge: Harvard University Press.

Schutz, A. (1945). On multiple realities. *Philosophy and Phenomenological Research*, *5*, 533–576.

Spitzer, M. (1990). On defining delusion. *Comprehensive Psychiatry*, *31*, 377–397.

Sullivan, H. S. (1953). *The interpersonal theory of psychiatry*. New York: Norton.

Szasz, T. (1976). Schizophrenia: The sacred symbol of psychiatry. *British Journal of Psychiatry*, *129*, 308–316.

Tatossian, A. (1997). *La Phénoménologie des Psychoses*. Paris: *L'Art du Comprendre* (*juillet 1997, Numéro double, hors série*).

Thornton, T. (2004). Wittgenstein and the limits of empathic understanding in psychopathology. *International Review of Psychiatry*, *16*, 216–224.

Wittgenstein, L. (1958). *The blue and brown books*. Oxford: Blackwell.

Woods, A. (2011). *The sublime object of psychiatry: Schizophrenia in clinical and cultural theory*. Oxford: Oxford University Press.

Chapter 10
Jaspers on Feelings and Affective States

Giovanni Stanghellini and René Rosfort

10.1 Introduction: Psychopathology, or the Enlightenment in Psychiatry

What is psychopathology? A rather sketchy, but not incorrect, answer is that psychopathology is a logos for pathos, i.e. a discourse about what troubles a person. Psychopathology provides a language to assess and make sense of the phenomena that express the vulnerability of the human person. Among the disturbing experiences that affect a person, emotions play a major role.

According to Jaspers, the founder of this discipline, psychopathology has two major aims. First, it offers 'clarification, order, formation' (GP, p. 33/38),[1] i.e. concrete descriptions, a suitable terminology, and systematic groupings that allow us to bring order into the chaos of disturbing mental phenomena as recounted by the patient and observed in her or his behaviour. Second, it aims at 'a psychopathological education' (GP, p. 44/50), i.e. endowing clinicians with a valid and reliable philosophical background, that is providing a philosophically sound methodology.

---

[1] We use the English translation of *Allgemeine Psychopathologie* (1997). With the aim of facilitating the process for readers who work with, or simply want to consult, the German original, we also refer to the pagination of the 7th edition of this work (1959). So in our references to Jaspers' text, the first page number refers to the English translation, whereas the number after the slanted stroke refers to the German original. When we disagree with the English translation, we have tacitly modified the text. The cross-reference will allow the critical reader to judge if our alternative is acceptable or not. To avoid ambiguity, we have chosen to include the German originals of central words and concepts in brackets in the text and in square brackets in direct quotations.

G. Stanghellini (✉)
Faculty of Psychology, Università degli Studi G. d'Annunzio,
Via dei Vestini 31, Chieti, Italy
e-mail: stanghellini@unich.it

R. Rosfort
Centre for Subjectivity Research, Købmagergade 44-46, 4,
1150, Copenhagen K, Denmark
e-mail: ros@cfs.ku.dk

T. Fuchs et al. (eds.), *Karl Jaspers' Philosophy and Psychopathology*,
DOI 10.1007/978-1-4614-8878-1_10, © Springer Science+Business Media New York 2014

Was Jaspers right about the relevance of psychopathology for psychiatry? We are convinced that he was. Since this is not the place to flesh out an argument for that conviction, we will merely list a number of reasons why we agree with Jaspers that psychopathology is an indispensable tool for any psychiatrist:

1. Psychiatry is a heterogeneous discipline. Its adepts approach the 'object' of their discipline from many different angles, as for instance neuroscience, depth psychology, sociology, and philosophy, each of which has its own language, methodology, and practice. Psychiatrists therefore need a common ground and a joint language. To Jaspers, disturbing mental phenomena are the main facts for psychiatry, and psychopathology—whose main focus is on abnormal experiences—is the shared language that allows clinicians with different theoretical backgrounds to understand each other when dealing with mental disorders.
2. Psychiatry addresses abnormal human subjectivity. Psychopathology attempts to define what is abnormal (rather than taking for granted commonsense views) as well as to grasp what is human in apparently non-human (e.g. irrational or nonsensical) phenomena.
3. Psychiatry aims at establishing rigorous diagnoses. Psychopathology is still highly useful in a field where the major disorders cannot be neuroscientifically defined as disease entities, but are exclusively syndromes that can be defined according to characterising symptoms such as, notably, abnormal subjective experiences.
4. Psychiatry is about understanding disturbed human experience, rather than simply diagnosing and classifying it. Psychopathology functions as a bridge between human sciences and clinical sciences, thus providing the basic tools to make sense of mental suffering.
5. Psychiatry is about caring for troubled human existence, rather than judging, marginalising, punishing, or stigmatising it. Psychopathology connects understanding with caring, and endeavours to establish an epistemological as well as ethical framework for this.
6. Psychiatry looks for a way to connect, or at least think together, first-person subjective experience with impersonal brain functioning. As Jaspers saw with admirable clarity, psychopathology is about bridging understanding (*Verstehen*) and explaining (*Erklären*) in research as well as in clinical settings.

A century or so after the birth of psychopathology, we can agree that 'psychopathology is the fundamental professional skill of the psychiatrist' (Oyebode 2008, p. 3). However, if we still need psychopathology, which psychopathology do we need? (Gross and Huber 1993). We think that there are three kinds of psychopathology, or better, three levels of psychopathological inquiry (Stanghellini 2009):

1. *Descriptive psychopathology*: The aim of this level is to systematically order, define, differentiate, and describe specific mental phenomena. These phenomena are thereby rendered accessible and can be described in specific terms. By grouping related phenomena on a purely phenomenological basis, the aim is to avoid any pre-established conceptual scheme or explicit theory about what these phenomena are. This is, of course, an ideal that demands a constant suspen-

sion of our 'natural' attitudes and pre-conceptions in order to let the phenomena themselves come to expression and, so to say, speak for themselves.

2. *Clinical psychopathology*: This is a pragmatic tool for connecting relevant symptoms and diagnostic categories with each other, and thus for restricting the scope of the clinical investigation to those symptoms that are useful to establish a reliable diagnosis. As Kurt Schneider (1967) defined it, it is an instrument for 'pragmatic diagnostic use', or the driving belt between the level of symptoms and that of nosographic syndromes (Rossi Monti and Stanghellini 1996).

3. *Structural psychopathology*: This must be considered the most ambitious level of psychopathology, namely that of reconstructing the overall meaningful structure of a syndrome. As Georges Lantéri-Laura puts it, 'instead of the trivialities of semiotics, one puts it [psychopathology] at a level of global understanding [...] at a level of synthetic knowledge' (1985, p. 604). It endeavours to attain to a global level of intelligibility, assuming that the manifold of phenomena of a given mental disorder is a meaningful whole and not just a collection of symptoms.

In the case of emotions, we do need a precise description of emotional experiences, including a sharp and comprehensive characterisation of feelings (such as anger, dysphoria, sadness, shame, jealousy, etc.). We also need to connect given psychopathological syndromes with more or less definite types of emotional experience to enrich our system of classification of mental disorders. Finally, we need an in-depth understanding of the life-worlds that different emotions bring about, and of the meaningful connections between feelings and cognition, perception, action, and values in each of these life-worlds.

10.2 Jaspers' Ambivalent Attitude to Emotional Experience

To Jaspers, emotional experience[2] is probably the fundamental topic in psychopathology. This can be argued by reading, for instance, his pages on the early stages of acute schizophrenia and delusional mood (*Wahnstimmung*)—an uncanny atmosphere of unattached feelings. In these pages, an alteration of mood (*Stimmung*) is at the origin of a deep metamorphosis of world experience:

> The environment is somehow different—not to a gross degree—perception is unaltered in itself but there is some change which envelops everything with subtle, pervasive and strangely uncertain light. A living-room which formerly was felt as neutral or friendly now becomes dominated by some indefinable atmosphere [*einer undefinierbaren Stimmung*]. (GP, p. 98/82)

---

[2]While in contemporary Anglophone philosophy there exists a significant conceptual difference between the term 'emotion' (intentionally—at times even cognitively—structured feelings with a more or less explicit propositional content) and the term 'feeling' (primarily referring to the perception of bodily changes), throughout this article we shall use the two words interchangeably as the translation of the German word '*Gefühl*'. As we shall see in the fifth section, we believe that there is a point to Jaspers' rather vague conceptual terminology for human emotional experience.

The following stages of schizophrenia, including perplexity (*Ratlosigkeit*) and the formation of delusions, are traced back by Jaspers to these uncanny experiences brought about by a change in the mood (*Stimmung*) of the person. Further, in the chapter dealing with the patient's attitude to his illness, he explains how these ineffable feelings of change amount to a pre-reflective awareness that something is not right:

> At the beginning of a mental illness some persons undergo an uncanny feeling of change [*unheimliches Gefühl der Veränderung*] (as if they had been bewitched, enchanted, or there may be an increase in sexuality, etc.). All this adds to the awareness [*Bewusstsein*] of impending madness. It is difficult to say what this awareness really is. It is the outcome of innumerous individual feelings, not a mere judgment [*Urteil*] but something actually experienced [*wirklich erlebt*]. (GP, p. 415/345)

Subtle changes in our pre-reflective embodied engagement with the world, a change in existential feelings (Ratcliffe 2008), an uncanny emotional atmosphere, rather than explicit reflective disturbances, are what mark the beginning of psychosis.

Also, for Jaspers, feelings are fundamental to a person's well-being and self-understanding. For some persons, it is through a change in feeling and mood that they become aware of their own self; for instance, a basic emotional experience such as suffering (*Leiden*) is a central component in the various limit-situations. The awareness that something is wrong or simply not as it should be disturbs the person, although he or she may not be able to say what is actually going on. In fact, it is precisely the elusive character of these objectless and cognitively impenetrable feelings (Goldie 2000, pp. 100–111) that is disturbing. Jaspers argues that persons undergoing such experiences often feel an 'almost inescapable need [*Drang*] to give some content to such feelings' (GP, p. 113/95), and goes on to provide a detailed description of how this emotional need can result in a cognitive enactment out of such objectless, but highly comprehensive feelings:

> These new and unfamiliar feelings press for some understanding on the part of the person who experiences them. Countless possibilities are contained in them which can be realised only when intuition, imagination, form [*Gestalten*] and thought [*Denken*] have created a coherent world. There is therefore always a path which leads from these immense feelings of happiness to recognition [*Erkennen*]. The experience of blissful feelings starts with a conscious clarity [*Klarsehens*] without there being no real content to present. The patients delightedly believe that they have grasped the profoundest of meanings. Concepts like timelessness, world, god and death become enormous revelations which when the state have subsided cannot be reproduced or described in any way—they were after all nothing but feelings. (GP, pp. 115/95–97)

Notwithstanding the central place of feelings in Jaspers' clinical and existential analyses, he does not provide a systematic and coherent theory of human emotions—neither in the GP nor in the minor psychopathological writings, not in *Psychologie der Weltanschauungen* or in his philosophical works. While he works hard, in the GP, to describe and categorise various feelings and affective states, to account for which categories of abnormal affective states are related to which nosographic symptoms, and to attempt to make sense of the connection between emotions and extra-conscious mechanisms, these efforts remain scattered in several places and amount to a fragmentary picture of human emotional experience. The reader can—so to speak—see the single trees but is not provided with a panoramic view of the whole forest. While he appears to be wary of extensive analysis of individual feelings and affective states, arguing that such an approach would most of the time 'only end in a vast array of trivialities' (GP, p. 108/91), he is outright dismissive of the possibility that feelings might teach us something about the cause and origin of mental disorders:

> Attempts have been made to let almost all abnormal phenomena derive from *feelings* [*aus Gefühle abgeleitet*]. If we use the term 'feeling' to denote everything for which common usage permits us to use the word, there is always some truth in this, but then it comes to very little if we go on to derive delusions, for instance, from feelings. Delusions of sense-lessness, sinfulness, and impoverishment were supposed to arise from a depressive affect in a rationally understandable way [*rational verständlich*], and it was generally supposed that the depressed patient concluded that there must be something which made him so miserable. People also wanted to explain delusions of persecution by the affect of distrust, delusions of grandeur by euphoric mood [*Stimmung*], but they did not realise that, though one may understand ordinary mistakes and over-valued ideas in this way, one can never do this with delusions [*Wahnideen*]. Furthermore, frightening hallucinations in sleep during fever or psychosis have been attributed to some kind of conditioned anxiety, and so on. We can, it is true, find meaningful connections [*verständliche Zusammenhänge*], and they can teach us something about the relationship of delusional content and previous experiences but nothing at all of how delusions, false perceptions, etc. could have come about in the first place. (GP, pp. 408–409/340)

So though feelings are central to the manifestation and subsequent development of a mental disorder, they are of no help whatsoever when it comes to understanding why or how a person suffers from such a disorder. In other words, Jaspers' attitude towards the role that emotions play in mental disorder appears to be rather ambivalent.

Now, we believe that explaining this ambivalence is imperative not only for understanding the role emotions play in Jaspers' psychopathology. It is also a necessary part of an argument for the relevance of Jaspers' psychopathology in contemporary psychiatry and clinical practice. But before venturing an explanation, we first need to take a careful look at what Jaspers actually has to say about emotions and affective states in the GP.

10.3   Feelings and Affective States in GP: An Overview

Jaspers' main description and analysis of emotions and emotional experience is limited to two paragraphs in GP, which add up to less than twenty pages. The first is found in Section One, § 5 (pp. 108–117/90–97), in the first chapter of Part One where Jaspers describes the phenomenology of individual features of our mental life. The section is entitled 'Feelings and Affective States' and is divided into a 'Psychological preface' and a 'Classification of abnormal affective states'. The second place is in Section One, (a)-(b) (pp. 367–372/305–310), in the second chapter of Part Two where Jaspers deals with meaningful connections in our mental life in view of extra-conscious mechanisms. This section is entitled 'Normal Mechanisms' and of particular relevance here are the first two subdivisions 'Experiential reactions' and 'After-effects of previous experiences'.

10.3.1 Previous Classification of Feelings

Jaspers introduces his treatment of feelings (*Gefühle*) and affective states (*Gemüt-szustände*) with a psychological prelude. Here he laments the state of emotion research at the time, which is lacking in clarity compared to research into sensation, perception, ideas, and even research concerning instinctual drive and act of will. In fact, he claims that both the word and the concept of 'feeling' remains highly confusing and appears to refer 'to everything for which we can find no other name'. At the same time, though, he is, as we have seen, sceptical of the trivialities brought about by scrupulous description and analysis of individual feelings, so instead he sets out to provide a synthesis of previous classifications of feelings. This amounts to the following catalogue:

1. *From a Purely Phenomenological Perspective*: We have three basic ways of distinguishing feelings: (a) feelings that are an aspect of conscious personality (*Persönlichkeitsbewusstsein*) and thus defining the self (*Ichbestimmtheit*) are distinguished from feelings that lend colour to object-awareness (*Gegenstandsbewusstsein*); (b) distinction by means of opposition, e.g. pleasure and displeasure, tension and relaxation, excitement and calm; (c) feelings without an object (*gegenstandslos*), i.e. how I feel in a given situation (*Zustandsgefühle eines Sichbefindens*), are opposed to those directed upon some object.
2. *According to Objects*: Feelings of fantasy (*Phantasiegefühle*), directed upon suppositions, are opposed to serious feelings (*Ernstgefühle*) directed upon actual objects. Also, feelings of value (*Wertgefühle*) that are either directed at the feeling person herself or at something extraneous, and can be distinguished as being either affirmative or negative (pride or humbleness, love or hate).
3. *According to Source*: This classification is made according to the different layers of our mental life (*Seelenleben*). Here we find four types of feelings (Scheler 1966): (a) localised feeling sensations, (b) vital feelings involving the whole body, (c) psychic feelings (e.g. sadness, joy), and (d) spiritual feelings (e.g. a state of grace).
4. *According to Significance*: The significance of a feeling with regard to life (*Leben*) or to the purposes of life (*Lebenszwecke*), i.e. feelings of joy can count as the expression of the promotion of a purpose in life, whereas feelings of distaste can count as expressing a hindrance.
5. *Particular Feelings vs. All-Inclusive Feelings*: Particular feelings (*partikulare Gefühle*) are those directed on specific objects or partial aspects of the whole, whereas in all-inclusive feelings (*Totalgefühle*), the separate elements are fused into comprehensive affective states (*Gefühlszustände*), e.g. irritable, 'feeling of being alive', etc.
6. *According to Intensity and Duration*: Here Jaspers follows what he calls 'the old and practical' division: (a) feelings (*Gefühle*) are the unique and original commotions of the psyche; (b) affects (*Affekte*) are momentary and complex emotional processes of great intensity with conspicuous bodily accompaniments and sequels; and (c) moods (*Stimmungen*) characterise the state of mind (*Zumu-*

tesein) or inner disposition (*innere Verfassung*) of a person; a mood is a result of prolonged feelings and colour the whole mental life while it lasts.

7. *Feelings vs. Sensations*: Feelings (*Gefühle*) are states of the self (*Zustände des Ich*) whereas sensations (*Empfindungen*) are elements in the perception of the environment and of one's own body (e.g. colour, tonal pitch, temperature). The latter is, furthermore, distinguished according to whether the sensations are object-directed (*gegenständlich*) or merely express the state of the body (*leib-zuständlich*). In between those extremes, we find sensations that are both object-directed and bodily expressions, i.e. feeling-sensations (*Gefühlsempfindungen*) in which feelings, affects, and drives constitute a whole as is the case with, for example, hunger, thirst, fatigue, sexual excitation.

10.3.2   Classification of Abnormal Affective States

After this cataloguing of previous classifications of feelings and affective states (leaving the reader rather dissatisfied if not confused), Jaspers goes on to provide a tentative categorisation of abnormal affective states. He starts out by making a fundamental distinction between two kinds: (a) the genetically understandable affective states (*genetisch verständliche Gemütszustände*), i.e. the abnormally exaggerated and particularly coloured affective states that can nevertheless be understood in view of some previous experiences or situations; and (b) the endogenous affective states that spring from something irreducible in the soul (*etwas seelisch Letztes*), i.e. affective states that escape our understanding and can be explained only in terms of extra-conscious causes (*ausserbewusste Ursachen*). He notices that language has enabled us to name many of these all-embracing abnormal affective states (*abnorme Gesamtzuständlichkeiten des Gefühls*) such as grief, melancholy, cheerfulness, and he concedes that certain typical states can indeed be recognised, for instance, the gloomy mood of depression or the silly, awkward blandness of hebephrenia. Once again, however, instead of examining the nature and phenomenological character of this emotional tonality, he chooses merely to examine the most particular and noteworthy 'out of the host of trivial affective states' (GP, p. 110/92). What is most characteristic of this part, though, is his attempt to connect each category of abnormal feeling with nosographic syndromes:

8. *Changes in Bodily Feelings*: Bodily feelings (*Leibgefühle*) are closely related to physical symptoms. They constitute a foundation for our entire feeling-state (*des gesamten Gefühlszustandes*), and often undergo a significant change in psychosis and personality disorders. We have, however, only slight knowledge of these vital and organic feelings (*Vital- und Organgefühle*) due to the fact that it is difficult to empathise (*kaum innerlich nachzufühlen*) with pathological changes in bodily feelings. He notes, without commenting further, that Kurt Schneider considers changes in vital feelings, located primarily in the limbs, chest, forehead and stomach, as the core of cyclothymic depression.

9. *Changes in Feelings of Capacity:* A feeling of insufficiency (*Gefühl der Insuffizienz*), e.g. being useless, incompetent, incapable of action, unable to think, remember, understand, and make a decision, are characteristic of depression, partly as primary phenomena and partly as feelings of actual insufficiency.

10. *Apathy:* We find the total absence of feelings (*Fehlen der Gefühle*) in acute psychoses where the person is utterly incapable of taking an interest in what goes on around him. He appears to be 'dead with wakeful eyes' and completely indifferent as to what befalls him. Accordingly, there is no incentive to action (aboulia), and the life of the person (*Seelenleben*) is entirely governed by what Jaspers calls object-consciousness (*Gegenstandsbewusstsein*), i.e. making sense of the world only in terms of rational understanding (*Verstand*). Due to the paralysing character of this feeling-state, the patient will die if he is not fed and cared for.

11. *The Feeling of Having Lost Feeling:* The feeling of having lost feeling (*Gefühl der Gefühllosigkeit*) is the odd experience of not having any feeling at all, which we find in psychopaths, depressives, and in the initial stages of all pathological processes. It differs from apathy by being a painful feeling of non-feeling (*Fühlen eines Nichfühlen*), a subjectively felt emptiness of feeling (*subjektiv empfundene Gefühlsleere*). And although the afflicted persons are convinced of not feeling anything, this non-feeling is characterised by an anxiety that becomes manifest in bodily symptoms.

12. *Change in the Feeling-Tone of Perception:* The change in the feeling tone of perception (*Gefühlsauffassung*) is particularly complex in acute psychosis. Here we find an increase of feeling towards normal objects as well as alterations of the character of feeling (*Gefühlscharakter*) resulting in abnormal feeling-sensations (*sinnliche Gefühle*). Things take on a life of their own in the sense that one can speak of 'a physiognomy of things' (*Physiognomie der Dinge*) expressing their psychic essence, e.g. cold and strange, clear and full of meaning, solemn and wonderful, divine and far removed, ghastly and spookish. Besides these feelings that are primarily object-directed, we can also find painful changes in empathic feelings (*Einfühlen in andere Menschen*) which can lead to either an abnormally strong empathy or the opposite where people appear as automata or soulless machines.

13. *Objectless Feelings:* Experiences that cannot be understood in terms of their development (*genetisch unverständlichen Erlebens*) manifest themselves in objectless feelings (*gegenstandslose Gefühle*). These feelings are free-floating, and '[i]f they are to become meaningful to the subject, these feelings must first search for an object or try to create one'. Anxiety (in depression) is one of these objectless feelings. Jaspers distinguishes two basic kinds of anxiety: (a) a specific feeling-sensation of the heart that manifests itself vitally, affecting one's body or parts of it; and (b) a basic state of the soul (*Seelenzustand*) that involves our being human (*Dasein*). Anxiety in general is closely related to bodily sensations such as feelings of pressure, suffocation, and tightness, comes in many shapes and degrees of intensity, and may result in slight, anxious tension as well as ruthless acts against oneself and others. However, Jaspers concludes that 'it is not possible to understand the existential anxiety any further

in a phenomenological perspective. It is the source of our existence (*Existenz*) and a fundamental feature of our being human (*Dasein*) as it manifests itself in limit-situations (*Grenzsituationen*)' (GP, p. 113/95). Anxiety often involves a lively feeling of restlessness (*Gefühl der Unruhe*) that can, however, also come about without anxiety. In psychosis, this feeling of restlessness is heightened to a tension and a pressure that is often experienced by the person as an unbearable massive weight of impressions. Jaspers also describes abnormal feelings of happiness (*abnorme Glücksgefühle*) as a multifarious objectless feeling-state, ranging from purely sensuous feelings of pleasure (*Lustgefühle*) to religious-mystical ecstasies of which the latter can be found primarily in schizophrenic persons.

14. *The Growth of Worlds from Objectless Feelings*: We have already mentioned this peculiar aspect of objectless feelings, namely, that they create an 'almost inescapable need to give some content to such feelings'. Here Jaspers explains that, for example, feelings of happiness often involve feelings of clarity, experiences of God (*Gotterleben*), and feelings of absolution (*Begnadungsgefühle*), which quickly drives the patient from the world of feeling into the concrete world of delusion, e.g. feeling holy, a child of God, the Messiah, a prophet, or Maria. These affective states are not only found in beginning schizophrenia, but also in epileptics or as a result of poisoning, and can also be found occasionally in healthy persons, for instance, in ecstatic mystics.

10.3.3   Extra-conscious Mechanisms

The concept of extra-conscious mechanism (*ausserbewusster Mechanismus*) is particularly interesting, since such mechanisms 'are the understructure of our mental life (*Unterbau des Seelischen*)' without which 'the meaningful connections (*verständliche Zusammenhänge*) could never be realised', and as such they function 'as an extra-conscious precondition of mental phenomena and of their effects on bodily function' (GP, p. 364/303). As of yet, Jaspers notes, there has been no successful description of these mechanisms in more exact bodily or biological terms. In fact, the mechanisms 'are not accessible to investigation', and we can only know about them indirectly—grasp 'a glimmer of meaning' (*einen Schimmer des Verständlichen*)—through the effect of their meaningful connections in our mental life. They remain purely psychological and theoretical concepts helping us to bring some order into mental phenomena that can be captured by neither a purely somatic nor an intellectualistic approach. One of the best guides to those hidden mechanisms, according to Jaspers, is still Nietzsche's analyses of their effects. Any attempt to go beyond this modest conception of the extra-conscious mechanisms still remains unverifiable speculation—as is the case with the Freudian theory of our unconscious life, even though such theories may sometimes bring about 'surprising insights'.

In order to avoid speculations of this kind or drown in the 'infinite world of human experiences', Jaspers deliberately confines his descriptions to how the extra-conscious mechanisms affect the 'different ways in which meaningful connections come about in actuality'. He proceeds to describe how normal mechanisms are at work in reactions to experience, after-effects of previous experiences, dreams, suggestion, and hypnoses (GP, pp. 367–381/305–317), and how abnormal mechanisms influence pathological experiential reactions, abnormal after-effects of previous experiences, abnormal dreams, hysteria, and psychosis (GP, pp. 381–413/317–344).

Of these detailed descriptions, the first two are those most germane to Jaspers' understanding of emotions:

1. *Reactions to Experience (Erlebnisreaktionen)*: Out of the endless variety of human experiences, Jaspers picks out the fundamental experiences (*Urerlebnisse*) that every human being undergoes through time, namely, experiences that momentarily shake or agitate a person and afterwards contribute to form his or her being (*Wesen*). He distinguishes between two basic forms of fundamental experiences:

   a. Violent emotional shocks (*heftigste Gemütserschütterungen*) caused by sudden experiences. These include feelings of terror, horror, and rage and are often the result of life-threatening situations such as a sexual assault, an earthquake, or death.
   b. Deep emotional changes (*tiefe Gemütsveränderungen*) growing slowly out of a persisting destiny (*Schicksal*). These prolonged emotional states may develop out of the vanishing of hope with increasing age, lack of positive experiences, lifelong captivity, the crumbling of self-deceptions, etc.

The violent emotional shocks bring a person into an emotional state and provoke experiences that appear abnormal when compared with humdrum everyday life. Such experiences can be considered normal so long as they can be controlled, do not have obscurely disturbing consequences, and remain within the range of what most people experience. These pliable criteria of normality are important to be aware of, for—as Jaspers writes—'human beings have an extraordinary capacity for extreme endurance'. The deep emotional changes, on the other hand, are normally connected with sexuality, erotic life, anxiety about one's life and health, money problems and material welfare, professional and social life, and not least with politics and religion. Understanding the deep emotional changes requires a different approach from the one used when dealing with violent emotional shocks. With regard to the latter, the extraordinarily intense character of the situation is normally the explicit cause of the emotional reaction, i.e. the reaction depends more on the situation and less on the individual person. Deep emotional changes are different because, to uncover meaningful connections in these more subdued and inarticulate feeling-states, 'we must apply ourselves to the particular content of each individual case' (GP, p. 367/305).

2. *After-Effects of Previous Experiences:* Here Jaspers starts with the apparently obvious observation that '[e]verything we experience and do leaves traces and slowly changes our disposition [*Veranlagung*]', and that a reversal of past experiences and actions is impossible. To emphasise that this is not a trivial observation, he enigmatically claims that '[i]n this lies the personal responsibility [*das persönlich Verantwotliche*] involved in every single experience'. He individuates

five kinds of paradigmatic after-effects of previous experiences [*Nachwirkung früherer Erlebnisse*]: memory traces, practice, mechanisation, habits, and the effects of complexes. And since he has already dealt with the first three earlier (Part One, Chap. 2, 'Objective Performances of Mental Life'), in this section he concentrates on the last two:

a. Habits (*Gewohnheiten*) dominate our life to a degree that we are rarely aware of. They are, according to Jaspers, '[o]ur second nature [*zweite Natur*]'; they render many aspects of our life unremarkable or unnoticed, for better or for worse; and 'the spontaneity of our psyche' retires in front of this monotonous work of our habits. They derive from repeated experiences and have a lasting effect on emotional responses.

b. The effects of complexes (*Komplexwirkungen*) are certain dispositions formed by the '[a]fter-effect of previous emotionally toned [*affektbetonter*] experiences, particularly unpleasantly-toned [*unlustbetonter*] ones', and complexes are 'supposed to characterise a particular, irrational after-effect arising from some experience in the past'. He describes four typical after-effects involved in complexes:

1. Affects—like habits—can be fully roused again through association as soon as one element of the original reappears;
2. Affects can displace themselves so that objects experienced together with unpleasant experiences may appropriate their particular feeling (*Gefühlscharakter*). This displacement accounts, among other things, for the countless subjective values that people without any apparent reason ascribe to particular objects.
3. Unpleasant experiences are dealt with (*verarbeiten*)—in one way or the other. Either we freely vent our emotional reactions to them (*Abreagieren*) or we deal with them intellectually (*intellektuell verarbeitet*).
4. Unpleasant experiences that are simply repressed or blocked out without any such intellectual processing tend to show exceptionally strong after-effects—although repression can also take place without any effect, particularly in 'indifferent and dull individuals'. The description of these extra-conscious mechanisms may immediately appear to be very similar to what psychoanalysis defines as defence mechanisms, but as we saw earlier, Jaspers prefers Nietzsche to Freud and his followers when it comes to the obscure forces at work in the human mind. One thing is certain, though: Jaspers does not underestimate the sway that such complexes hold over a person. In fact, he claims that '[c]omplexes have the tendency to dominate the person [*Mensch*] to such an extent that the person no longer has complexes, but the complexes have him' (GP, pp. 371–372/309).

10.4 Jaspers' Asymptotic Understanding of Emotional Experience

Without any doubt, Jaspers' psychopathology of emotional experience has many strong points which make it a valuable basis for further analyses and conceptualisations. He has made us aware that emotions are central to understanding mental disorders. His argument for the crucial importance of suffering in mental illness shows that in order to understand mental disorders, we need to describe and understand, when possible, the subjective character and development of emotional experience, how emotions are connected with nosographic syndromes, and finally the person's attitude (*Stellungnahme*) to his or her emotional experience. In this sense, Jaspers admirably laid the foundation for psycho-patho-logy as a discourse (*logos*) that endeavours to articulate the emotional suffering (*pathos*) that troubles the human mind (*psyche*).

Although his analysis of emotions is kaleidoscopic and remains incomplete, Jaspers manages to show that the phenomenological perspective of descriptive psychopathology and the pragmatic perspective of clinical psychopathology cannot stand alone. They need to be supported by a more comprehensive, structural view of human nature if the clinician is not to fall prey to unwarranted prejudices or intellectual short-cuts, i.e. either 'the brain mythologies' (*Hirnmythologien*) or the speculative 'anti-reason' (*Widervernunft*) of psychoanalysis (GP, p. 18/16; Jaspers 1950, pp. 17–24, 1951, pp. 221–230). This is the philosophical ambition behind the GP, already present in the first edition but becoming more and more explicit as Jaspers' philosophy develops (Kirkbright 2008). We return to this structural level of his approach in a moment, but first we will evidence Jaspers' achievement in regard to the descriptive and the clinical levels psychopathology defined in the beginning.

Jaspers' insistence on phenomenology is basically an attempt to make a discourse about feelings, i.e. *not to treat them as cognitive phenomena per se*, but rather to use cognition to finely describe, rigorously define, and classify them systematically. This is of indisputable value to descriptive psychopathology, since there is always the risk of over-intellectualising when it comes to emotions (Goldie 2000, p. 41), that is to say, reading emotional experience as a result of cognitive problems rather than as a disturbance in our pre-reflective engagement with the world, other people, and ourselves. This emphasis on the significance of the emotional dimension of mental illness is one of Jaspers' most important contributions to contemporary descriptive psychopathology. And while we have come a long way since the GP, there is still much work to be done when it comes to describing, defining, and classifying the various aspects of emotional experience. It remains an open question to what extent we may speak of a dividing line between the cognitive and the affective aspect of human experience. It is certain, though, that if it is there, it is a highly blurred and unstable line that requires a constant phenomenological effort to distinguish the various feelings, emotions, and moods that are at work in human experience (e.g. Strasser 1956; Schmitz 1992; Fuchs 2000).

Jaspers not only provides an outline of how to proceed along these descriptive lines; his analyses are also of clinical value, since they attempt to bridge between descriptive and clinical psychopathology by coupling various abnormal feelings (e.g. abnormal vital feelings) with nosographical syndromes (e.g. major depression). His pages on *Wahnstimmung* (GP, pp. 98–104/82–87), for instance, are still a classic and unsurpassed *topos* in phenomenological psychopathology. A particularly important is the demonstration that the afflicted person's experience of suffering (*Leiden*) is the core of our understanding of mental illness. In this way, Jaspers succeeded in showing that emotional experience cannot be considered merely as a more or less accidental by-product of neurological or rational disturbances.

These descriptive and clinical achievements notwithstanding, Jaspers' treatment of emotions is not satisfactory. What we seem to lack is a development of the structural level of a psychopathology of emotional experience. Jaspers does not provide us with a comprehensive theory of emotion that can help us understand not just the descriptive or clinical aspect of human emotional experience, but more generally the role emotions play in overall meaningful structure of pathological syndrome. However, without connecting the dots, so to speak, he does provide us with interesting 'hints' in that direction.

One of these 'hints' is the outline of how to connect objectless feelings with the growth of 'private worlds', which marked an important advance in our understanding of mental suffering that is still highly relevant today. Narratives of existential suffering and pathology serve as evidence of the need to have the person pinpoint her disturbing feelings of strangeness, non-familiarity, and alienation. The interplay between these unattached, free-floating feelings and the patient who takes her stance in front of them is the cornerstone of the *dialectic model* in psychopathology (Stanghellini 1997a, b; Stanghellini and Rosfort, in press; Stanghellini et al., forthcoming); i.e. the growing of 'private worlds' out of non-intentional feelings is at the heart of the dialectical understanding of delusions and other fundamental psychopathological phenomena.

Another of these hints is Jaspers' rather sketchy attempt to connect extra-conscious mechanisms with conscious feelings and cognitions, especially in the part on normal mechanisms. The intimate connection between the involuntary source of emotions and the way they structure the person's field of experience and life-world is at the heart of contemporary research on emotions (e.g. Stocker 1996; Pugmire 1998; Goldie 2000; Solomon 2007; de Sousa 2011), and is linked with the theme of the limits of human understanding. Jaspers' psychopathology is an *asymptotic kind of knowledge* that tries to push understanding to its extreme limits without ignoring its limitations. Articulating emotions contributes to make intelligible what is cognitively impenetrable, or unintelligible in terms of rationality.

When these two hints are held together, they bring out the mind-numbingly complex interplay of necessity (fate) and moral accountability that lies at the heart of any pathology of the mind—as well as of any psychotherapy. To what extent can a person be held responsible for his own recovery? What is the relation between freedom and nature in mental suffering? Can we find a sparkle of freedom in the obscure regions of mental suffering, and if we can, how do we help the patient to deal with the accompanying responsibility to articulate, make sense of, and eventually cope with that which troubles his fragile and vulnerable sense of being a person? This last aspect of Jaspers' structural outline of the role emotions play in psychopathology discloses, we would argue, the reason for his reluctance to formulate a theory of emotions. The question of responsibility is fundamental to psychotherapy, because the way in which a clinician answers this question in the form of her approach to care and therapy (drug prescription, explanatory models, diagnostic criteria, etc.) reveals her—more or less articulate—philosophical understanding of human nature. The therapeutic engagement, in other words, reveals how descriptive and clinical psychopathology cannot avoid—in the therapeutic procedure—employing a basic structural view on mental illness that depends on some conception of what it means to be a human person.

When it comes to understanding human nature and personal responsibility, emotions are perhaps the most notoriously obscure of our mental phenomena, and we believe that Jaspers' philosophical awareness of this obscurity is the reason for his ambivalence towards human emotions. As mentioned earlier, emotional experience remains at the heart of his thinking, but not even his explicit philosophical writings provide us with a theory of emotions. We do not believe that this is simply the result of a careless neglect on Jaspers' part. On the contrary, the unwillingness to construct an overall theory of emotion is part and parcel of the peculiar combination of philosophy and science that informs and shapes his thinking about human nature—in psychopathology as well as philosophy. Jaspers operates with what has been called an 'empiric-methodological Cartesianism' (Wiehl 2008, p. 15; see also Wiehl 2007) characterised by a strict distinction between scientific explanation (*Erklären*) and philosophical understanding (*Verstehen*). Without going into the long and complex debate about this methodological dualism in Jaspers thinking, we will simply note that while Jaspers acknowledges and respects the inescapable explanatory significance of the biological aspect of human nature, he nevertheless works with a philosophical conviction that the freedom and responsibility of every single human person is inexorable and plays a fundamental role in mental suffering (remember the enigmatic statement about personal responsibility above).

In the next section, we will explain how this 'anthropological dualism' (Wiehl 2008) makes a philosophical understanding of human nature impossible. This, in turn, will enable us to make sense of his ambivalent stance towards human emotions.

10.5 Human Nature and Emotional Experience

In Part Six, written for the fourth edition in 1946, Jaspers famously argues that we are faced with the obligation (*Forderung*) to integrate our knowledge of human nature with our psychopathological, because science demands a systematic and holistic approach (GP, pp. 748–750/625–626). The problem is, however, that this is not possible in a scientifically satisfactory way, since 'in the end being human [*Menschsein*] itself remains an open question, and so too does our knowledge of it' (GP, p. 749/626).

Jaspers was well aware that this refusal to provide a comprehensive theory might give rise to objections to his work, among which the most obvious would be that '[t]his psychopathology does not give any concretely united [*gegenständlich geschlossenes*] picture of the whole; everything is dismembered or else stands rigidly parallel. The multiplicity of the material and of the different approaches is confusing. No picture of the sick human being [*Menschseins*] emerges' (GP, p. 747/624). Jaspers explains the reasons for his approach as follows: (a) what counts is whether the differentiations between phenomena are sufficiently clear; (b) the non-systematic structure is motivated by a conscious rejection of succumbing to any one approach; and (c) he intends to oppose all dogmatic theories of being (*Seinsdogmatik*). In other words, we should not look for a systematic design of human emotional experience 'showing how everything we know has its place somewhere within this construct or as part of it' (GP, p. 748/625). Rather, what we need to organise, writes Jaspers, is '*the way we gain such knowledge*' (GP, p. 748/625). Jaspers adopts an eloquent metaphor: 'A synthesis is not like an outline [*Entwurf*] of a continent but more like an outline of possible ways to explore it' (GP, p. 749/626). What we need is a *method* rather than an 'ontological theory of human life' (GP, p. 749/626). Jaspers has epistemological as well as ethical reasons for his scepticism of strong metaphysical claims about emotions, and about human nature in general.[3] Since we can know human nature 'only through ourselves—that is only through our contact [*Umgang*] with human beings' (GP, p. 748/625), we cannot aspire to arrive at an utopian epistemological 'view from nowhere' from which we are able to construct a scientifically warranted theory of human nature. The best we can hope for is a critical awareness of ourselves and of the methods we adopt to establish this human contact is quintessential. And from an ethical perspective, whenever we generalise single observations trying to establish a general theory, we renounce on the individual expressions of freedom that we experience through the contact with each single person.

The question of responsibility remains the crux of any attempt to explain and understand what emotions really are, how they influence our thought and actions, and eventually how we should cope with our emotions—in health as well as in illness. This inescapable connection between emotions and responsibility means that any explanation of emotions always involves a basic understanding of human nature—even if this understanding is not clearly formulated. This can be illustrated if, for a moment, we turn to a fundamental debate in contemporary philosophy of emotions. This debate concerns what emotions really are, and it is conducted from the perspectives of two incompatible types of explanations. On the one hand, we find the so-called feeling theories (e.g. Prinz 2004; Damasio 2003) that argue for an explanation of human emotions in terms of core evolutionary themes (e.g. survival and reproduction) and physiological changes in our body. On the other, we have the so-called cognitive theories (e.g. Solomon 2007; Nussbaum 2001) arguing for an explanation in term of intentional structures and cognitive operations in the light of ethical and societal norms. The principal difference between the two approaches

---

[3] For a historically careful and admirably clear philosophical treatment of Jaspers' critical stance towards the philosophical anthropologies of his day, see Lehnert (2006).

is that the cognitive theories opt for a view of emotions as constituted primarily by personal factors, while the feeling theories advocate a picture of human emotions as primarily informed and shaped by cross-species, evolutionary themes and anonymous biological values. These two kinds of explanations of human emotions entail two fundamentally different pictures of what it means to be human. The cognitive theories present us with a conception of human nature as being primarily a person whose existence is informed and orientated primarily by rational strategies and ethical standards, while the feeling theories insist that a human being is simply a biological organism functioning on a par with every other living organism in nature that knows nothing of rationality or ethical ideals.

The gist of what it means to be human in the cognitive theories is expressed with unabashed vigour by the late Robert Solomon:

> [T]ypically, our emotions are both unplanned and more or less dictated by circumstances and it would make little sense to insist that we are responsible or ought to take responsibility for our emotional responses. But even so, there is a self-fulfilling prophecy involved here that cannot be easily denied [...] When we look into our emotional life with the idea that we are or might be responsible and ask ourselves those probing questions, "what am I doing this for?" "What am I getting out of this?" we often see aspects of our strategic behavior that would otherwise escape us. By contrast, if we look into our emotional life with the idea that our emotions are forces beyond our control that happen to us, we are prone to make excuses for ourselves and resign ourselves to bad and destructive behavior that otherwise might be controlled. (Solomon 2007, p. 199)

This picture of a human being as a person ultimately responsible for his or her emotions is countered by Jesse Prinz, who argues for a biological understanding of human nature. Prinz does not deny that human beings are moral creatures, nor does he reject the inherent relation between emotions and moral values. In fact, he goes further than most cognitive theorists of emotions would be prepared to go by arguing bluntly that 'moral values are emotional values' (Prinz 2012, p. 329). On Prinz' account, however, emotions are not constituted by our cognitive engagement with the world, but by pre-reflective somatic signals in the physiological landscape of the body; or to put it differently, for Prinz, 'somatic signals are both necessary and sufficient for emotions' (Prinz 2007, p. 60). Emotions have their own impersonal life, and just as each person has her individual bodily constitution, shaped by core evolutionary themes and more proximate cultural factors, so her basic emotional constitution is developed in ways that are out of her control. A person may simply have what Prinz calls 'a calibration file for amusement that contains representations of others' misfortune'. The automatic function of such an emotional calibration leads him to conclude that emotional experience and emotional responses cannot be assessed or evaluated by the obfuscated ideas of personal responsibility, let alone by ethical standards:

> It is not wrong to feel amusement when one encounters something that matches the contents of your amusement file. Nor is it right. Once a calibration file has been set up, we cannot help but react to its contents. This is one source of emotional passivity. The response to items in our calibration files is automatic, and falls outside the jurisdiction or normative assessment [...] There is a sense in which the most heinous passion is as innocent as seeing an afterimage. (Prinz 2004, p. 240)

Our intention with this brief excursion into a contemporary debate in philosophy of emotion is to show that explaining human emotions involves a conception of what human nature is that, as we have seen, Jaspers believes lies beyond the scope of human understanding.

10.6   Conclusion: Responsibility and Personal Suffering

As we have already seen, Jaspers is sceptical of attempts to arrive at a comprehensive theory of human nature. In fact, a central pillar in his philosophy is exactly that an individual human being can never be explained by a general theory. The individual is a unique person who thinks, feels, and behaves in ways that escape our attempts to understand that individual through a theoretical approach. We may explain the particular aspects of an individual person, but we may never fool ourselves into believing that such explanations can lead us to an understanding of that person:

> The human being as a whole never becomes an object of understanding [Erkenntnis]. Being human [Menschsein] cannot be systematised. Whatever the complex unity in which we think we have caught a human being, he himself has always escaped us. All knowledge of the individual has its own particular aspect; it always demonstrates one reality but not the reality of human nature. It is knowledge in suspense and not final. (GP, p. 767/641)

What is at work here is Jaspers' notorious 'theorem of incomprehensibility' (Baeyer 1979) that Wolfgang Blankenburg has elegantly explained in the following way: 'Where understanding ends, nature begins—be that in physiological form (e.g. fatigue or sleep) or in pathological processes (i.e. in form of an illness that destroys the life of the mind [Seelenleben]. In short: Where understanding ends, we have to explain' (Blankenburg 1986, p. 143).

Jaspers approaches human nature with what has been called a 'methodological particularism' (Rinofner-Kreidl 2008). This approach, he believes, is particularly warranted in psychopathology, where the suffering person risks becoming a mere 'object for medical interference [Objekt ärztlicher Einwirkung] in the sense that all behaviour [Tun] is considered a means to an end', that is to say, in our capacity of trained clinicians and psychotherapists we are always in risk of neglecting the experience of the patient, in particular if we treat the person 'according to certain fundamental opinions about human beings (that normally remain obscure), according to conventional rules and common ideas about what is desirable, what is useful, and about human happiness' (Jaspers 1956, p. 125). By turning the suffering person into an object for medical explanation, we have already implicitly decided upon the extent to which that person can be held responsible for his or her suffering. We thereby explain away the autonomy of suffering and occlude the fragile dialectics of rationality and biology at the heart of mental disorders. The person's responsibility for his or her illness is always an open question that cannot be understood, but can only be approached in a careful exchange with the patient. We must, in other words, respect that human suffering is ultimately incomprehensible due to the obscure complexity of biology and rationality in human nature, while constantly trying to improve our understanding and explanation of what it means to suffer. In this way, the 'theorem of incomprehensibility' can be understood as Jaspers' attempt to safeguard the autonomy of the suffering person, without neglecting that a person's sense of responsibility becomes severely disrupted in mental disorders.

Where does this leave us with regard to Jaspers' ambivalence concerning emotions and emotional experience in the GP? Now, as we have seen, there are few aspects of human experience and behaviour that warrant the 'theorem of incomprehensibility' as evidently as that of feelings and affective states.

First, explaining emotional experience in terms of a theory of emotions entails an understanding—be that articulated or not—of human nature. Jaspers thinks that such an understanding is impossible. To understand a person in the light of a theory would imply objectifying human complexity and sacrificing the individual person to our own norm of what a person is supposed to be or should be. What we need, according to Jaspers, is not an all-encompassing theory, but much more modestly a palette with different shades of colour that may allow the clinician to recognise the kind, the tonality, and the intensity of emotional experience at play in the single individual.

Second, emotions are the most embodied of our mental phenomena. We must acknowledge that it is close to impossible when it comes to emotional experience to disentangle what is purely biological (thus un-understandable) from what is affected by our intentional and cognitive capacities.

Third, emotional experience is intimately subjective. Feelings may be irrational, stupid, alienating, or inappropriate, but still they are part of who we are. They are inescapable part of our character and thus that which makes us the unique individual that we are. Also, feelings are closely related to personal values and societal norms. All this makes them particularly difficult to handle from the perspective of an objective approach.

Fourth, the question of responsibility becomes explicit with regard to emotional experience. Formulating a theory of emotions would necessarily mean taking a stance with regard to the extent to which a suffering person can be said to be responsible for her emotions. The question of the responsibility of the person in front of her emotions must remain open. No general theory can help us understand the concrete individual existence of a human person, i.e. what 'the real, living existence of a human being' (Jaspers 1956, p. 19). Nobody can choose her emotions, nonetheless, at least in some cases, we can decide whether to act accordingly to an emotion or not. The possibility (or impossibility) to decide depends on the proportion between the quality and the intensity of an emotion and the person's capacity to cope with it and make sense of it. This proportion, or disproportion, depends on many *personal* factors that escape an impersonal theory and conceptualisation, as for instance life-history, cultural and intellectual individual resources, personal values, present situation, societal constraints, etc.

Fifth, and most important, understanding the other person's troubled emotional experience is not just an epistemological problem that can be solved relying on a general theory that does the job for us. Making sense of the other person's suffering is an *ethical* problem that necessarily implies feeling and being responsible for the way *I* as a clinician understand it.

References

Baeyer, W. R. v. (1979). *Wähnen und Wahn.* Stuttgart: Enke.
Blankenburg, W. (1986). Unausgeschöpftes in der Psychopathologie von Karl Jaspers. In J. Hersch, J. M. Lochman, & R. Wiehl (Eds.), *Karl Jaspers: Philosoph, Arzt, Politischer Denker* (pp. 127–160). Munich: Piper.
Damasio, A. R. (2003). *Looking for Spinoza. Joy, sorrow, and the feeling brain.* New York: Harcourt.
de Sousa, R. (2011). *Emotional truth.* Oxford: Oxford University Press.
Fuchs, T. (2000). *Leib, Raum, Person. Entwurf einer phänomenologischen Anthropologie.* Stuttgart: Klett-Cotta.
Goldie, P. (2000). *The emotions: A philosophical exploration.* Oxford: Oxford University Press.
Gross, G., & Huber, G. (1993). Do we still need psychopathology, and if so, which psychopathology? *Neurology, Psychiatry and Brain Research, 1,* 194–200.
Jaspers, K. (1950). *Vernunft und Widervernunft in unserer Zeit.* Munich: Piper.
Jaspers, K. (1951). Zur Kritik der Psychoanalyse. In K. Jaspers (Ed.), *Rechenschaft und Ausblick: Reden und Aufsätze* (pp. 221–230). Munich: Piper.
Jaspers, K. (1956). *Philosophie. Band I: Weltorientierung.* Berlin: Springer.
Jaspers, K. (1959). *Allgemeine Psychopathologie,* 7. unveränderte Aufl. Berlin: Springer. English edition: Jaspers, K. (1997). *General Psychopathology* (trans: Hoenig, J., & Hamilton, M. W.). Baltimore: Johns Hopkins University Press.
Kirkbright, S. (2008). Ein kritischer Vergleich zwischen den verschiedenen Ausgaben von Karl Jaspers' Allgemeine Psychopathologie. In S. Rinofner-Kreidl & H. A. Wiltsche (Eds.), *Karl Jaspers' Allgemeine Psychopathologie zwischen Wissenschaft, Philosophie und Praxis* (pp. 21–29). Würzburg: Königshausen & Neumann.
Lantéri-Laura, G. (1985). Psychopathologie et processus. *L'Évolution Psychiatrique, 50*(3), 589–610.
Lehnert, E. (2006). *Die Existenz als Grenze des Wissens. Grundzüge einer Kritik der philosophischen Anthropologie bei Karl Jaspers.* Würzburg: Ergon.
Nussbaum, M. C. (2001). *Upheavals of thought: The intelligence of emotions.* Cambridge: Cambridge University Press.
Oyebode, F. (2008). *Sims' symptoms in the mind: An introduction to descriptive psychopathology.* New York: Saunders Elsevier.
Prinz, J. J. (2004). *Gut reactions: A perceptual theory of emotion.* New York: Oxford University Press.
Prinz, J. J. (2007). *The emotional construction of morals.* Oxford: Oxford University Press.
Prinz, J. J. (2012). *Beyond human nature: How culture and experience shape our lives.* London: Allen Lane.
Pugmire, D. (1998). *Rediscovering emotion.* Edinburgh: Edinburgh University Press.
Ratcliffe, M. (2008). *Feelings of being: Phenomenology, psychiatry and the sense of reality.* Oxford: Oxford University Press.
Rinofner-Kreidl, S. (2008). Zur Idee des Methodenpartikularismus in Jaspers' Psychopathologie. In S. Rinofner-Kreidl & H. A. Wiltsche (Eds.), *Karl Jaspers' Allgemeine Psychopathologie zwischen Wissenschaft, Philosophie und Praxis* (pp. 75–93). Würzburg: Königshausen & Neumann.
Rossi Monti, M., & Stanghellini, G. (1996). Psychopathology: An edgeless razor? *Comprehensive Psychiatry, 37,* 196–204.
Scheler, M. (1966). *Der Formalismus in der Ethik und die materiale Wertethik. Gesammelte Werke. Bd. 2.* Bern: Francke Verlag.
Schneider, K. (1967). *Klinische Psychopathologie* (8th ed.). Stuttgart: Georg Thieme Verlag.
Schmitz, H. (1992). *Leib und Gefühl. Materialen zu einer philosophischen Therapeutik* (2nd ed.). Paderborn: Junfermann.

Solomon, R. C. (2007). *True to our feelings: What our emotions are really telling us*. New York: Oxford University Press.

Stanghellini, G. (1997a). *Antropologia della vulnerabilità*. Milano: Feltrinelli.

Stanghellini, G. (1997b). For an anthropology of vulnerability. *Psychopathology, 30*(1), 1–11.

Stanghellini, G. (2009). The meanings of psychopathology. *Current Opinion in Psychiatry, 22*(6), 559–564.

Stanghellini, G., & Rosfort, R. (in press). *Emotions and personhood: Exploring fragility—Making sense of vulnerability*. Oxford: Oxford University Press.

Stanghellini, G., Fulford, K. W. M., & Bolton, D. (forthcoming). Resources for a person-centered 2 of schizophrenia. Building on Karl Jaspers' understanding of the patient's attitude towards his illness. *Schizophrenia Bulletin*.

Stocker, M. (1996). (with Hegeman, E.) *Valuing emotions*. Cambridge: Cambridge University Press.

Strasser, S. (1956). *Das Gemüt: Grundgedanken zu einer phänomenologischen Philosophie und Theorie des menschlichen Gefühlsleben*. Freiburg: Verlag Herder.

Wiehl, R. (2007). Philosophie und Wissenschaft bei Karl Jaspers. *Jahrbuch der Österreichischen Karl Jaspers Gesellschaft, 20*, 9–30.

Wiehl, R. (2008). Die Philosophie in Karl Jaspers' Allgemeine Psychopathologie. In K. Eming & T. Fuchs (Eds.), *Karl Jaspers—Philosophie und Psychopathologie* (pp. 3–18). Heidelberg: Winter.

Chapter 11
Jaspers Concept of "Limit Situation": Extensions and Therapeutic Applications

Christoph Mundt

11.1 Introduction

The interest in Jaspers' concept of limit situation was aroused by the conceptual debate about precipitations of psychiatric syndromes, particularly depressive episodes as a model of limit situations, and their prevention (cf. Mundt et al. 2009). British Psychiatry emphasized the objectifying approach up to an ultimate conceptual restriction of life events to entries and exits in the life history of a person. These criteria were the most reliable ones predicting onset or in case of "fresh start events" remission of depression. Opposite to the 3rdPP of those studies, the phenomenological approach took the 1stPP on patients' strivings or specific apprehensions. The two perspectives relate to each other in a complementary way.

Over the last 10 years, Jaspers' concept of limit situation has been re-evaluated under psychopathological, psychological, and psychotherapeutic aspects. This treatise will comprise those reformulations which help to elucidate the detrimental impact of life events and lasting distressing life situations on mental health. Furthermore it is meant to contribute to better understanding of the salutogenetic mechanisms of psychotherapeutic crisis intervention. Also limits of the concept will be discussed for its use in clinical context. Since the term was not conceived for psychopathological but for philosophical use, adaptation to psychopathological and psychotherapeutic terms was needed. Furthermore, its limits as a concept of understanding psychopathology had to be determined.

According to Jaspers (1954, pp. 229–280, 416–418; 1965; 1973) limit situations are characterized by inevitable antinomies which prevent a person going on as usual. A personal solution is necessary to accustom which implies change or development. Jaspers' typing of limit situations declares them as super-individual challenges intrinsic to existence, thus unavoidable, and requiring a personal

C. Mundt (✉)
University of Heidelberg, Voßstr. 4, 69115, Heidelberg, Germany
e-mail: christoph.mundt@med.uni-heidelberg.de

T. Fuchs et al. (eds.), *Karl Jaspers' Philosophy and Psychopathology*,
DOI 10.1007/978-1-4614-8878-1_11, © Springer Science+Business Media New York 2014

response which engenders maturation. In a first approach, four, later five, categories were conceived.

11.2 The Antinomies

Fight is defined as the necessity to take a decision in contradictious constellations
or highly ambivalent states of mind. As an example, Jaspers mentions individual
freedom be basically limited by the freedom of the other. Without fighting, the
individual, according to Jaspers, runs into complacency, i.e., relinquishes potential
development. We could add: or falls into depression if developmental potential of
the person is wasted.

Jaspers says that fight usually is disliked, misperceived as an ultimate action as
though the fight for the sake of fighting should be appreciated. However, fight for
the concrete existence is unavoidable. Man lives but is doomed to die, needs to se-
lect, to overcome or reconcile contentions. Since living without fight is impossible,
fight lends dignity and strength to the individual.

Guilt is another central aporia leading to limit situations since any human being
has to leave options aside while acting in any decision whatsoever. Jaspers refers
here not so much to ethical problems we deal with in our ethical committees or in
forensic psychiatry but to existential guilt, i.e., lagging behind one's own abilities
and aspirations. Augustine, Luther, and Kierkegaard were particularly aware of existential guilt. Guilt out of antinomies is experienced silently. It makes a difference
whether man confronts himself or others, or judges himself in an absolute way.
Several social procedures of pre-emptive redemption have been introduced in different religions to heal this existential guilt inflicted upon oneself by the alter ego.
Jaspers considers several dualistic systems of guilt, as remorse, forgiving, and the
penitential systems of religions as attempts to relieve existential guilt. The psychopathology of delusional guilt in some severe depressive states demonstrates a great
deal of these tormenting phenomena (Tellenbach 1980).

Jaspers made a separate category of *haphazard* (also translated as incident,
chance, accident, coincidence). He says the world is both at random and necessarily
given, chaotic and coherent. Again religions have tried to overcome these antinomies, i.e., by the Christian belief in predestination.

To the better or worse, haphazard may influence human fate. It is suffered not
constellated and it requires taking a stance. By posing the unforeseen, it forces
the individual to decide, to use the freedom left to exert will and constitute value.
Trauma research has evidenced that it matters whether it is man-made or caused incidentally (Fiedler 2008). Man-made torture seems to be different from the category
of limit situation by a haphazard accident. Severe trauma can reduce the capability
of a person to cope with a situation to a degree that the ability to respond positively
is no longer pertained.

Death respectively *finality in life* and *of life* is another category of limit situation. It is the contrast to striving, endeavor, development, and reproduction. Jaspers

has conceived this category in a radical sense implying not only individual but also finality of mankind and the universe. It is with this category of limit situation that a political notion can be felt in Jaspers writings when he acknowledges the soldier's fear of death as existential limit situation as if it were not man-made. This notion probably arisen vis-à-vis the World War I may be seen critically today. Finality as such and imminent death as a natural entity are existential limit conditions; death posed by politics is not intrinsic to existence.

The category of *suffering* (pathos) originally was meant by Jaspers to be part of all other categories. Later it was conceived as a separate, independent, and predominant category. Its meaning gravitates about the Greek term pathos, i.e., existential forms of passivity, being the object not active part in a process. Suffering or pathos in this sense is an existential feature not evadable, suspended to a certain degree but never absolutely in self-efficacious acting. Jaspers concludes that man generally dies before his objectives are finalized. One may cope with this limit condition rather than situation by believing in eternal life or by negating all meaning and purpose in a stance of nihilism.

There are paradigmatic ways of reacting to these antinomian structures of existence: insecurity, denial, or several forms of evading Man's foremost way to protect himself against limit situations is the accommodation or even retreat in a "protective shelter" (my home is my castle). Jaspers uses this metaphor to characterize the role of religious faith and ideological convictions, personal styles of living, and protective relationships to put off limit situations. He calls this type of existence to "crawl under" in a "stronghold within boundaries" because this type of existence has to pay off with restricted development. The term expresses contempt since Jaspers considers the challenge of limit situations to be taken. Limit situations destroy the home and make it uninhabitable. Jaspers uses the metaphor of a mussel that has lost its shell. Limit situations according to Jaspers enlighten the paradoxical structure of existence and they call for what has been named existential turn up, i.e., to reach a higher level of self-awareness and depth of feeling in case the limit situation is mastered.

11.3 Transfer to Psychopathology and Psychotherapy

Phenomenologically oriented psychopathologists have resumed Jaspers concept with different transcriptions to particular syndromes. The standard limit situation stipulated by Tellenbach (1980) for the entry into melancholic depression is the lagging behind one's self set standards and being hemmed in these standards unable to modify or question them. The protecting mussel shell then turns to a prison.

Another equivalent paradigmatic failure to master a limit situation in psychoses may be the principal indeterminacy of the definition of interpersonally exchanged meaning exemplified, e.g., in language disorders of psychotic patients. The indeterminacy of meaning of any language as manifested in translation (Quine 1960; Schönknecht and Mundt 2013) is not a fault or mishap but essential to the creative use of language. Schizophrenia patients with their under-structured perceptive, cognitive, and emotional organization may lose track of common sense meaning if addressed with a multiply determined joke or irony in a conversation as in the comprehensive context of existential challenges, a paradigmatic limit situation.

11.4   From the Static to the Dynamic Model of Situation in Psychopathology

Glatzel (1978) has presented a little known concept of interactional psychopathology which attributes to the social other (partner, work mate, psychotherapist) some co-responsibility for the patient's limit situation both in causing and healing. Furthermore he suggested a dynamic model of limit situation influenced by gestalt psychological principles consisting of four stages. Situation in this sense is not "outside" the self but merges perception and intention to a unity of these two components. On a first stage, restriction of meaningful perceptual elements sharpens the focus in case of pathological development, i.e., to a delusional perception. On a second stage, the delusional definition of the situation loses the future bound openness of perception and intention. On a third stage, the situation becomes a monothematic paranoid complex and on the fourth stage the definition of situation loses its perceptual common sense context and becomes definitely delusional.

The turn from static to dynamic models of situation differentiates impression, expression, and dynamics. This model implies a circular impressive–expressive process open for both suffering and intentional acting (cf. Weizsäcker's concept of "gestalt circle," i.e., the interdependence of acting and perceiving; Weizsäcker 1940). In contrast Schneider (1976) conceived situation as the entirety of its factual features perceived in a one way communication by the patient.

Phenomenological authors emphasize the intuitive notion of a situation (in Schmoll and Kuhlmann 2005): The notion of details implies the whole (Blankenburg); protentions are deflected by the unexpected gaze (Husserl); the practically relevant world of values predetermines the notion of situations (Scheler); situation as unity is a creation in which the private floats along the common sense (Heidegger); there is no private reality, situation always entails private and common world, conjunction of meaning and acting (Arnold Gehlen).

Other philosophers emphasize the political notion of limit situations and their implications for individual and collective acting. World War I may have inspired them as Jaspers possibly was. Simmel spoke of 'absolute situation' ('kein wenn und aber,' no turn or twist, straight forward); each generation gets their own 'situation' (Hans Lipps); he differentiates situation vs. setting (-site-condition-state of affairs); the historian philosopher Rothacker differentiates the objective and perceived situation; and permanent situations and permanent answers to them. Plessner emphasizes the timeliness of dealing with a situation, the occasion to join in to "master" the situation, its "eternal unpermeability." Bollnow defines situation as an existential constraint to be corrected and dissolved: as body in a surrounding, as person in a plight, only as existence in a situation; what is needed to be rescued is shelter, abatement, and patience. Merleau-Ponty considers existence as making the factual situation one's own, situation being open to interpretation, needing explication and personal appropriation. Habermas stipulates that the common sense world is always intuitively present as a source for definitions of situations. The latter are salient to the perception by topics and aims for acting. Habermas has been criticized for neglecting the pre-reflective, diffuse knowledge of situations and their handling. Schmitz has suggested a classification of situations which unfolds a spectrum of very different challenges emerging from them: diffuse, chaotic, sharply profiled, variegated ones. Drawing on Heidegger he emphasizes the importance of their signal significance as availability ("Zuhandenheit") and signal function as seduction or prestige. Schmitz also discriminates situations according to their content-related significance like impressive situations experienced, i.e., while travelling, they are entire-diffuse or in contrast segmented, never to be grasped as a whole at a time. This latter statement in turn is contrasted by Blankenburg: The whole of the situation is always co-represented and perceived in the detail of situation (Schmitz 2005).

Schmidt-Degenhardt emphasizes the complexity of situation and considers it as possibly bridging the gap endogenous-reactive. Furthermore, he adopts Lewin's field theory as a tool to disentangle person, world, and situation and yet taking them as a functional unity which contrasts Jaspers separation of person and situation. Referring to Weizsäcker and Zacher, he also pays attention to psychosomatic disorders as a signal of "the truth of the unconscious" which may indicate the "unlived life," i.e., a situation desired but over since not used when due. A critical aspect of Schmidt-Degenhard's phenomenological work—similar to Binswanger's—may be that situation is highlighted entirely from the perspective of ambivalence, jeopardy of integrity, overwhelming affect but not as a psychotherapeutic tool with the perspective of growth, consolation, and liberation.

The most elaborate dynamic model of limit situation was presented by Kick and Dietz (Dietz and Kick 2005; Kick and Dietz 2008). They discriminate three phases: In the first phase, the challenge of novel ways of behavior is still buffered by convention or repression, evading, and symptoms. In the second phase, the actual crisis intensifies ambivalences and despair. Retreat, reactive down regulation of feelings, or engagement may give relief and some security. The so-called life-serving barriers—pain, shame, despise, and moral or conscientiousness—guide the transition to the third phase of either manifest psychopathology or restructuring with new values. This sequence has been exemplified by the authors by referring to ancient Greek mythology.

Fuchs (2009) differentiates two different applications of the term *Grenzsituation*: trauma and normal healthy life. In trauma the edifice is broken, existence is without shelter. In normal life, daily living may become an ordeal: "Existential vulnerability." This is particularly visible in schizophrenia patients. Hyper-reflexivity in schizophrenia patients is known as an attempt to compensate for the lack of intuitive pre-reflective common sense. Fuchs speaks of reduced limit situation competency. Withdrawal does not help either since disengagement reduces existence: the "engagement calamity" (Kaegi 2009). Life without development is not conceivable (Cesana 2009), it is unlimited, inconclusive, not to be resolved with objective knowledge. Cesana objects Jaspers' thesis that limit situations are intrinsic to existence and came to awareness already at the beginning of self-reflexive cultural life (Achsenzeit). He attributes it to our specific historical cultural state in Western Europe.

Another paradigm of psychopathology in and by limit situations is the psychosomatic manifestation of symptoms. Following Weizsäcker, Stoffels (2005) spoke of the "faltering of the body" as an equivalent of faltering of the mind in limit situations specifically toxic to the patient. The dedicated clinician opposed the philosopher psychiatrist Jaspers that existential turn up could be brought about by mere self-reflection. He claimed that it needs acting as well, otherwise the process of change gets stuck. This stipulation also applies to the psychoanalytic procedure.

Are limit-situations pacemakers for therapeutic change in the sense of Jaspers' concept of potential enlightenment emerging from the situation? Video-recorded psychotherapeutic sessions support the notion that transference actions which come to mind by a coincidence of procedural and declarative notion can induce lasting change of interaction patterns. Also mirroring of affects repressed by the patient but felt by proxy through the therapist can induce lasting change (Krause 2009). One may consider these therapeutic moments as provoked micro limit situations.

11.5   Trauma: Part or Counter-Part of Limit Situation?

There are extreme forms of harming the self, the existence, which go beyond what is usually subsumed under the heading "trauma". The extreme experiences of concentration camp survivors describe the "ego being reduced to itself, its pure closed stream of consciousness; life with its living and material objects is excluded" (Segev 2009), an attitude responding to the situation and trying to protect the remaining self-parts to survive, perhaps similar to a stoic position. Segev rejects the importance and existential force of death as almost celebrated according to his view by Heidegger, Jünger, and also Gadamer in his late work. Segev holds against the relevance of death saying that in concentration camps only dying is relevant, not death. There is fear of certain ways of dying but not of death. Death he claims is an "empty term" in concentration camp. It is much more the loss of dignity and significance, the enforced abiding with utter humiliation that causes what he called "wrath of existence." Jean Amery (1976) a survivor too who wrote a monograph on suicide decided by himself when to die. It may be experienced as the ultimate dignity after what concentration camp survivors have gone through.

Research with holocaust victims described an unease of many survivors with existential philosophical terms being applied to existing in a concentration camp. Not death but dignity is the point, they say. Hence philosophical categories which signify living under fairly free conditions although distressing, i.e., by facing vital decisions may appear as barren and alien to them (Segev 2009; Amery 1976).

Modern trauma research claims that trauma results from dissociation not from the situation or an objectively measurable life event (Fiedler 2008). First an intended forgetting is attempted along with a hypnoid way of dealing with the trauma reminiscences, e.g., in BPD patients. Intended forgetting can successfully be done but often fails and engenders states of dissociation. Fiedler parallels trauma and limit situation to a certain degree without referring to it. There are three overlapping concepts:

1. being caught in a situation not constellated by the victim;
2. the situation is an aporia, i.e., it can happen to anybody and there is no escape;
3. it makes the victim loose her edifice (habitation).

Also Fiedler develops the concept of trauma entirely out of the phenomenon of dissociation. He considers dissociation as an advantage to survive trauma. Typical constellations according to his literature survey are life threat, resistance, wish for support, but no way out. Feelings of loss, threat, punishment precede dissociation.

Vinar and Vinar (1997) have specified trauma by torture: It is done intentionally by humans not by blind nature; it may make the victims disappear as in Chile; it extinguishes the victims' social existence including knowledge of their suffering and plea; if torture happens in conjunction with genocide this is even intensified; and if a response should be elicited by torture, the responsibility for the suffering is allocated to the victim. The authors describe sequelae down to the third generation with submissive attitudes, with frequent alienation proceeding to dissociative states, and extremely low self-esteem. Humiliation has been shown to be more harming than natural catastrophes which were not intended by men, elicit compassion and support, and do not wreck trust in humans in general. Particularly harming is sequential traumatization which reinforces generalized expectancies and the vegetative hyper-reactivity to stress. Ameliorating factor may be a sense of coherence, personal influence, and acknowledgement of the suffering (Müller-Hohagen 1997; Andreatt 2006).

Although there are transitions, the extreme trauma by torture should be differentiated from limit situation:

- Trauma is experienced as constellation (Glatzel 1976) not as situation which would be entangled with the experiencing individual by co-constituting.
- The quality of subjective experience is severely damaged, in particular the qualities of mine-ness, self-hood, agency, same-ness, identity.
- Dissociation manifests the lack of mutual molding between subject and situation. And continuous spells of dissociation keep this interdependence being disrupted.
- Damage of subjectivity ensues from these criteria to a degree that prevents the existential stimulus of a limit situation reaching a subject as sustaining as to be able to use the challenge for an existential turn up in the sense of Jaspers.

11.6   "Soft" Limit Situations: Walking the Line by Travelling and Art

Jens Clausen (2007) has collected reports about reactive psychotic episodes in conjunction with travelling. He comprises his findings in 13 hypotheses. Several of them hover about the loss of acquainted routine, the unaccustomed language, alien patterns of conventions and behavior in daily living, and loss of protective bonding. It makes a difference whether the traveler wants to stay or soon will return, whether there are reliable bonds at home to be expected upon return or emigration is definitive (cf. the emigration triggered exacerbation of psychoses in Ödegaard's studies of the 1970s). However, the self may as well undergo a change to its advantage and gain complexity or it may reassure provincial prejudice. Over-identification occurs as ridiculous and as a failure to master this limit situation as avoiding indulgence would be. Psycho-pathological crises abroad are double alienations undermining the integrity of the self twofold: by the host culture and by the illness. Travelling may be a paradigm for hu-man life in general being a continued limit situation given the vulnerable openness of human mind which we have to pay off with for the gift of changeability and creativity.

In post-structuralism, the paradigm of travelling serves as a technique of tamed alienation (Rotzoll 2009). Since limit situations set off change and development man is attracted by them as well as intimidated. Trespassing the border to novel experiences may incidentally happen or was purportedly sought under drug influ-ence, i.e., by Baudelaire for poetry, some painters of the Collection Prinzhorn for painting, and so-called automatic writing by surrealists. Alfred Kubin is an example that this stimulated soft limit situation may transmute to mannerism instead to real creativity (Rotzoll 2009).

11.7   Summary and Conclusion

Point of departure for this overview on Jaspers' term limit situation and the psy-chopathological aftermath was the finding that situations with specific toxicity for vulnerable individuals can set off psychiatric illness. Opposite to the quantitative life event research Jaspers' existential view refers to the first-person-perspective psychopathology and opens a perspective for psychotherapy. Personality and situa-tion merge in one context. Even the premorbid personality can be obsessed by antic-ipating a specific limit situation. The attempt to prevent it may restrict the personal development and yet be not even successful towards an "acquiescence of being."

Psychopathological and psychotherapeutic research have transformed Jaspers' rather static philosophical concept into a clinical and dynamic process model. There are many psychopathological equivocations to Jaspers' term "Gehäuse" which we have translated as edifice. In psychopathology neurotic defense mechanisms refer to it, Reich's concept of character shield is an equivocation, and psychotic autism represents a specific pathological manifestation of it. The paradigms of travelling and art in particular the mannered branches and surrealism cultivate controlled alienation as a means to generate creativity.

Trauma research suggests that certain traumata as torture need to be segregated from the concept of limit situations since in these conditions the subject is harmed to an extent which prevents constructive or even defensive dealing with those extreme situations. The subject addressed by this type of limit situation is no longer apt to respond to it in a meaningful way enabling "existential turn up" and development ("Seinsaufschwung").

Critique of Jaspers' concept of limit situation may put forward the following theses:

- The social other needs to be conceived and analyzed as an acting part in antinomies, the one of freedom foremost, also death and finality as examples of man-made not necessarily intrinsic existential limit situations. Death is of course universal and existentially given but man caused killing is different from natural death in that it asks for responsibility and liability.
- By considering the social other as mediator of limit situations psychiatry would include the most relevant source of precipitating crises as well as for finding a way out of them by relational resources.
- The social and political dimension of limit situation could be integrated, again with the aspect of limit situations man made to others.
- The psychotherapeutic setting could gain insight by using transference crises as guided soft limit situations. The same applies to affect by proxy or "now moments" of coinciding procedural and declarative insight in behavioral fallacies to be focus of attention in psychotherapy. Jaspers' restrictive attitude to psychotherapy and his hierarchical concept of the therapeutic relationship prevented him to follow up this strain.
- Guided chaos is a chance for fresh start. In somatic medicine "crisis" was and is an ambiguous state turning to the better or worse (cf. Schnitzler's theatre play "Dr. Bernhardi"), in psychopathology the "turning point" (John Strauss) or fresh start event in life event research on depression, in cultural life the confrontation with novel views and styles of thinking and perceiving by travelling and exposing oneself to the unforeseeable.

References

Amery, J. (1976). *Hand an sich legen*. Stuttgart: Klett-Cotta.

Andreatt, M. P. (2006). *Die Erschütterung des Selbst- und Weltverständnisses durch Traumata. Auswirkungen von primärer und sekundärer Traumaexposition auf kognitive Schemata.* Kröning: Asanger.

Cesana, A. (2009). Selbstsein. Jaspers` Philosophie der Existenz und der Prozess der Subjektivierung. In A. Hügli, D. Kaegi, B. Weidmann (Eds.), *Existenz und Sinn. Karl Jaspers im Kontext* (pp. 73–94). Heidelberg: Winter.

Clausen, J. (2007). *Das Selbst und die Fremde. Über psychische Grenzerfahrungen auf Reisen.* Bonn: Psychiatrie-Verlag.

Dietz, G., & Kick, H. (Eds.).(2005). *Grenzsituation und neues Ethos. Von Homers Weltsicht zum modernen Weltbild*. Heidelberg: Winter.

Fiedler, P. (2008). *Dissozitive Störungen und Konversion. Trauma und Traumabehandlung.* Weinheim: Beltz.

Fuchs, T. (2009). Existentielle Vulnerabilität. Ansätze zu einer Psychopathologie der Grenzsituationen. In A. Hügli, D. Kaegi, B. Weidmann (Eds.), *Existenz und Sinn. Karl Jaspers im Kontext* (pp. 37–56). Heidelberg: Winter.

Glatzel, J. (1976). Zum Begriff „Situation" in der Psychopathologie. *Archiv für Psychiatrie und Nervenkrankheiten, 221*, 361–368.

Glatzel, J. (1978). *Allgemeine Psychopathologie.* Stuttgart: Enke.

Jaspers, K. (1954). *Psychologie der Weltanschauung* (4th ed.). Berlin, Göttingen, Heidelberg: Springer.

Jaspers, K. (1965). *Allgemeine Psychopathologie* (8th ed.). Berlin, Heidelberg, New York: Springer.

Jaspers, K. (1973). *Philosophie: Band II. Existenzerhellung* (4th ed.). Heidelberg: Springer.

Kaegi, D. (2009). Leiden als Grenzsituation. In A. Hügli, D. Kaegi, B. Weidmann (Eds.), *Existenz und Sinn. Karl Jaspers im Kontext* (pp. 57–71). Heidelberg: Winter.

Kick, H., & Dietz, G. (Eds.). (2008). *Verzweiflung als kreative Herausforderung. Psychopathologie, Psychotherapie und künstlerische Lösungsgestalt in Literatur, Musik und Film.* Berlin: Lit.

Krause, R. (2009). Psychodynamische Intervention. In M. Hautzinger & P. Pauli (Eds.), *Enzyklopädie der Psychologie: Band 2. Psychotherapeutische Methoden* (pp. 161–222). Göttingen: Hogrefe.

Müller-Hohagen, J. (1997). Auf den Spuren des Traumas. Perspektiven aus der praktischen psychologischen Arbeit. In W. Wirtgen (Ed.), *Trauma. Wahrnehmen des Unsagbaren. Psychopathologie und Handlungsbedarf* (pp. 39–58). Heidelberg: Asanger.

Mundt, Ch., Schroeder, A., & Backenstrass, M. (2009). Altruism versus self-centredness in the personality of depressives in the 1950s and 1990s. *Journal of Affective Disorders, 113*, 157–164.

Quine, W. v. O. (1960). *Word and object.* Cambridge: MIT Press.

Rotzoll, M. (2009). Perlen aus „kranken Muscheln"? Die Bedeutung des „Wahnsinns" für das „Genie" in Selbstzeugnissen von Künstlern aus dem frühen 20. Jahrhundert. In D. v. Engelhardt & H.-G. Gerigk (Eds.), *Karl Jaspers im Schnittpunkt von Zeitgeschichte, Psychopathologie, Literatur und Film* (pp. 345–373). Heidelberg: Mattes Verlag.

Schmitz, H. (2005). Was ist ein Phänomen? In D. Schmoll & A. Kuhlmann (Eds.), *Symptom und Phänomen. Phänomenologische Zugänge zum kranken Menschen* (pp. 16–28). Freiburg: Alber.

Schmoll, D., & Kuhlmann, A. (Eds.). (2005). *Symptom und Phänomen.* Freiburg: Alber.

Schneider, K. (1976). *Klinische Psychopathologie* (11th ed.) Stuttgart: Thieme.

Schönknecht, P., & Mundt, Ch. (2013). Quine's indeterminacy of translation and the schizophrenic basic disturbance. *Psychopathology, 46*(2), 88–93.

Segev, A. (2009). Die Wut der Existenz – ein phänomenologisches Experiment im KZ. In A. Hügli, D. Kaegi, & B. Weidmann (Eds.), *Existenz und Sinn. Karl Jaspers im Kontext* (pp. 229–237). Heidelberg: Winter.

Stoffels, H. (2005). Situationskreis und Situationstherapie. Überlegungen zu einem integrativen Konzept von Psychotherapie. In D. Schmoll & A. Kuhlmann (Eds.), *Symptom und Phänomen. Phänomenologische Zugänge zum kranken Menschen* (pp. 166–184). Freiburg: Alber.

Tellenbach, H. (1980). *Melancholy.* Pittsburgh: Duquesne University Press.

Vinar, M., & Vinar, M. (1997). Folter-Attacke auf das Menschsein. In W. Wirtgen (Ed.), *Trauma. Wahrnehmen des Unsagbaren.Psychopathologie und Handlungsbedarf* (pp. 59–74). Heidelberg: Asanger.

Weizsäcker, V. v. (1940). *Der Gestaltkreis. Theorie der Einheit von Wahrnehmen und Bewegen.* Leipzig: Thieme.

Chapter 12
Psychopathology and Psychotherapy in Jaspers' Work and Today's Perspectives on Psychotherapy in Psychiatry

Sabine C. Herpertz

12.1 Introduction

In his first edition of *Allgemeine Psychopathologie* (1913), Karl Jaspers looked upon psychotherapy as a kind of art, with the personality of the psychotherapist being the main factor of effectiveness. According to Jaspers, those personalities turn out to be good psychotherapists who have natural authority, that means, who have developed a capability to make decisions on the basis of instinctive conviction rather than by scientific reasoning. A further valuable predisposition is that a good psychotherapist has a philosophical outlook towards the other as someone "being in his world", the notion of world being understood as an integration of a subject's inner and outer world. Consistent with modern knowledge of the significance of good matching between patient and therapist, Jaspers already claimed: "He (the psychotherapist) is usually only good for a certain circle of people for whom he is well suited" (Jaspers 1997, p. 809). For Jaspers, psychotherapy is the attempt to help the invalid by means of psychic communication, so that he[1] can explore his inner world in its depths. This process enables the patient to retrieve degrees of freedom, not in an instrumental sense but by providing him with perspective (Schlimme et al. 2012). Consequently, the psychotherapist has characteristics of a philosopher, and successful psychotherapy is regarded as a process of clarification that results in an individual becoming himself ("das philosophierende Selbstwerden"; Jaspers 1973, p. 668). Following Jaspers, at best psychotherapy becomes an existential communication between companions in fate.

As indications of psychotherapy, Jaspers listed psychopathies or, personality disorders, mild psychoses, and all "subjects who feel ill and suffer from their psychic

---

[1] Insofar as the masculine form is used in this text, it is assumed that this refers to both genders on equal terms.

S. C. Herpertz (✉)
Klinik für Allgemeine Psychiatrie, Zentrum für Psychosoziale Medizin,
Universitätsklinikum Heidelberg, Voß-Str. 2, 69115 Heidelberg, Germany
e-mail: eva-maria.goetz@med.uni-heidelberg.de

T. Fuchs et al. (eds.), *Karl Jaspers' Philosophy and Psychopathology*,
DOI 10.1007/978-1-4614-8878-1_12, © Springer Science+Business Media New York 2014

state" (Jaspers 1997, p. 835). Probably due to his own weak physical condition, he also recognized physical illnesses as indicators for the need of psychotherapy assuming that they are often overlaid with neurotic symptoms. Against the backdrop of his time, he differentiated the following methods of psychotherapy: suggestion, cathartic methods for after-effects of experiences sometimes bringing forgotten events to consciousness, autogenic training and other relaxation techniques, and re-education (including a precise structuring of daily life). Regarding methods that specifically address personality he suggested psychoeducation, rational methods of persuasion, appeals to will-power, as well as ways of understanding the contradictions between the conscious personality and his own unconscious motives. In a narrow sense, psychotherapy was restricted to the highest level of medical treatment and was differentiated from technical-causal treatment, dietetical treatment inspiring self-help, and educative treatment, which aimed at changing the patient's lifestyle.

The following contribution searches for methodological sources in Jaspers' work that may inspire our current perspectives on psychotherapy and the diagnostic process that precedes it. It was Jaspers who claimed that insight into the methodological confinement of psychotherapeutic methods and knowledge needs to be a basic competence of psychotherapists.

12.2   Diagnostics in Today's Psychotherapy

Within today's concept of psychotherapy diagnostics is not a static, temporally limited procedure but a dynamic process. It is further needed for the primary case formulation that precedes commitment to a treatment plan and that later subsumes additional information that has been collected through therapeutic steps (Freyberger and Caspar 2007). With increasing dissemination of disorder-oriented methods of psychotherapy during the last decades, diagnostics have even gained in importance, starting from the detailed descriptive assessment of psychopathological symptoms that then leads to a nosologic diagnosis or to several diagnoses (i.e. comorbidities). This approach is supplemented by a functional-behavioral analysis or related concepts in psychodynamic psychotherapy that illuminate each facet of the patient's problem and take various domains of inner processing into consideration, such as cognitions, emotions, behavior, and physiology. Beyond these steps, the diagnostic process includes further characteristics of the patient: his concept of illness and treatment, strength of motivation to change, resources and impediments of change, degree of self-awareness and self-reflection (whether the patient can take a stance towards himself and recognizes motives for his behavior), and—of particular importance—capabilities such as interpersonal competence, reality testing, self-regulation, and self-identity, which reflect the level of structure functioning (Herpertz et al. 2012). In addition, the complex structure of motives and conflicts between them have to be detected, or to use Grawe's language of plan analysis (1998), the inconsistencies have to be identified that are induced by discordancies among motivational schemata, respectively, aims of approach and avoidance and/or incongruencies with actual life experiences.

To summarize, the methodological approach in current individual case concepts of psychotherapies needs a differentiated and explicit case formulation that consists of both, on one hand, observations and interpretations and, on the other hand, results from a complex diagnostic process that is established and refined in the course of psychotherapy. Such an individual case formulation needs an objective approach with the psychotherapist as an independent observer who assesses both symptoms and problems and conducts a functional behavior analysis. In addition, we need to learn in detail about the subjective experiences of the patient and his ideas about the genesis of the symptoms and problems, as well as his ideas for solving them. The assessment of a detailed life-history will help psychotherapists gain this information. Finally, we need the psychotherapist to enter a profound relationship with his patient, responding to the patient's thoughts and feelings, learning about discordancies among motivational schemata and incongruencies with actual life experiences. In psychodynamic therapy, but also in modern disorder-related approaches such as the Cognitive Behavioral Analysis System of Psychotherapy (CBASP; McCullough 2000), one makes use of the therapeutic relationship as a diagnostic instrument.

In addition, experimental psychopathology, but also neurobiological methodology, functional neuroimaging in particular, can help to reduce the gap between the first- and third-person perspectives as neuronal correlates of a patient's subjective experiences may help the psychotherapist to better understand the inner experiences of his patient and to pose the right questions in psychopathological assessment. Investigating neuronal correlates of psychotherapeutic effects can help to get a more in-depth idea of how psychotherapy works. However, neurobiological methodology—at least at the current stage of knowledge—is restricted to group effects and thus can only enhance our knowledge of patients' typical modes of experiencing their environment, while failing to provide information on a single subject's experiences.

12.3   Jaspers' Method of Psychopathology

By addressing these issues, Jaspers' method of psychopathology can be regarded as extensive, multi-level diagnostics. Jaspers' approach to diagnostics is particularly helpful for psychotherapy since it is understood as a complex process that is not distinct from psychotherapy, but is rather entangled with psychotherapy, i.e., is an integral part of psychotherapy itself. Furthermore, it is suitable to be communicable to the patient, which is another necessary precondition for psychotherapy. Jaspers claimed a strict dualism of methods between explaining and understanding (Jaspers 1913) and differentiated three methodological levels in the diagnostic process of psychopathology:

- *Objective psychopathology*: observes psychic symptoms from the perspective of an independent observer, and includes also somatic symptoms and meaningful phenomena found in expressive gestures etc.
- *Phenomenology or subjective psychopathology*: based on static understanding. This comprises of the representation and concrete description of subjective phenomena in the sense of conscious experiences and the appreciation of objective causal connections "from without".
- *Genetic understanding*: understanding of psychic events "from within" by empathizing, putting oneself in the patient's shoes and taking his perspective. Principles of genetic understanding stand in contrast to causal explaining, on the one hand, and interpreting ("deuten"), on the other hand. Genetic understanding is based on the analysis of meaningful connections, "psychic events emerge out of each other" (Jaspers 1997, p. 357); i.e., it interprets connections between meaningful facts, thereby establishing internal causality on the basis of self-evidence (and not inductively obtained from theory).

This kind of diagnostic process leads to circular movements from particular facts to the whole and back again from the whole to the facts. According to Jaspers, the process of understanding meaningful connections subsumes three aspects: content, form, and self-reflection. With some striking parallels to Grawe's theory of inconsistencies, Jaspers understands meaningful contents as drives, creative urges, motives, and subjective goals that provide pleasure, help to avoid displeasure, or, in rare cases, help to achieve displeasure. The analysis of such meaningful contents investigates a person's attitudes towards typical life situations of existential significance, such as death, illness, guilt, etc. The analysis of meaningful contents also explores how a person deals with his physical and mental capabilities and their deficiencies, with his social rank or relationships. It investigates mechanisms of defense, regardless of whether a person faces reality or denies it through self-deception. As part of the analysis of contents, Jaspers also considered symbols as carriers of comprehensive meanings. He claimed that symbols cannot be really understood from within but are carriers of comprehensive meanings within either collective archaic images or individual dreams as unique historical symbols.

In order to understand the form of meaningful connections, Jaspers evaluated the degree of integration of opposing tendencies (e.g., self-direction and safety, self-will and social sense, will to power and urge to submit, and dialectical modes such as tension and release). In his opinion, integration succeeds in cases when the opposites are connected in constructive tension.

Finally, self-reflection according to Jaspers meant self-awareness, identity in the actual situation and in the world. Self-reflection "turns something given into something accepted, mere happening into history, and the sequence of a life into a biography" (Jaspers 1997, p. 348). Therefore, reflection—according to Jaspers—produced an awareness of the self as a whole with persisting drives, motives, and values, while simultaneously it subsumed self-observation, self-understanding, and self-revelation.

According to Jaspers, the method of understanding begins with a comprehensive intuition of meaning. The more that meaningful connections could be brought together with facts, i.e., objective data with the reports of subjective experiences, the more one could assume the reality of such a connection. Every step in understanding is considered linked to objective phenomena. This process included understanding (normal and abnormal) extra-conscious mechanisms (e.g., habituation, memory, after-effects of previous experiences, dreams or suggestion) alongside cases of normal mechanisms, and abnormal psychogenic reactions (e.g., reactive psychosis, hysteria, or delusion-like ideas) alongside cases of abnormal mechanisms. Jaspers posited that this process of understanding could be described as a circular movement. The certainty of understanding increases with the extent to which phenomena are concordantly interpreted. The scientific practice of the psychology of meaning wants to differentiate carefully between that which is understood empirically and that which is understood as a self-evident possibility.

12.4   Jaspers and Psychoanalysis

In Jaspers' view, it was a merit of psychoanalysis that it drew strong attention to the inner life-history of individuals and, as a psychology of meaningful connections, intensified their ability to observe. Jaspers and Freud shared the belief that everything a subject experiences leaves its trace by slowly changing dispositions and that man's conscious life is only the topmost layer of a wide realm of sub-conscious and extra-conscious events.

However, Jaspers was unequivocally a powerful critic of Freud. The text by Oskar Pfister (1952), a coeval with Freud, which was published in *Psyche* 1952 ("Karl Jaspers als Sigmund Freuds Widersacher"), is a peculiar contemporary document detailing their dispute. Jaspers opposed the prominent role of sexuality and sexual drive in psychoanalysis and, although he shared Freud's assumption that dream-contents have meanings, Jaspers argued against the importance attached to dream-interpretations and did not share Freud's view that dreams are completely determined and meaningful.

The main critique, however, at least in his early writings raised methodological arguments with regard to the psychoanalytic approach. It was the lack of careful differentiation between observing and understanding in psychoanalysis that became the starting point for Jaspers' critique of psychoanalysis. According to him, psychoanalysis starts with certain individually valid observations as a deductive method that leads to hypotheses within a theory which are unproven and improvable. This procedure results in a confusion of meaningful and causal connections. Freudian investigations are constructions of extra-conscious events and even "use meaningful connections as a basis for building theories about the original causes of the whole course of psychic life" (Jaspers 1997, p. 539). In contrast, Jaspers' assessment of meaningful mechanisms was not performed in the nature of a logical deduction and did not provide a theory. Jaspers' meaningful mechanisms must rather be understood as psychological concepts that aim at bringing some order into psychic and psychopathological phenomena in an individual case.

Jaspers' skeptical attitude towards basic philosophical assumptions in psycho-analysis played increasingly a central role in his later writings. Jaspers spoke of an "analogous method to that of archaeology, where one tries to find some connections between the prehistoric fragments and so rebuild the ancient world" (Jaspers 1997, p. 361). He claimed that Freud gave up the differentiation between realities of objective and subjective being (as ontological manifestations of the plurality and unity of being) for an abstract and determined total explanatory system of man. The methodological confusion of "understanding" and "explaining" was one of the central reasons which attributed the character of a faith to schools of psychotherapy (Schlimme et al. 2012). Responding critically to the psychoanalytic theory of psychosis, Jaspers asserted that psychoanalysis wanted to understand everything, ignoring the reality of organic illness and psychosis. In this way, psychoanalytic theories, according to Jaspers, tended to be too simplistic by trying to reduce the variety of meaningful connections to basic rules. The individual's personal contents were thought to become meaningful in terms of what happened to mankind generally and, in this way, evolved into a psychological myth.

Finally, Jaspers' critique of psychoanalysis culminated in the problematic accusation that psychoanalysis was the third disguise of mankind beside Racial Theory and Marxism (Jaspers 1932/1999).

12.5   Implications for Today's Education in Psychotherapy

Jaspers appears to have had a rather low enthusiasm regarding education in developing a helpful therapeutic relationship. However, his texts may help developing psychotherapists deepen their understanding of what psychotherapy requires on the level of intersubjectivity, which is:

- Understanding the patient's psychic experience from within.
- Understanding a patient through circular moves from facts to the whole of the person and back.
- Building a relationship of empathic communication that aims at clarification and, thereby, increases the patient's degrees of freedom instead of regarding him as the product of determination.
- Differentiating what is observed empirically from what is understood as a self-evident possibility.
- Smoothly moving from one perspective to the other, accompanied by the continuous reflection of the method applied.

Complementing other methods and techniques, psychotherapists may learn from Jaspers the importance of not neglecting an understanding of meaningful connections that help patients better achieve a self-determined life.

References

Freyberger, H.J., & Caspar, F. (2007). Diagnostik und Psychotherapie. In S. C. Herpertz, F. Caspar, C. Mundt (Eds.), *Störungsorientierte Psychotherapie* (pp. 55–75). Munich: Elsevier.

Grawe, K. (1998). *Psychologische Therapie*. Göttingen: Hogrefe.

Herpertz, S.C., Schnell, K., & Falkai, P. (2012). Einleitung. In S. C., Herpertz, K. Schnell, & P. Falkai (Eds.), *Psychotherapie in der Psychiatrie* (pp. 13–18). Stuttgart: Kohlhammer.

Jaspers, K. (1913). *Allgemeine Psychopathologie* (1st ed.). Heidelberg: Springer.

Jaspers, K. (1932/1999). *Die geistige Situation der Zeit* (5th ed.). Berlin: de Gruyter.

Jaspers, K. (1973). *Allgemeine Psychopathologie* (9th ed.). Heidelberg: Springer.

Jaspers, K. (1997). *General Psychopathology* (trans: J. Hoenig & M. W. Hamilton). Baltimore: Johns Hopkins University Press (German edition: Jaspers, K. (1959). *Allgemeine Psychopathologie*, 7. unveränderte Auflage. Berlin: Springer).

McCullough, J. P. Jr. (2000). *Treatment for chronic depression: Cognitive behavioral analysis system of psychotherapy (CBASP)*. New York: Guilford.

Pfister O. (1952). Karl Jaspers als Sigmund Freuds Widersacher. *Psyche, 6*, 241–275.

Schlimme, J. E., Paprotny, T., & Brückner, B. (2012). Karl Jaspers. Aufgaben und Grenzen der Psychotherapie. *Der Nervenarzt, 83*, 84–91.

Index

T. Fuchs et al. (eds.), *Karl Jaspers' Philosophy and Psychopathology*,
DOI 10.1007/978-1-4614-8878-1, © Springer Science+Business Media New York 2014

Printed by Publishers' Graphics LLC